INSIDE
HARVARD

**A Student-Written Guide
to the History and Lore
of America's Oldest University**

Second Edition

Presented by
Crimson Key Society

ACKNOWLEDGEMENTS

Dedicated with love from Crimson Key Society to the memory of Wendy H. Chang, Harvard Class of 2012.

This guidebook is the result of years of collaboration between Crimson Key Society and our esteemed publishers at Harvard Student Agencies Publications. We cannot thank them enough for their unyielding support, professionalism, and experience which impacted all aspects of the book. A very special thanks to Joe Gaspard, Michael Goncalves, Laura Gordon, Meagan Hill, Ashley Laporte, Dan Lee, Jim McKellar, Joseph Molimock, Sara Plana, Mark Warren, Lauren Xie and Roland Yang. This book would certainly not exist with you!

We'd also like to give a very special thanks to Dean Thomas A. Dingman, Dean Paul McLoughlin, and Dean Cory Way, who went above and beyond their roles as CKS's Faculty Advisers to become invaluable mentors for this project during the creation of both the first and second editions.

Last, but certainly not least, thanks are in order for Alexandre Terrien, Harvard Class of 2011 and the Guidebook and Marketing Manager on the Crimson Key Society Executive Board in 2009 and 2010. It was Alex who produced *Inside Harvard* by means of his unparalleled optimism, enthusiasm, and dedication. He is an inspiration to all of CKS and has shown us the incredible things we can create when we pool our talents and energy. Alex, thank you for working so hard at making your vision a reality that we will all always be able to take pride in!

ABOUT
CRIMSON KEY SOCIETY

Founded on April 14, 1948, the Crimson Key Society (CKS) was formed to provide the Harvard Athletic Association with an organization responsible for meeting incoming athletic teams and providing accommodations for their members. By 1955, campus tours had become the focus of the Society's efforts. Today, CKS welcomes all new students at the beginning of each year by organizing Freshman Week with the Freshman Dean's Office. Throughout the year, CKS leads historical tours of the Harvard campus. CKS also offers special tours during reunions, helps with Freshman and Junior Parents' Weekends, and assists the University in various capacities during Commencement Week and the annual ARTS First celebration.

To be sure, each of us experiences Harvard's legacy in individual ways. One CKS member includes this personal anecdote on his tours: he was checking out a book in Widener Library and found a note inside the pages from the last user of the book, signed in 1922, wishing him good luck on his paper. Other tour guides talk about a different note—the list of the previous room's occupants that was waiting on the desk of their first dormitory room at Harvard. Some lists contain the names of former United States Presidents; others include accomplished writers, artists, and activists. It's funny to think that one day we, too, may appear among these names.

We not only introduce you to America's oldest academic institution, but we also welcome you to a place we will always consider our home. As members of CKS, we remember our University's tradition every time we give a tour of campus and in every sentence that we have written in this guidebook. It is our hope that through the pages of this book, we may share with you Harvard's history as well as a sense of the community of which we are privileged to be a part. This guidebook is not an exhaustive history of Harvard, nor is it a complete architectural survey. Instead, we have aimed to provide an accurate and compelling picture of Harvard today, through the eyes of students. This book is an especially useful supplement to an actual tour of the campus, which we hope you have the opportunity to take with us.

FELIX COOK

Crimson Key Society on the steps of Widener Library with President Faust

CONTRIBUTORS

Grace Baumgartner '11
While at Harvard, Grace lived in Winthrop House and concentrated in History & Literature. Her favorite part of CKS was giving tours to Harvard alums, as she learned as much from them as they did from her. Specifically, Grace once gave a Women's History tour to the Class of 1974 that included the first female president of Crimson Key. She has returned to live and work in her native Boulder, Colorado.

Johnny Bowman '11
From Los Angeles, California, Johnny was a Sociology concentrator and a member of Pforzheimer House. His favorite part of Harvard was telling lies, falsehoods, and 100% fictionalized yarns while giving Crimson Key historical tours of Harvard Yard. He now lives and works in New York City.

Andrea Brettler '14
Andrea lives in Leverett House and is studying Human Developmental & Regenerative Biology. She was born in London but has spent the majority of her life New York City. One of her favorite moments at Harvard was storming the freshman dinning hall with the wonderful members of Crimson Key Society to publicize the annual screening of *Love Story*.

Caroline Burke '13
Caroline is concentrating in Social Studies. At Harvard she is a proud resident of Dunster House, but she is originally from Barrington, Rhode Island. She loves running Freshman Orientation with Crimson Key and cheering for the Crimson at Harvard football games!

Katie Chang '11
At Harvard, Katie concentrated in History & Literature with a secondary field in Visual and Environmental Studies while residing in Lowell House. She grew up in Taiwan but now lives in New York City. Katie's favorite part of CKS was greeting parents and new students at 5am on freshman move-in day.

Matt Coe '12

Matt is a Psychology concentrator who hails from Los Angeles, California. As a member of Kirkland House, his favorite parts of CKS are the wonderful people that make up its membership. His claim to fame is that he is the only member that has been free of Friday classes for his entire Harvard career.

Lee Ann Custer '10

Lee Ann studied History of Art & Architecture, was lucky enough to live in fair Currier House, and served as President of Crimson Key in 2009. Her favorite part of Harvard was the best friends she made while on the Crimson Key Executive Board. A native of Cincinnati, Ohio, she currently lives in New York City.

Kyle Dancewicz '11

Kyle was a History of Art & Architecture concentrator from Peabody, Massachusetts who lived in Cabot House. His favorite part of Harvard was his experience with the Hasty Pudding Theatricals. He is now living in New York City.

Alexandra Dowd '11

A Dallas, Texas native, Alexandra lived in Lowell House and concentrated in Psychology. Her favorite parts of Harvard were meeting her best friends and dancing at Lowell Bacchanalia every year. She is now living and researching in New Haven...yes, at Yale!

Cody Evans '12

Cody has served as both President and Treasurer of the Crimson Key Society. Originally from North Oaks, Minnesota, he is concentrating in Economics and lives in Pforzheimer House. Cody's favorite part of Harvard was serving on the CKS Executive Board for two years.

Taylor Freret '12

Taylor is a Chemistry concentrator who lives in Mather House. She hails from Los Altos, California. Her favorite part of Crimson Key Society is giving tours. Seeing how excited tourists are to be on Harvard's hallowed ground reminds her just how lucky she is to be a student on this campus.

Haley Fuller '14

Haley is an Economics concentrator and a proud member of Adams House. Originally from Holland, Massachusetts, she loves dancing on The Crimson Dance Team, talking about the John Harvard Statue on her tour, and welcoming incoming classes to Harvard with fellow members of the Crimson Key Society.

Ana P. Gantman '10

Ana was a Philosophy concentrator in Currier House. Her favorite part of Harvard was whispering messages into the archway over the entrance to Sever Hall, as it is a conduit of sound! Ana has returned to her native New York City where she is pursuing a Ph.D. in Psychology.

Jenya Godina '13

Jen is a History and Literature concentrator in Winthrop House. Originally from Moscow, Russia, she now lives in Boulder, Colorado, where she enjoys skiing and drinking massive amounts of tea. Her favorite part of Harvard is loitering for hours at Sunday brunch.

Kathleen Goodwin '13

A Social Studies concentrator, Kathleen hails from Winchester, Massachusetts, just 5mi. away from the Radcliffe Quad where she lives in Cabot House. Her favorite part of her Harvard experience is serving the University with Crimson Key Society and appreciating being part of a community of the most motivated and talented students in the world.

Zach Hamed '14
Zach is a Computer Science concentrator living in Leverett House. Originally from New York City, he enjoys serving on the Executive Board of Crimson Key and being involved with entrepreneurship and startups on campus.

Mark Khanin '12
Mark is a History of Science Concentrator in Lowell House. Originally from Edison, New Jersey, his favorite part of Crimson Key Society is welcoming the freshmen at the beginning of each year.

D. Patrick Knoth '11
Patrick was a History & Literature concentrator in Dunster House. His favorite part of Crimson Key was giving a tour of Harvard Square aboard a bright green Duck Tour trolley. Now working in New York City, Patrick is originally from Shaker Heights, Ohio.

Adam Lathram '10
A Psychology concentrator from Alamo, California, Adam lived in Quincy House. His favorite part of Harvard was being involved in many organizations on campus, especially Crimson Key Society. He is now living in New York City.

Ken Li '12
A native of Los Angeles, California, Ken studies Anthropology and Film/Video and lives in Winthrop House. A couple of his favorite things at Harvard are the Film Archive and the dining hall's New England Clam Chowder.

Eeke de Milliano '11
Eeke lived in Lowell House and concentrated in Government. She hails from the Netherlands but has spent the majority of her life in Africa. Her favorite part of Harvard was serving as both the Treasurer and President of Crimson Key Society. Eeke now lives and works in New York City.

Daniela Nogueira '11
Daniela was a Government concentrator from Durham, North Carolina. Her favorite part of her Harvard experience was the courage and determination of her roommates in Kirkland House. She is now living in the Palestinian city of Nablus.

Alix Olian '11
A Social Studies concentrator, Alix lived in Lowell House. Her favorite part of Harvard was serving as an Editorial Chair of the The Harvard Crimson and Secretary of Crimson Key Society. Alix is now back in her native Illinois, living and working in Chicago.

Samantha Peretore '11
A native of "the middle of nowhere," New Jersey, Sam concentrated in Psychology and lived in Lowell House. Her favorite parts of Harvard were both the incredible opportunities and the peers she learned from and grew with. She is now living in San Francisco.

Alexandra Perloff-Giles '11
A History of Art & Architecture concentrator from San Francisco, California, Lexie was a resident of Winthrop House. Her favorite parts of Harvard include the Sackler Art Museum and the infinite number of coffee shops in the Square. She is now in Paris getting her Master's in Art History.

Mike Polino '11

Mike was a History of Science concentrator in Lowell House and is originally from Annapolis, Maryland. His favorite Harvard memory was spending an afternoon in Widener Library without any homework to do. He is now living in Los Angeles.

Tara Raghuveer '14

Tara is from Kansas City, Kansas. She lives in Currier House, concentrating in Social Studies. Her favorite part of Harvard is its inspiring array of academic, extracurricular, and social challenges. Her favorite part of Crimson Key is the wonderfully diverse community of students who conquer those challenges everyday, remaining jolly and symmetrical all the while.

Alexandre Terrien '11

Alex was a History & Literature concentrator and lived in Quincy House. His favorite aspect of Harvard was the unique combination of never-ending fun with a vibrant intellectual environment. He is now living and working in his native Paris.

Todd Venook '13

Todd is a Social Studies concentrator in Quincy House and is originally from San Francisco, California. He loves the Harvard-Yale Game and the Charles River. As a member of Crimson Key, he can be seen dancing in floral pants at the annual *Love Story* screening and giving frequent tours of the Yard.

Lanier Walker '14

Lanier is originally from Montgomery, Alabama. At Harvard she lives in Currier House and concentrates in English. Her favorite part of Crimson Key Society is wearing her red sweatshirt as she gives tours and spending time with the most symmetrically faced people on campus.

Scott Yim '13
A native of Methuen, Massachusetts, Scott is a Biomedical Engineering concentrator in Quincy House. His favorite part of Crimson Key is giving tours to people from all over the world.

Lillian Yu '11
Lillian concentrated in History & Literature with a secondary in Film Studies. She is from Ellicott City, Maryland and was a resident of Quincy House. She struggled to choose a favorite part of her Harvard experience but decided on the people. She's now living and working in San Francisco.

Thank you to the CKS members and Harvard students who assisted in the creation of this book:

Lucy Baird
Hana Bajramovic
Natalie Chapman
Felix Cook
Cecelia Cortes
Kristina Dominguez
Sam Galler
Kylie Gleason
Conner Griffith
Gus Hickey
Michael Hoffman

Timur Kalimov
Alan Kirkpatrick
Lina Lavitsky
Emma Lind
Laurel McCarthy
Austin Meyer
Joe Morcos
Amelia Muller
Becca Nadler
Natalia Paine
Brian Paison

Andreas Randow
Mariel Sena
Catherine Sheils
Peter Shields
Noah Silver
Brittan Smith
Alex Tremblay
Marianna Verlage
Matthew Woodward

A special thank you to:

Jim Aisner
Lois Andreasen
Sanders Bernstein
Andrew Berry
Robin Carlaw
Heather Cartwright
Maxwell Child
Patrick Chung
Daniel Coquillette
Linda Cross
Jeff Cruikshank
Dwight Livingston Curtis
Sara Davis
Kyle DeCicco-Carey
Patrick Dethridge
Paul DiMattia
Kit Dodgson
Tim Driscoll
David T. Ellwood
Alison Franklin
Michelle Gachette

Susan Hamilton
Luciana Herman
Anne Hubbard
Justin Ide
Melodie Jackson
Kathleen Jarvinen
Brian Kenny
Judith H. Kidd
Thomas Lentz
Robb London
John Longbrake
Blue Magruder
Asis Martinez
Tim McCarthy
Robin G. McElheny
Barbara Meloni
Martha Minow
Terry Murphy
Jeff Neal
Jackie O'Neil
Jon Page

David A. Paine
Frank Peretore
Janis Peretore
Ben Prosky
Bill Purcell
Julie Rafferty
Michael Rodman
Michael Rutter
William Sahlman
Andrew Schlesinger
Justin Schoolmaster
Sarah Speltz
Karla Strobel
Gina Vild
Joe Villapiano
Kristie Welsh
Benjamin Wood
John Woodward
Beverly Woodward

HARVARD UNIVERSITY
Office of the President

Massachusetts Hall
Cambridge, Massachusetts 02138

t. (617) 495-150(
f. (617) 495-855

PRESIDENT FAUST'S
FOREWORD

Crimson Key Society (CKS) has welcomed one and all to Harvard's campus with excitement and enthusiasm for over 60 years. An organization composed of students involved in every corner of Harvard's campus—and hailing from all over the world—CKS members are united in their appreciation of Harvard and desire to share their experience with others. Each fall CKS greets the arriving freshmen and their families on move-in day, and every day they escort visitors to Harvard around the Yard on free and informative public tours that are delivered with unfailing good humor and energy. Now, in the same welcoming spirit, they present the latest edition of their guidebook so that all of us, whether we work or study at Harvard, or are reading from elsewhere, have a detailed guide to the University.

As Harvard University celebrates its 375th anniversary, the members of Crimson Key Society continue their commitment to Harvard with the publication of this new edition of the guidebook. Its pages provide unique insight about what students value at Harvard and reflect how honored we all are to be part of this historical institution.

Sincerely,

Drew Gilpin Faust

PRESIDENT'S OFFICE
Harvard University President Drew Gilpin Faust

HARVARD COLLEGE

EVELYNN M. HAMMONDS
DEAN OF HARVARD COLLEGE
BARBARA GUTMANN ROSENKRANTZ
PROFESSOR OF THE HISTORY OF SCIENCE
AND OF AFRICAN AND AFRICAN AMERICAN STUDIES

UNIVERSITY HALL, FIRST FLOOR
CAMBRIDGE, MASSACHUSETTS 02138

A NOTE FROM THE DEAN

For more than 60 years, Crimson Key Society (CKS) has provided invaluable services to Harvard University. This new Guidebook embodies the values and knowledge of CKS and is yet another example of its exemplary and long-standing commitment to the Harvard community. A model work of collaboration, the project is not only the product of a strong partnership between CKS and Harvard Student Agencies (HSA), but was developed by no fewer than 30 students, all deeply committed to different aspects of the College. Thanks to their dedication to this project, this book exists to guide visitors, prospective students and their families, as well as current students and faculty, through a compelling view of Harvard's history and life on campus today.

On behalf of the College, I would like to congratulate the Crimson Key Society on this incredible achievement!

Sincerely,

Evelynn M. Hammonds

Evelynn M. Hammonds, Ph.D.
Dean of Harvard College
Barbara Gutmann Rosenkrantz Professor of the History of Science and of African and African American Studies

DEAN'S OFFICE
Dean of Harvard College Evelynn Hammonds

TABLE OF CONTENTS

HARVARD LEXICON

The Berg: Annenberg Hall, the freshman dining hall inside Memorial Hall. As a freshman one finds the Berg a bit annoying because of the long food lines and poorly placed bathrooms, but as an upperclassman you reminisce about how great it was on a regular basis.

Blockmates: during the spring, freshmen can "block" with up to seven other people who become their blockmates. This process is rarely without drama and often involves tears. Your blocking group will be randomly placed into one of 12 upperclassmen houses (the 13th is for the small number of students who live off-campus). It is also possible to "link" two blocking groups together, ensuring that the two linking groups will be in the same neighborhood of three nearby houses.

Brain break: begins at 9pm in undergraduate Houses. Snacks are available for hungry students in dining halls.

"Yeah! Brain break! Let's go! Tonight's options: white bread and wheat bread."

Citation: certificate of proficiency in a foreign language. Typically requires six advanced classes in that language.

Senior: What do you think you are going to concentrate in?
Freshman: I'm concentrating in Molecular and Cellular Biology, with a secondary field in Classics and a citation in Chinese.
Senior: Yeah, when I was a freshman I thought I was going to be a Neurobio concentrator with a secondary field in Literature.
Freshman: What are you now?
Senior: Gov.

Class Day & Commencement: the two graduation ceremonies. Occurring on back-to-back days at the end of the year, they involve all graduating students and thousands of guests and attract prominent speakers like J.K. Rowling, Bill Gates, and Bill Clinton.

Comp (origin: competency; false-but-sort-of-true cognate: competition): the process that students undertake in order to join certain student organizations on campus. Many student groups devise elaborate comps. Some accept all students who complete the comp; others use it to weed out potential candidates. Can be a verb or a noun.

"I want to comp the Crimson, but the comp takes all semester and I still value my social life."

Concentration and secondary field: Harvardian for "major" and "minor."

Coop: pronounced like "chicken coop," Harvard's bookstore and one of the places to go for H-emblazoned paraphernalia.

Dean: Harvard royalty. It is rumored that some Deans are still loyal to the British Crown.

Expos: Expository Writing, the only freshman year requirement; see Lamonster.

Final club: Harvard old boys' (and more recently, girls') club akin to a fraternity or sorority. There are eight male clubs and five female clubs on campus; see Punch.

The Game: the annual Harvard versus Yale football game that closes the Ivy League season every November. The locations alternates each year and tailgating begins in the early morning and lasts all day.

Gap year: a year taken off from school before starting at Harvard. You better have traveled to at least five developing countries and vaccinated 10,000 children during yours or you're going to feel pretty inadequate when everyone starts comparing "gap yah" stories in the Berg.

GenEd: since 2009 Harvard students have been required to complete eight General Education requirements (this is a revamp of what was once called the Core). Ranging from "Aesthetic and Interpretive Understanding" to "Science of the Physical Universe," GenEds are widely regarded as the classes with the easiest grading and most busy work.

H-bomb: "dropping the H-bomb" means mentioning that you go to Harvard. Most often dropped in bars.

Harvard Time: seven minutes past the hour; when classes start at Harvard. A practice sure to make all Harvard students perpetually late for the rest of their lives upon graduating.

HoCo: House Committee; social committee of a House, the pertinence of this group depends on how social the House is.

House: there are 13 upperclassman Houses at Harvard, modeled after the colleges at Oxford and Cambridge. Most are named after Harvard Presidents (excepting President Leonard Hoar for obvious reasons).

Housing Day: think "sorting" at Hogwarts. Housing Day is when freshmen find out which upperclass House they have been placed in. Current members of each House pick up freshmen from their rooms early in the morning (some future Quadlings cry at this point...tears of joy, of course) and everyone congregates in the Berg to celebrate.

HUPD: Harvard University Police Department, pronounced "hup-dee." These officers are always on your side and beloved by all students.

The Kong: an inexpensive Chinese restaurant, bar, and comedy club on Mass Ave. A late night favorite (now open until 3am) among Harvard students and home to the Scorpion Bowl, the drink that you never realize was a bad idea until the next morning during your 9am Spanish class.

Lamonster: what you'll look like when you emerge from Lamont Library after pulling an all-nighter to finish your final Expos paper.

Noch's: Pinocchio's, a pizzeria off JFK Street that serves world-famous Sicilian slices and does the majority of its business between midnight and 2am on Saturday nights.

Primal Scream: a Harvard tradition. At the end of each semester, the night before exams start, students gather at midnight and run a naked lap around the Yard, encouraged by the Harvard Band and hundreds of cheering onlookers.

PAF: Peer Advising Fellow, an upperclass adviser assigned to each freshman. These are the people who will tell you that taking LS1a, Math21b, Ec10, and CS50 all at once in your first semester will only land you in the Emergency Room no matter how good at time management you think you are.

Proctor: a non-undergraduate live-in freshman adviser, akin to an RA.

Punch: the four-round selection process for membership in a final club. The two months of the fall semester when everyone always seems to be in formal wear regardless of the day of the week or time of day.

The Quad (origin: Radcliffe Quadrangle): dreaded by some for its distance from the Yard, the Quad is the home of three upperclass Houses: Pforzheimer, Currier, and Cabot. The Quad is a 10min. walk from the Yard, enough to cause some freshmen to dread being "Quadded" on Housing Day, despite the Houses' plentiful singles.

Freshman girl: My boyfriend says if I get Quadded we're breaking up. He's not ready for a long distance relationship.

Reading period: the week preceding exams. Without a regular class schedule, students spend the week sleeping and frantically catching up on the semester's missed lectures.

Safety School: Yale. The cheapest joke used by a visiting professor but it is usually good for at least a few perfunctory laughs from the audience.

Section: in large lecture classes, a weekly discussion section of about 14 students is usually also required. Taught by TFs and can range the spectrum from a dissapointing use of time to absolutely essential for passing the class.

Shopping Week: during the first week of each semester, classes are open to all students, who can enter and leave as they please before deciding which classes to take.

Teaching Fellow (TF): teaching assistant, usually a graduate student. The bigger the class, the more the TF can make or break your grade.

Tutor: not usually someone who helps you with your homework, but always someone who breaks up your dorm room party if it's occurring on a Wednesday night. Tutors live in upperclass Houses and serve as supporters, advisers and House rule enforcers.

UC: Undergraduate Council, Harvard College's student government. The President/Vice President Elections are held every fall and are taken extremely seriously by many students and extremely lightly by others. 2009's ticket included Robert Long '11 and David Johnson '11 with a campaign slogan that read "Long-Johnson: Erecting a better Harvard." The two students were not elected.

Veritas: Harvard's motto which means "truth" in Latin. Overused in spinoffs like "Veritaffles," the Belgian waffles with Harvard's crest in the center that you can make at Sunday brunch, and "Visitas," the name for the prospective student visiting weekend in April.

Walk of Shame: the walk back to your room after a night spent in someone else's, most often in the clothes you wore the previous night. Depending on the circumstances, also known as the Stride of Pride. From the Quad to the river, it's more like a 5k. Mather to Currier or vice versa holds the record for longest distance often completed in heels or in costume over uneven brick sidewalks.

The Yard: Harvard Yard, the oldest part of campus. The Yard is home to most freshman dorms and the highest concentration of tourists in the Boston area. Harvard professors are contractually encouraged to graze their livestock here.

Z-listed: The Harvard Admissions Office technique of asking an undisclosed number of accepted high school seniors to wait a year before beginning their freshman year; see Gap Year.

HISTORY
OF HARVARD

EARLY HISTORY

A ROCKY BEGINNING

Founded on October 28, 1636, just 16 years after the Pilgrims arrived at Plymouth Rock, Harvard University is the oldest institution of higher education in the United States. Its founding was preceded in North America only by two Spanish universities in Mexico and a French college in Quebec. Located in what was then called Newetowne, Massachusetts, Harvard was established by vote of the Great and General Court of the Massachusetts Bay Colony and was originally called "The College of Newetowne," or simply "The College."

In 1637, one year after the establishment of Harvard, the newly selected overseers of the College purchased an acre of land from Newetowne. This plot, christened the "College Yard," has grown over nearly four centuries into the Old Harvard Yard of today. The College Yard was the home of the first three buildings of the College: Goffe House, Peyntree House, and the first Harvard Hall.

Just a year later, John Harvard, the wealthy but otherwise insignificant minister of Charlestown, Massachusetts, did something that would change the College forever: he died. In his will, he left the College about 400 volumes and half of his estate, which was valued at £779. This was Harvard's first sizable donation and the reason the University carries John Harvard's name today.

BY THE NUMBERS

9	Students in the first Harvard class, under the tutelage of 1 master
5	Total number of Native American students educated at Harvard's Indian College, founded in 1655
8	Presidents of the United States with Harvard degrees (John Adams, John Quincy Adams, Rutherford B. Hayes, Theodore Roosevelt, Franklin Delano Roosevelt, John F. Kennedy, George W. Bush, and Barack H. Obama)
44	Harvard faculty members who have won the Nobel Prize

FUN FACT

In the 17th century, student tuition could take the form of wheat, malt, Indian corn, barley, rye, apples and parsnips, casks of butter, honey, firewood, sides of beef, hogs, calves, sheep, and chickens.

Nathaniel Eaton served as the first headmaster of the newly formed college, but his tenure was brief. A strict and even cruel disciplinarian, Eaton was removed from office in 1639 for severely beating several students and feeding them poorly.

In 1640, Reverend Henry Dunster was elected Harvard's first President and began a 14-year term that established Harvard as a fiscally and administratively sound institution.

PRESIDENT DUNSTER

Dunster carried out Harvard's first fundraising drive, and among the donors was Ann Radcliffe (whose married name was Lady Mowlson) who donated funds in 1643 for Harvard to create its first scholarship. Her gesture was recognized

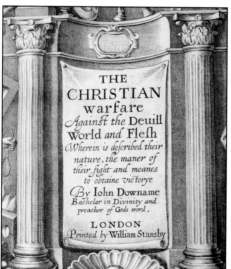

OFFICE OF PUBLIC AFFAIRS
The Christian Warfare Against the Devil, World and Flesh, *the only remaining part of John Harvard's original donation to the College*

1775-6
College exiled to Concord during revolutionary activity

1776
College successfully petitions Continental Congress for damages done to Harvard buildings by revolutionary troops

1782
Medical School founded

1807
President Kirkland appointed; advocates for educational reform and less classical education, establishes Law School

1816
Divinity School
founded

FUN FACT

In 1825, a riot took place outside Lehman Hall after tuition was raised from $20 to $25.

1829
President Quincy
appointed;
oversees
building of
Observatory and
Gore Hall

over 250 years later with the naming of Radcliffe College (p. 44), the women's liberal arts college that was for many years Harvard's sister school.

On June 9, 1650, President Dunster obtained a charter from the Massachusetts Court, placing the institution under the sole direction of the President and Fellows of Harvard College, known today as the Harvard Corporation. This seven-member board, consisting of the President, the Treasurer, and five other fellows, is the oldest corporation in the Western hemisphere and continues to act as the principal governing board of Harvard.

1867
School of
Dental Medicine
founded

Despite his success as President, Dunster was dismissed in 1654 due to pressure from Boston ministers who considered his views on baptism heretical. Dunster believed that there was no scriptural basis for infant baptism, a divergence from Puritan beliefs that proved too great to be tolerated.

1869
President Eliot
appointed; Law
School institutes
case method

THE TURN TO SECULARISM

Although Harvard was not founded exclusively for training ministers, many graduates did enter the clergy, and the early Presidents of Harvard were traditionally clergymen. Indeed, Dunster's immediate successors, Charles Chauncy, Leonard Hoar, Urian Oakes, and John Rogers, were all ministers before their appointments at the College. Harvard's early motto was *"Veritas Christo et Ecclesiae"* ("Truth for Christ and the Church") and the mission of a Harvard education was to: "Let every student be plainly instructed and consider well that the main end of his life and studies is to know God and Jesus, which is eternal life. And therefore to lay Christ at the bot-

1872
Graduate
School of Arts
and Sciences
founded

1879
Society for
the Collegiate
Instruction
of Women
founded;
becomes
Radcliffe College

FUN FACT

The only student to graduate from the Indian College was Caleb Cheeshahteaumuck, Class of 1665. He died one year later of tuberculosis.

ARCHITECTURAL SPOTLIGHT:
MASSACHUSETTS HALL

Massachusetts Hall, south of Johnston Gate in the Old Yard, is the oldest Harvard building still standing and the second oldest academic building in the country (the oldest is Christopher Wren's Administration Building at the College of William and Mary in Virginia). Funding was provided by the Province of Massachusetts in 1718, and in 1720 the building was erected under the supervision of President Leverett to provide additional dormitory rooms.

During the Revolutionary War, 640 soldiers of the Continental Army were billeted in this building, which was originally planned to house 30 students. The soldiers, unfortunately, were not very good houseguests, as they melted down the metal rooftops and doorknobs to use for ammunition. The College returned to Cambridge in June 1776 only to discover the damages that had been done to its buildings by the revolutionary troops. Harvard successfully petitioned the Continental Congress in Philadelphia for compensation, becoming the first institution to file and win a lawsuit against what is now the United States government.

FRESHMAN DEAN'S OFFICE
Massachusetts Hall

Mass Hall was remodeled in 1870, at which point all of the original studies were removed to accommodate lecture rooms, reading rooms, and offices. The lower hall was the famous "Workshop 47" from 1916 to 1924; Professor George Pierce Baker used this space to test the plays written for his course, English 47. Today, the upper floor houses freshmen while the lower two floors house the offices of the President and high-ranking officials of the University.

tom as the only foundation of all sound learning and knowledge."

In 1655, Harvard established the Indian College to educate Native Americans. A two-story structure in Harvard Yard at the present-day site of Matthews Hall, the Indian College housed a printing press that produced the first Bible in North America—a translation of the Bible into the Wampanoag language by John Eliot, the "Apostle to the Indians."

LEGEND HAS IT: THE STORY OF EPHRAIM BRIGGS

According to Harvard legend, one cold January night in 1764, a student named Ephraim Briggs was working late in the library, taking notes for an essay due the following day from a book propped open before him—a real page-turner called *Christian Warfare Against the Devil, World and Flesh* by John Downame. He had checked out the book in October of 1763 and was only just now getting the chance to write about this surely extremely interesting text. The next morning, when he went to return the book, he found a pile of ashes where the library had been: Harvard Hall had burned down during the night.

This presented Briggs with a moral dilemma: whether to return the book, which was now the last remaining book of the original John Harvard donation, or to keep the book—and the secret of its long overdue status—to himself. He decided to take the high road, and Briggs returned the book to the President of the University, Reverend Edward Holyoke. Legend states that President Holyoke thanked Briggs profusely—and proceeded to expel him. Harvard students have had their revenge, however: the Holyoke Center, which houses Harvard University Health Services as well as various administrative offices, is generally considered among the least attractive buildings on campus.

ARCHITECTURAL SPOTLIGHT: HARVARD HALL

The first building built on Harvard's campus was actually Harvard Hall, not Massachusetts Hall. The first Harvard Hall, completed in 1642, was a poorly constructed wooden structure that had rotted and fallen into disrepair by 1677. The second attempt at Harvard Hall was built that year on the site where the present Harvard Hall now stands. It contained classrooms as well as a dining room, a kitchen, a chapel, and the largest library in the colonies with a collection of over 5000 volumes, including the original John Harvard donation. The building also housed the country's first experimental physics laboratory, where Benjamin Franklin attended lectures by John Winthrop, grandson of the first Puritan governor, and the University's first mineralogical collection.

In January 1764, a smallpox epidemic in Boston forced the General Court of the Colony to convene in Harvard Hall. The Court had planned to use the building for several months, but on the night of January 24, 1764, a fire destroyed Harvard Hall, including the John Harvard collection housed inside.

FRESHMAN DEAN'S OFFICE
The third and current Harvard Hall

The blaze, which threatened nearby buildings, including the newly constructed dormitory Hollis Hall, was believed to have started with a small fire left burning overnight in the library.

The present-day Harvard Hall was designed by Francis Bernard, Governor of the Massachusetts Bay Colony. Completed in 1766, it is the fifth oldest structure in the Yard and the seventh oldest at the University.

1936
Graduate
School of
Design founded;
Graduate
School of Public
Administration
(later Kennedy
School) founded

Over the next 15 years, only five Native American students were educated at the College, and the building, originally intended for the sole use of Native Americans, housed mostly English students. By 1693 the building had fallen apart, and Harvard received permission to tear the structure down.

The fourth President of Harvard College was Dr. Reverend Leonard Hoar, Class of 1650. A strict educator, Hoar ordered the prison-keeper to publicly whip Thomas Sargeant, a senior who had spoken blasphemously against the Holy Ghost; this punishment was deemed far too severe for the crime, and it incited public controversy. Over the next few years, Hoar mismanaged the College and only nine bachelor's

1938
School of Public
Health founded

1946
Harvard and
Radcliffe classes
combined

1953
President Pusey
appointed

1969
Student strikes
at Harvard
protesting
Vietnam War

1971
President Bok
appointed

FUN FACT

In 1818, some Hollis Hall residents formed the "Med. Fac." This society, rife with ceremony and ritual, revolved around the delivery of mock medical lectures. The first article of their constitution stated:

Article Fyrste: This, the Harvard Lodge of Independent Order of Odd Fellows so called to express in a manner at once lucid, melodious, and concise, its relation and character, shall be a society dedicated to FUN. With the god of mirth for its patron it is instituted for the sake of embringing intellectual amusement with many a hearty laugh.

Titles of officers included the Grand Master, the Ignoble Grand, a Sub-Ignoble, a Despicable Clerk, a Sacerdotal Scavenger, an Infernal Satellite, a Sublunary Doomster, a Receptional Vampire, a Ladaverous Spectre, a Danitor Orci, a Medicinal Tormentor, and a Celestial Imp. The organization was ordered dissolved in 1834 after the College received a handsome gift, a set of surgical instruments from the Tsar of Russia, who was expressing his gratitude for his Med. Fac. diploma. The society continued underground for the rest of the century and was credited with the demolition of the College Pump in 1901. The Med. Fac. may have been a predecessor to the *Harvard Lampoon*.

ARCHITECTURAL SPOTLIGHT: THE JOHN HARVARD STATUE

The bronze statue of John Harvard that stands in front of University Hall was cast in 1884 by Daniel Chester French, who also sculpted the Lincoln Memorial and the Minuteman statue in Concord, Massachusetts. The John Harvard statue was originally placed in front of Memorial Hall but was moved to its current location 40 years later. The statue is often referred to as the "statue of three lies"; while the inscription reads "John Harvard, Founder, 1638," all three of these assertions are false. Firstly, the College was actually established by the Massachusetts Bay Colony, and was only later named after John Harvard in recognition of his donation to the fledgling university. Secondly, the College was founded in

FRESHMAN DEAN'S OFFICE

1636, not 1638. Finally, the seated figure of the statue is not really John Harvard.

When the statue was cast, no one could find a single image of Harvard— they had apparently all been destroyed in the Harvard Hall fire of 1764. No one knows quite how the model was selected, but the face chosen to represent John Harvard was that of Sherman Hoar, Class of 1882. One theory holds that Hoar was a descendant of Rev. Leonard Hoar, who served as President of the University from 1672 to 1674. It is a tradition at Harvard to name upperclassman Houses after former Harvard Presidents, but because "Hoar House" wouldn't fly for obvious reasons, Hoar was honored instead with the selection of Sherman as the model for the statue. Most, if not all, images of John Harvard seen today—including his US postage stamp—are in fact of Sherman Hoar.

degrees were awarded from 1672 to 1676. Four members of the Corporation resigned in protest and Hoar finally stepped down in March of 1675.

In 1682, Reverend Increase Mather, who had presided over many of the Salem witch trials, became the fifth Presi-

ALUMNUS ILLUMINATED: HENRY DAVID THOREAU

Henry David Thoreau, Class of 1837, was an author, philosopher, poet, naturalist, and leading figure in Transcendentalism. According to legend, Thoreau refused to pay the $5 fee for a Harvard master's degree, quipping, "Let every sheep keep its own skin." After graduation, Thoreau taught briefly at Concord Academy before being dismissed for refusing to administer corporal punishment. At the suggestion of Ralph Waldo Emerson, Thoreau began keeping a journal and publishing

with the Transcendentalist publication, the *Dial*. His essay "Civil Disobedience," which he wrote after spending a night in jail for refusing to pay the poll tax, is a defense of individual resistance in the face of unjust civil government and has become a classic text of modern political theory.

Harvard University Archives, HUD 237.714 (page 107)

On July 4, 1845, Thoreau began a two-year retreat into the woods that he described in his 1854 meditation on nature, *Walden, or Life in the Woods*. A staunch opponent of slavery, Thoreau publicly condemned the Fugitive Slave Act and rose to defend abolitionist John Brown. Thoreau was one of the first American backers of the Darwinian theory of evolution and an early advocate of publicly protected wilderness and nature reserves. His philosophical writings anticipated modern-day environmentalism.

> **FUN FACT**
>
> Immediately after the disastrous fire of 1764, which destroyed Harvard Hall, the University bought a fire engine, which was kept near Hollis, in Holden Chapel. Some Hollis residents opportunistically formed the Engine Society, a volunteer firemen's organization. Since fires at Harvard were infrequent, the society made many practice runs, hooking the engine to the Old College Pump and aiming at unpopular professors and inviting open windows.

dent of Harvard College. Throughout his 16-year term, he continued to serve as pastor of Boston's historic North Church, and his presidency reignited the religious conflict between the colonial Boston community and Harvard. A strict and conservative disciplinarian of the Congregational Church, Mather wished to incorporate religious examinations into the admissions process, but the rest of the College administration had different ideas. In the 1680s Harvard endorsed a religious liberalism radically opposed to the conservative and powerful Boston ministry. In addition, the General Court passed an order in 1701 stating that "no man should act as President of the College, who did not reside in Cambridge." Mather, a lifelong resident of Boston, refused to move to Cambridge and was therefore dismissed from office. Samuel Willard, Class of 1659, was appointed as his replacement; despite only officially holding the office of Vice President, Willard was authorized to live in Boston. An infuriated Mather and his son, Cotton Mather, Class of 1678, moved on to become instrumental in founding the college that is today Yale University. Harvard, unlike much of the Boston community, was becoming more secular. John Leverett, Class of 1680, who took office in 1708, was the first University President not to come from the clergy, and under his tenure, Harvard further loosened its ties to Puritanism.

HARVARD AND THE REVOLUTION

Revolutionary activity erupted on campus in 1768, when students gathered at the "Rebellion Elm," a tree outside Hollis Hall, to decry the passage of the Townshend Act. That year, the senior class voted to defy British law and boycott tea. Two years later, when the General Court of the Massachusetts Bay Colony moved into Harvard Hall to escape mob influence in Boston, Harvard students were able to witness the speeches of great revolutionary orators like James Otis. The ardor of these speeches sparked the formation of several secret organizations for students to develop their oratory skills: the Speaking Club (1770), the Mercurian Club (1770), and the Clintonian Club (1774). All of these oratory groups eventually merged into the Hasty Pudding Club, an organization which evolved into what is today a social club and a theatrical company.

ARCHITECTURAL SPOTLIGHT:
HOLDEN CHAPEL

Early in Harvard's history, Thomas Hutchinson, Class of 1727, went to London determined to raise support for a chapel, which the University did not have. There he befriended Samuel Holden, a wealthy Englishman interested in religious causes. When Holden died in 1740, his will stipulated that part of his estate be used for "true religious advancement." Mrs. Holden donated £400 for the building of Holden Chapel, which was completed in 1744. Located on the northwest side the Old

KEVIN LIN

Yard in the Lionel-Mower quadrangle, Holden Chapel is a strikingly beautiful example of Georgian architecture. The designer, who was most likely English, is unknown. The beautiful coat of arms on the gable above the door is the coat of arms of Mrs. Holden's family.

The third-oldest building in the Yard, Holden was used as a chapel until 1766, when the new Harvard Hall absorbed that function. Holden then began its life as Harvard's "catch-all" building. For a brief period, it was the seat of the Province House of Representatives. Later it was used as a military barracks. In the late 18th and early 19th centuries, it was the site of the Medical School and nearly all undergraduate lectures. Since 1810, the chapel has served as a storehouse, fire engine house, clubhouse, chemical laboratory, museum auditorium, and classroom. Today, Holden Chapel is the headquarters for several choral groups on campus: the Harvard Glee Club, the Collegium Musicum, and the Radcliffe Choral Society.

As conflict with the British intensified, Harvard students became increasingly revolutionary. The Martmercurian Band, a militia-like organization of Harvard students, was formed in 1770. On April 19, 1775, six of the group's members participated in the confrontation with British troops at Lexington. Students boldly defied British law and were even known to write their theses on untaxed paper.

At the onset of the Revolutionary War in 1775, the colonists demanded the use of Harvard facilities for military purposes. The Committee of Safety, revolutionary Boston's equivalent to our current Department of Defense, ordered Harvard students to return home and commandeered the College's buildings. The Corporation decided to move all students and tutors to Concord, Massachusetts, 20 miles from Cambridge, on October 4, 1775.

While Harvard was in Concord, the College conferred its first degree of law. An honorary degree was presented to George Washington on April 3, 1776, one month after the British evacuation of Boston.

Despite the interruption, the 43 members of the Class of 1776 graduated on time. Several pursued positions in public office: Christopher Gore became Governor of Massachusetts and a United States Senator, and Samuel Sewall became Chief Justice of the Massachusetts Supreme Court.

After the Revolutionary War ended in 1781, Harvard was still a very small private college: only five professors and six tutors led a student body of 200. The transformation of this small college into the vast, bustling university of today began with the presidency of John Thornton Kirkland.

PRESIDENT KIRKLAND

Appointed in 1810, Reverend Kirkland initiated a policy of educational reform. He strengthened the Medical School and established the Divinity School in 1816 and the Law School in 1817. Finally, Kirkland transformed the Yard from an "unkempt sheep-commons"—treeless and cluttered with a brew house and privies—into the majestic lawn of today.

In 1817, a food fight erupted in University Hall that involved some of the United States' most distinguished sons. Afterward, President Kirkland punished four notably unknown students. Many of those who went unpunished met under the Rebellion Elm to suppor their fellow students, including Ralph Waldo Emerson; Josiah Quincy Jr., son of the Congressman Josiah Quincy, Class of 1790; George Washington Adams, son of the Secretary of State John Quincy Adams, Class of 1787; and George Otis, son of the Senator Harrison Gray Otis, Class of 1783. President Kirkland asked Quincy, Adams, and Otis to leave town for a few days and not to return to the Rebellion Elm. Of course, they disobeyed; Quincy wrote in his journal: "Resistance to tyrants is obedience to God." Most of the sophomore class ended up facing consequences from President Kirkland in the end.

PRESIDENT QUINCY

President Josiah Quincy, a former mayor of Boston, continued Kirkland's policy of growth. During his presidency (1829-1845), Quincy supervised the construction of the Observatory and of Gore Hall, a library building designed to hold Harvard's 40,000 volumes.

Harvard also owes its seal to President Quincy. Researching for his massive two-volume history of the College, Quincy stumbled upon a 1693 hand-drawn version of the seal, with three open books and the letters V-E-R-I-T-A-S. Despite the opposition of the Calvinists, who held that replacing the old "Christo et Ecclesiae" with the new "Veritas" was a sign of the Unitarians' infidelity, the Harvard Corporation adopted the 1693 sketch as the new official seal that remains today.

In the period between the Revolutionary and Civil Wars, Harvard began to leave its mark on American history. Some of the first truly American scholars chose Harvard as their home. The poet Henry Wadsworth Longfellow and naturalist Louis Agassiz both served as Harvard professors during the 1800s.

THE CIVIL WAR

The Civil War was a subject of much debate at Harvard, and hundreds of students and alumni served in both the Union and Confederate forces. Latin professor Charles Beck, who lived in the yellow clapboard Warren House (now home to Harvard's Celtic department), was an ardent abolitionist during the years leading up to the Civil War. Warren House is equipped with a trap door that leads through a secret passageway into a 16 square foot room, suggest-

President Kirkland, Harvard Art Museums/Fogg Museum,
Harvard University Portrait Collection,
Gift of Lemuel Shaw to Harvard College, 1842, H15

ARCHITECTURAL SPOTLIGHT:
UNIVERSITY HALL

Though Charles Bulfinch is most famous for having designed the intermediate rotunda and the dome of the U.S. Capitol, he is also the architect of the Massachusetts State House on Beacon Hill, Harvard's Stoughton Hall, and the Federalist-style University Hall. Built on the eastern edge of the Old Yard where Professor Wigglesworth once let his cow graze, University

KEVIN LIN

Hall was completed in 1816 after three years of construction. Originally designed to house a dining hall, the University chapel, and the offices of the President, University Hall no longer contains any of these facilities. The dining hall was moved in 1849 after food fights among undergraduates became alarmingly frequent events. The chapel was relocated in 1858 to the newly constructed Appleton Chapel, while the offices of the President moved to Massachusetts Hall in 1945.

University Hall was forcefully occupied in 1969 by a student group of protesters, although the building itself was largely undamaged. To prevent future occupation by students, glass doors and an elaborate security system were installed in University Hall. While demonstrating for Harvard's divestment in South Africa in the early 1990s, students circumvented the system by hiding out in the bathroom. Today, University Hall houses the offices of the Dean of the College and other senior administrators.

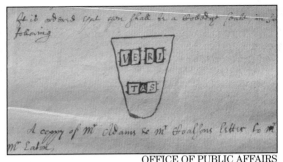

OFFICE OF PUBLIC AFFAIRS
Veritas seal, hand-drawn by President Quincy

ing that the building was once part of the Underground Railroad. In the 1940s workers uncovered the "slave-quarters," as this basement room came to be known, where they found rotting drapes and carpet, a metal bed, and a small dresser with a photograph of a cow. The secret passages received a great deal of student attention before they were finally sealed to prevent any injuries.

Many prominent Harvard affiliates were involved in the Civil War. Along with his classmate N.P. Hallowell, Robert Gould Shaw (who actually withdrew before graduating to join the military) led the 54th Massachusetts Regiment, the nation's first all-black military division, and orchestrated the conscription of black men into his personal regiment. He died alongside his men charging Fort Wagner in South Carolina in 1863, and is now commemorated both in Memorial Hall and in a statue facing the Boston State House. Senator Charles Sumner, who was famously caned on the Senate floor by Charles Preston for his speech, "The Crime Against Kansas," was also a Harvard graduate, Class of 1830.

FUN FACT

A story often shared on campus tours is of John Harvard statue's seal, located on the left side of the pedestal and depicted on the cover of this book. In contrast to the present-day seal which shows "VE," "RI" and "TAS" written on the open pages of three books, the statue's seal contains one book that is face down below the other two open. The downturned book is often interpreted as a reflection of the Puritan belief that not all knowledge can be gained from the written word. At Harvard, it holds that we often learn just as much after we have put our books away.

ALUMNUS ILLUMINATED:
RALPH WALDO EMERSON

An instrumental figure in the so-called "New England Renaissance" of the 19th century, Ralph Waldo Emerson, Class of 1821, was an essayist, philosopher, and lecturer. Like his protégé Henry David Thoreau, Emerson was a key figure in Transcendentalism, a movement rooted in the idea that truth may be revealed through personal experience in nature rather than illuminated by God. Emerson entered Harvard at age 14, at which point he began to keep journals filled with his thoughts, poems, and drawings, a practice that he continued throughout his life. Emerson spent a few years teaching before entering Harvard Divinity School, and he later became a minister at Boston's Second Church. Emerson resigned his post in 1832, however, to devote himself to lecturing and writing.

Ralph Waldo Emerson,
Harvard University Archives,
HUP Emerson, Ralph Waldo (17)

His Phi Beta Kappa speech at Harvard in 1837, entitled "The American Scholar," which called for America to cease looking to Europe for ideas, was dubbed "America's Intellectual Declaration of Independence" by Oliver Wendell Holmes. A speech addressed to the eight graduating seniors of the Harvard Divinity School the following year was less well received, however; his refutation of Biblical miracles caused controversy as one Divinity School professor decried his words as the "latest form of infidelity." In the 1850s, Emerson put his rhetorical power to use in the service of abolitionism, greater freedom in worship, broader university education, and increased economic rights for women. Emerson's writings, among which *Nature* and his two collections of essays are best known, reflect his belief that people can transcend the world of the senses to apprehend the spiritual unity of man with nature and the divine.

ARCHITECTURAL SPOTLIGHT:
JOHNSTON GATE AND GUARDHOUSE

Johnston Gate, the main entrance to the Old Yard, was built in 1890 and is the oldest of the Yard's 26 gates. Located between Massachusetts and Harvard Halls, the gate serves as the major vehicular entrance to the Yard for the majority of the year. Twice each year, however, the gate is closed to vehicles. On Opening Day, the gate is used to usher in the entering freshman class, while on Commencement Day, the graduating senior class processes out through the gate. The gate was constructed in accordance with the will of Samuel Johnston, Class of 1855, who provided the funds for the construction of the gate's stone pillars.

Located just inside Johnston Gate is the smallest building in Harvard Yard, the guardhouse. Though not much bigger than a phone booth, the guardhouse is the most expensive building per square foot on Harvard's

JUSTIN SCHOOLMASTER
Johnston Gate under the snow

campus, costing a whopping $57,000 to build. The architect, Graham Gund, was forced to develop approximately 80 designs before he satisfied the demands of the Cambridge Historical Commission. Constructed of pine and cedar and highlighted by arched windows and a slanted roof, the guardhouse is meant to convey a colonial charm.

PRESIDENT ELIOT

Charles William Eliot was a Harvard chemistry professor before he became president in 1869. After having revitalized the Medical School (p. 91) with new funds and curriculum improvements, he founded the Graduate School of Arts and Sciences in 1872 and the Business School (p. 211) in 1908. At that time only at Harvard and Johns Hopkins could a student extend his formal liberal arts education beyond the undergraduate level without traveling to Europe.

Notwithstanding his vast renovation of the graduate schools, Eliot did not ignore the heart of the University, the undergraduate College. Several new disciplines of academia were added to the curriculum: economics, government, social ethics, psychology, geology, fine arts, classical and American archaeology, and ethnology. The admissions requirements of the College were stiffened, but Greek was dropped as a prerequisite for admission. Perhaps the most significant of Eliot's contributions to the College was the addition of the elective system, as Harvard once again led the way in American education.

By the time Eliot retired, he had raised the University's endowment from $2.3 million to $22.5 million, allowing it to expand enrollment from 2000 to 3000 students. In 1890, he oversaw the construction of Johnston Gate, the main entrance to the Old Yard and the oldest Yard gate standing. Between 1869 and 1909, Harvard's faculty increased from 49 to 278. Eliot's presidency also saw such noted professors as Henry Adams and Edward Channing in history; Charles Eliot Norton in fine arts; English scholars George Kittredge, Barrett Wendell, and Bliss Perry; and the four greats of the philosophy department, William James, George Herbert Palmer, Josiah Royce, and George Santayana.

ARCHITECTURAL SPOTLIGHT: WADSWORTH HOUSE

For two weeks in 1775, General George Washington used Wadsworth House in Harvard Yard as his headquarters. Built in 1726 as a home for President Benjamin Wadsworth, the building is Harvard's second-oldest standing building and was home to Harvard Presidents until 1849. It is said that plans to oust King George's troops from Boston took form in Wadsworth's parlor. At the turn of the 20th century, the

SCOTT YIM

house was used to accommodate student boarders, most notably Ralph Waldo Emerson, Class of 1921. During World War I, the Navy occupied the house—save for the preacher's quarters—as part of its Officer Training School.

ARCHITECTURAL SPOTLIGHT:
MEMORIAL HALL

After the Civil War ended, the 136 Harvard affiliates who died fighting for the Union were commemorated with the erection of Memorial Hall. Oliver Wendell Holmes, Sr., a poet and the Parkman Professor of Anatomy and Physiology at Harvard, composed a hymn for the ceremony:

ALEXANDRA DOWD

> *While o'er their marbles the mosses are creeping,*
> *Stealing each name and its record away,*
> *Give their proud story to Memory's keeping,*
> *Shrined in the temple we hallow to-day.*
> *Hushed are their battle-fields, ended their marches,*
> *Deaf are their ears to the drum-beat of morn—*
> *Rise from the sod, ye fair columns and arches*
> *Tell their bright deeds to the ages unborn.*

The omission of the names of Harvard students and affiliates from the Confederate army has been the subject of some controversy, but no changes have been made to the memorial.

Memorial Hall was not, however, designed solely as a memorial. At the same time that a group of Harvard alumni raised a staggering $370,000—a sum equal to one twelfth of the endowment of the University at the time—toward the erection of a memorial, Charles Sanders, Class of 1802, bequeathed $40,000 for a space to be used for Commencement, Class days, and other occasions. These two projects were combined in the construction of Memorial Hall, designed by William Robert Ware, Class of 1852, and Henry Van Brunt, Class of 1854, and the cornerstone was laid in October of 1870. All of the paintings and drawings that currently hang in Memorial Hall relate to the Civil War period.

During Eliot's administration, another college was founded several blocks north of Harvard Yard. This college, originally called the Society for the Collegiate Instruction of Women, later became Radcliffe College (p. 44).

PRESIDENT LOWELL

Abbot Lawrence Lowell succeeded Eliot as president in 1909. Lowell, a former lawyer and professor of government, reinforced the concepts of a residential college and a complete liberal arts education. The endowment increased by more than $100 million, and more buildings were erected in this period than during the entire preceding history of the University, including the newly founded Graduate School of Education. In 1928, Edward S. Harkness, a Yale graduate, gave Harvard $10 million for the establishment of the seven Georgian residential houses near the Charles River (p. 123).

300 YEARS

Harvard's 300th anniversary was celebrated in 1936 with the opening of the New Yard, called "Tercentenary Theater." The New Yard, now home to Convocation in September and Commencement exercises in June, is bounded by Sever Hall, Widener Library, University Hall, and Memorial Church, which was dedicated on Armistice Day 1932.

President Eliot, Harvard Art Museums/Fogg Museum, Harvard University Portrait Collection, Gift of Uriel H. Crocker, Arthur T. Lyman, and other members of the Class of 1853 to Harvard College, 1876, H86

ARCHITECTURAL SPOTLIGHT: MARBLE DRAGON STATUE

It was also on the occasion of the Tercentenary Celebration that the marble dragon statue in front of Boylston Hall was presented to Harvard by Fred Sze, President of the Harvard Club of Shanghai, on behalf of Harvard alumni in China. Carved during the reign of Emperor Chiach'ing (1796-1820), the statue was originally presented by the emperor to one of his provincial governors as a mark of imperial favor and appreciation. Today, the phallic statue spends most of the year hidden from view, wrapped up to protect it from the elements.

FRESHMAN DEAN'S OFFICE

The marble dragon statue with Widener Library in background.

WORLD WAR II

During World War II, Harvard became a great center for research and training. Thirty five percent of Harvard's faculty were on active duty during the war. Back on campus, many others conducted research vital to the war effort. Loeb House, the residence of Harvard Presidents from 1909-1971, was used by the Navy for the offices of the V-12 School. The building was run as a ship: men stood 24hr. watches and classes for the midshipmen were held over the same mahogany tables at which the Board of Overseers had dined in years past. Misbehaving seamen were assigned to scrub the "deck" (the oak floors) and polish the "brightwork" (the gold mirrors). The seamen must have neglected their duties, however; when the Navy moved out, the University had to spend $50,000 to "sweep out the cigarette butts and clean the poetry off the bathroom walls."

GROWING AND DIVERSIFYING

During the second half of the 20th century Harvard actively worked to end its reputation as a bastion of white male elitists and became truly notable for its promotion of diversity in all realms. During this period Harvard also experienced remarkable monetary and infrastructural growth.

During World War II President James Bryant Conant oversaw the integration of classes between Harvard and Radcliffe. As far as we know, the boys

FUN FACT

What does it take to teach a class at Harvard? Tweed suits and bowties? Glasses resting on a perpetually upturned nose? Try LSD and a criminal record. Timothy Leary, a former lecturer in clinical psychology, is most famous for his promotion and endorsement of acid. This interest did not, however, lead to tenure at the (otherwise quite liberal) university. In 1963, after Leary had spent five years at Harvard, President Pusey announced that his salary would be terminated because he had "failed to keep his classroom appointments and has absented himself from Cambridge without permission."

The real reason for Leary's dismissal was most likely his study and use of LSD and other psychedelic drugs. Leary famously bragged that he had learned more about his brain in the hours after taking mushrooms than he had in his entire career of studying psychology. Some have even suggested that Leary brought underground drugs to Harvard through his academic work—so many volunteered to participate as subjects in Leary's research that some had to be turned away, a rare problem for research psychologists to grapple with. To fulfill the remaining curiosities, a black market for psychedelics took shape on campus.

Three years after leaving Harvard, Leary founded the League for Spiritual Discovery, a religion that encouraged its followers to take LSD. (Conveniently, the League shared an acronym with its holy sacrament.) Following his 1969 arrest in California for possession of marijuana, Leary brought his case to the Supreme Court and successfully argued that the Marijuana Tax Act was unconstitutional. Leary died in 1996, and in 1997 some of his ashes were sent into space.

weren't too upset to come home from war and find women in their classes. Helen Keller, the world-famous pioneer of handicapped learning, graduated from Radcliffe College in 1908, and received an honorary degree from Harvard in 1955, becoming the first woman to gain such a distinction. President Conant also worked to promote National Scholarships for talented students without the financial means to afford a college education, a commitment that Harvard has continued to uphold.

President Nathan Marsh Pusey, inaugurated in 1953, initiated what would become a $20 million campaign, the Program for Harvard College, to increase Harvard's endowment and make higher education a reality for a much broader demographic of students. It also funded the construction of three new under-

ARCHITECTURAL SPOTLIGHT: THE CAMBRIDGE FIREHOUSE

In 1933, the City of Cambridge purchased a small triangle of land between Broadway and Cambridge Streets from Harvard, seeing the site as a perfect location for a firehouse. In the terms of the sale, Harvard stipulated that the firehouse be built in the expensive Neo-Georgian style in order to fit in with the overall aesthetic of the campus.

SCOTT YIM

Harvard's extravagant architecture came back to haunt it in September of 1956, when the tower of Memorial Hall burst into flames. The Cambridge Fire Department, just across the street, was unable to extinguish the fire right away because the bell tower was taller than its ladders, and the tower clock was destroyed.

graduate houses, William James Hall, the Holyoke Center, and many more invaluable additions to the College and Graduate School campuses. In 1965, the endowment reached $1 billion.

PUSEY AND PROTEST

Pusey began his presidency with political controversy when he and Senator McCarthy publicly clashed, making national news headlines. McCarthy is quoted saying of Pusey, "He is what could best be described as a rabid anti-anti-Communist." It wasn't until the end of his tenure that Pusey was forced to contend with political clashes within the Harvard community. On April 8, 1969, 300 members of Harvard's chapter of Students for a Democratic Society (SDS), a prominent national anti-war group, tacked a list of demands to the door of President Pusey's home. These demands included the dissolution of Harvard's Reserve Officers' Training Corps (ROTC), the lowering of rents on Harvard-owned apartments in Cambridge, and the prevention of demolishing residential areas in Boston's low-income neighborhoods for the building of new Harvard complexes. On April 9, 30 students invaded University Hall and forcibly removed all Harvard faculty and administrators, including physically lifting Dean Archie Epps and carrying him down the stairs. By the

FUN FACT

John F. Kennedy, Class of 1940, spent his freshman year in Weld Hall. When the President returned to Harvard in February 1961 for a Board of Overseers meeting, he had just completed a campaign that pointed out the need for a national "depressed-areas" bill. Accordingly, the students of Weld—which badly needed renovation—greeted the President-elect with a sign that read, "Jack, Weld is a depressed area."

same evening approximately 500 students had joined the protestors inside the building. The next night 400 police officers broke up the protest and arrested approximately 100 students. While the majority faced minor criminal charges, 23 were suspended from the University, and three students were permanently expelled. Though not the first public protest in Harvard's long history, it was undoubtedly a national news story that brought enormous attention and pressure on Pusey; he announced an early retirement in February 1970.

PRESIDENTS BOK AND RUDENSTINE

Derek Bok transitioned from Dean of Harvard Law School to President of the University in 1971. Bok is remembered for both the creation of the Core Curriculum and his commitment to diversity in Harvard admissions. Thanks to Bok, Harvard's financial aid policy has been equal-access and gender blind since 1975; he revolutionarily advocated for equal numbers of male and fe-

President Conant, Harvard University
Archives, HUP Conant, James B. (39)

FUN FACT

Perhaps the most famous film shot on Harvard's campus was the 1970 tearjerker *Love Story,* written by Erich Segal '58. In the film, Emerson Hall home to the Philosophy Department in the New Yard, is called Barrett Hall after the main character, Oliver Barrett IV.

The movie was filmed amid protests at the height of the "peace and love" era at Harvard. In order to capture the aristocratic, old-boy Harvard that Segal had envisioned, the actual Harvard student popula- tion was seques- tered in their dormitories while preppily clad ex- tras milled around the Yard for the filming. Popular frustra- tion among stu- dents at the time

FELIX COOK

Crimson Key Society students promoting their viewing of Love Story

led to a ban on filming movies on Harvard's campus, this prohibition lasted until 2007, when *The Great Debaters* was shot in Sanders Theater. Most films supposedly set at Harvard are actually shot in cities like To- ronto or colleges like UCLA and John Hopkins University, or even prep schools like Phillips Andover. At Harvard, it has become an annual tradi- tion for the Crimson Key Society to dress up in 1970s attire, screen *Love Story,* while providing a mocking commentary for the amusement of the incoming freshman class.

male students on campus. In 1979 Bok announced the Harvard Campaign, the largest capital campaign in Harvard's history. In the 1980s, with Bok's sup- port, funding and initiatives for the arts expanded, including the arrival of the American Repertory Theater (p. 193).

President Neil L. Rudenstine was inaugurated in 1991 and served Harvard through the turn of the century. Rudentstine continued to increase the endow- ment and increase both undergraduate and graduate financial aid. He also worked to unite the different schools and departments of Harvard into a more cohesive institution through University-wide academic planning. Harvard became deeply committed to research funding, resulting in the development of a new Cholera vaccine at Harvard Medical School in 1995. Under Rudenstine, Radcliffe and Harvard officially merged into a single institution—now both male and female graduates receive a Harvard diploma at Commencement instead of the "Harvard-Radcliffe" co-signed diploma given to previous female graduates.

RECENT HISTORY

PRESIDENT SUMMERS

The most controversial President in recent Harvard history, Lawrence Summers led the University until 2006 when he resigned in the wake of a lack-of-confidence vote by Harvard faculty. Unfortunately, Summers' tenure has been tainted by a series of controversies that have come to overshadow his numerous accomplishments while in office.

In October 2001, Summers famously condemned African-American Studies Professor Cornel West, alleging that his rap album was an embarrassment to a university that prides itself on intellectual rigor and scholarship. Summers also reproached West for canceling classes for three weeks to work on Bill Bradley's presidential campaign, and complained that he was contributing to grade inflation. West subsequently left Harvard for Princeton.

Summers became the subject of public controversy again in January 2005 when, at a Conference on Diversifying the Science & Engineering Workforce organized by the National Bureau of Economic Research, he addressed the question of why women are underrepresented among science and engineering faculty at universities and research institutions. In the previous year, men accounted for 28 of 32 faculty tenure appointments at Harvard. Among the potential explanations that Summers suggested for this imbalance, he cited "issues of intrinsic aptitude, and particularly of the variability of aptitude." This suggestion immediately drew accusations of sexism, spurring public controversy.

On March 15, 2005, members of the Faculty of Arts and Sciences declared their "lack of confidence" in Summers' leadership in a vote of 218 to 185, with 18 abstentions. Among Summers' defenders was popular psychologist Steven Pinker. In an interview with *The Harvard Crimson*, in which he was asked if Summers's remarks were "within the pale of legitimate academic discourse," Pinker replied: "Good grief, shouldn't everything be within the pale of legitimate academic discourse, as long as it is presented with some degree of rigor? That's the difference between a university and a madrassa." Many members of the Harvard Corporation also jumped to Summers's defense, with the notable exception of board member Conrad Harper, who resigned in protest in July 2005. Among students, Summers enjoyed the support of the majority: according to one *Crimson* poll, 57% of students opposed his resignation, while only 19% supported it.

A third issue of concern among Harvard faculty members was Summers' support of economist Andrei Shleifer, who was accused of using his knowledge of the Russian economy to make lucrative personal investments despite leading a Harvard group under contract with the U.S. government to advise the Russian government. According to a January 2006 article in *Institutional Investor*, Summers protected Shleifer from disciplinary action by the University.

Summers' tenure was not without its successes, however. Among his accomplishments was a series of building projects, including the 2003 opening of the largest building in the school's history—the $260 million, 525,000 square foot New Research Building at the Harvard Medical School. Other building projects included the Center for Government and International Studies (CGIS), the New College Theater, and the Laboratory for Integrated Science and Engineering. During this time, Harvard was also accumulating land in Allston, which it plans to eventually transform into new University facilities.

Summers also expanded Harvard's international reach and significantly increased financial aid, both for undergraduates from low-income families with the implementation of the Harvard Financial Aid Initiative in 2004 and for graduate and professional students pursuing careers in public service.

On February 21, 2006, Summers announced his intention to resign, and June 30, 2006 marked his last day in office. Former University President Derek Bok was called upon to serve as Interim President while the University undertook a nationwide search for a new President, and Summers, for his part, was awarded the Charles W. Eliot University Professorship.

"Believing deeply that complacency is among the greatest risks facing Harvard, I have sought for the last five years to prod and challenge the University to reach for the most ambitious goals in creative ways," Summers said in a statement when he resigned. Summers served as the Director of the National Economic Council under Barack Obama's administration until November 2010. He then returned to Harvard and resumed his post at the Kennedy School of Government.

PRESIDENT FAUST

Enter President Drew Gilpin Faust. A calm, well-liked consensus builder, Faust could hardly paint more of a contrast to her predecessor. So far, President Faust's tenure has primarily involved coping with the financial crisis, but she has also increased Harvard's commitment to undergraduate financial aid and turned her attention to arts at the University.

Faust took office as Harvard's 28th President—and first female head—on July 1, 2007. A historian of the Civil War and the American South, Faust had previously served as the founding Dean of the Radcliffe Institute for Advanced Study. Prior to taking her position at Radcliffe, Faust was a professor of history and director of the Women's Studies Program at the University of Pennsylvania, where she taught for 25 years. Born in New York City and raised in Virginia's Shenandoah Valley, Faust graduated magna cum laude from Bryn Mawr in 1968, before earning her Ph.D. in American civilization from the University of Pennsylvania in 1975. Faust has written six books, including her most recent, *This Republic of Suffering: Death and the American Civil War*, which the *New York Times* hailed as one of the "10 Best Books of 2008." President Faust is married to Charles Rosenberg, a professor in the History of Science Department at Harvard; they have two daughters.

In January 2011 the University launched "Harvard on the Move," a Faust-sponsored initiative to promote exercise and health awareness on campus. The program organizes community walks and runs around Cambridge and Boston, and faculty lectures on nutrition and exercise evolution.

President Faust has been spotlighted for her decision to end Harvard's 40 year ban on the ROTC program. In March 2011, following the December repeal of the "Don't Ask Don't Tell" Policy that prevented openly gay or lesbian Americans from military service, Faust announced the return of the ROTC program to Harvard. Faust has also worked hard to continue the popular support of the "Green is the New Crimson" sustainability movement inspired by Al Gore's visit to campus in 2008.

HARVARD'S EXPANSION INTO ALLSTON

On June 2, 2005, Harvard released a report outlining options for a major expansion of its Allston campus—which is currently home to the Business School, the Harvard Stadium and gym facilities, and IT services—that would feature new sites for at least four new undergraduate houses, new academic buildings for the Graduate Schools of Education and Public Health, a massive new science complex, and the Harvard Stem Cell Institute.

This expansion would be no simple feat. Not only would it require space—which would be created by moving existing houses and stores—but Harvard would also have to create a new transportation system. Among the proposed solutions are a bridge between Winthrop House and Harvard Business School, a tunnel extension from the bus and subway station in Harvard Square under the river to Allston, and two pedestrian bridges flanking the Lars Anderson Bridge.

Alas, as Harvard's endowment shrank dramatically in the fall of 2008, so too did its enthusiasm for the Allston expansion. In February of 2009, President Drew Faust issued a letter in which she announced that Harvard would put its building plans on hold and reassess the Allston project goals for financial viability at a future date.

Progress has since resumed but the original projected completion dates of the new complexes, labs and residential buildings are being pushed further into the future. The Harvard Allston Work Team, a group of 14 Harvard faculty members and administrators, published a letter in September 2011 which detailed plans for a Health and Life Sciences Center as well as proposed construction on a residential and retail complex. Allston residents have expressed continued frustration at the lack of concrete information available about the Expansion project and the current vacant lots and abandoned construction sites. However, President Faust has continued to declare Harvard's commitment to completing projects that will benefit both the Allston and Harvard communities.

ADMISSIONS AND DIVERSITY

AT HARVARD

IT'S TRAINING MEN:
EARLY HARVARD ADMISSIONS

High grades, perfect SAT scores, glowing recommendations, extracurricular activities, a significant experience to write about in the personal essay, and an intriguing interview. That's a start. For the most part, though, admission to Harvard remains clouded in mystery. What do admissions officers really care about? Do they want legacies, athletes, geniuses, or something completely different? How do these gurus decide who gets in and who gets sent the solemn envelope framing the five little words that crush dreams: "We regret to inform you…"?

Harvard is a subject of interest and speculation for a number of reasons, but the shrouded admissions process is probably the one that is most analyzed, debated, and criticized. "What is that X factor that got you into Harvard?" many visitors ask their student guides as they are led through the Old Yard. Most reply that there is no single qualification that gets you into Harvard. Indeed, the Harvard College admissions process involves multiple essays, an interview for most candidates, teacher recommendations, and an all-in-all thorough review of an immense number of qualified candidates by the committee. Harvard's admissions website states:

Applicants can distinguish themselves for admission in a number of ways. Some show unusual academic promise through experience or achievements in study or research. Many are "well rounded" and have contributed in various ways to the lives of their schools or communities. Others are "well lopsided" with demonstrated excellence in a particular endeavor—academic, extracurricular or otherwise. Still others bring perspectives formed by unusual personal circumstances or experiences.

BY THE NUMBERS

6.2	Percent of Harvard College freshmen ('15) applicants that were accepted: 2,158 from a total of 34,950
25	Religions represented by Harvard chaplains, from Buddhists to Zoroastrians
61	Percent of Class of 2015 freshmen receiving financial aid
85	Home countries represented by the Class of 2015

In the end, only about 6% of freshmen applicants are admitted (even less for transfer applicants); almost all are in the top 10-15% of their graduating high school classes. It is clear that the admissions office seeks to create a unique freshman class, and with the help of a huge financial aid initiative, Harvad has been able to produce previously unprecedented diversity on campus.

FINANCIAL AID

Harvard's commitment to a diverse, qualified student body is exemplified in its robust financial aid policy. The first American university to introduce financial aid, Harvard has consistently awarded more financial aid each year than any other private university worldwide. In 1643, Lady Anne Radcliffe Mowlson (p. 7) gave £100 to Harvard to pay for the tuition of students with limited means, marking the first recorded issuance of financial aid in America.

Actual money was scarce in the colonies, perhaps because the New World lacked a mint, and "tuition" often meant payment in agricultural products, boots, hardware, and other useful commodities.

Harvard has been higher education's most prolific sugar daddy for centuries. In the 1700s, Harvard provided over a third of its student body with financial aid packages. Around the turn of the 20th century, Harvard created the Winter Coat Fund, which still exists today, to provide funding to low-income students for winter clothes. In 1934, Harvard President James Bryant Conant established the National Scholarship Program, dramatically expanding Harvard's ability to enroll students with limited financial means.

Today, Harvard is one of only six colleges that offers need-blind admissions and full-need financial aid to all of its students both American and international, along with Dartmouth, MIT, Princeton, Yale, and Amherst. "Need-blind admissions" is a policy of admitting applicants regardless of their financial background, while "full-need" financial aid means the college meets what it determines to be the full economic need of the admitted student through scholarship aid. Of these colleges, Harvard was the first to offer need-blind admissions and full-need financial aid to international students.

In 2007, Harvard College announced sweeping changes to its financial aid plan. Families earning under $60,000 are no longer expected to contribute anything toward their child's tuition. The only small contribution requested is from students themselves, who are asked to come up with between $2000 and $3000, which they can do by applying for scholarships, working, or requesting a loan. Families earning anywhere from $60,000 to $180,000 per year contribute as little as 0% and at most 10% of their annual income. Moreover, student loans have been eliminated such that no student will graduate in debt due to obligatory loans. In 2011-2012, Harvard College awarded $166 million in financial aid to over 60% of its students, with over 20% of students required to pay nothing at all. The admissions office website states: "It now costs the same or less for 90 percent of families in the U.S. to send their daughters or sons to Harvard than to their flagship public university."

However, this commitment to diversity and expanded opportunity was not the case throughout most of Harvard's history.

DIVERSIFYING

For the first two centuries of Harvard's history, the student body was fairly homogenous. The Harvard type of yore is a caricature by today's standards. White, Protestant, and male, yesteryear's Ivy Leaguer had the time and the resources to put "work" aside and hit the books.

Thanks to the leadership of Charles William Eliot (p. 22), who served as Harvard's President from 1869 to 1909, the University entered the 20th century as one of the most diverse academic institutions in the country. President Eliot firmly believed that "the poorest and the richest students are equally welcome here, provided that with their poverty or their wealth they bring capacity, ambition, and purity." As socioeconomic diversity at Harvard increased, however, distinctions between the rich and poor only grew starker. Wealthy students with eyes for opulence lived along the "Gold Coast", the strip of luxurious apartments on Mount Auburn Street, while the less affluent students retreated to the Yard—a middle-class sanctuary that generally lacked heating and plumbing.

Although Eliot made great efforts to make the University accessible for everyone, many wished for it to remain a place for the wealthy, Protestant white men with whom the University had an extensive history. The admissions process in the early 1900s reflected this: although the only requirement was to pass a simple entrance exam, Harvard reserved the right to admit on "conditions." That is, if you could not pass this exam, Harvard could admit you on other grounds. By 1907, more than 55% of the student body represented such "conditional acceptances." Furthermore, the entrance exam was based on a traditional curriculum that included Latin and Greek, languages taught only in private schools.

Despite these conditions, President Eliot made the admissions process far more open and welcoming than it had ever been before. In the years immediately after his resignation, it seemed as if his successor, President Abbott Lawrence Lowell, would do the same. Lowell instituted the "New Plan," which, in its repeal of Greek and Latin entrance prerequisites, better served the interests of public school students. By 1913 New Plan students outnumbered Old Plan Students. Despite the increased openness of admission policies, poor and rich students ate separately, lived separately, and mixed in different social circles. Former President Eliot complained about the "snobbish separation" that the New Plan was creating on campus. Furthermore, President Lowell's implied promise of diversity quickly turned sour as his anxieties about the changing character of the "Harvard man" led to secrets and scandal.

BUILDING "CHARACTER"

PRESIDENT LOWELL, LIES, AND SCANDAL

In the early decades of the 20th century, World War I and the subsequent Red Scare contributed to the growth of a particularly paranoid brand of American anti-Semitism to which even Harvard, the seat of American intellectualism, was not immune. President Lowell worried that an influx of Jewish Harvard students would scare off other top applicants. Lowell bluntly remarked that his ideal action in the face of growing religious diversity would be "to state frankly that we thought we could do the most good by not admitting more than a certain proportion of men in a group that did not intermingle with the rest, and give our reasons for it to the public." Lowell was convinced that the "Jewish Problem" could be swept under the carpet by implementing a discreet quota. To Lowell's outrage and dismay, the number of Jews on campus expanded. By the spring of 1922, more than 20% of the student body was Jewish.

Under Lowell's guidance, the Committee on Admission and the Harvard faculty passed a motion in a 56-44 vote that required faculty to "take into account the... proportionate size of racial and national groups in the membership of Harvard College." Lowell got his way, marking a dramatic departure from Harvard's commitment to non-discrimination.

CONTINUED ADMISSIONS PROFILING

Lowell's new admission standards quickly took root. When the explicit quota system became too overt, the admissions office created in 1922 what would become the standard for admissions at colleges all across the country: a definition of merit based on character and background, not just academics. Just as prospective students today submit personal essays, letters of recommendation, and family histories, applicants to Harvard in the 1920s and 1930s were required to answer questions on race, religious affiliation, mother's maiden

President Lowell. Harvard University Archives, HUP Lowell, Abbott Lawrence (17)

ALUMNI ILLUMINATED

Though far from an exhaustive list, famous LGBT Harvard alumni include poet and philosopher George Santayana, New York City Ballet founder Lincoln Kirstein, composer and conductor Leonard Bernstein, and poets John Ashberry and Frank O'Hara.

name, and father's birthplace. Moreover, admissions officers focused on selecting applicants who they presumed would become "successful members of the University," institutionalizing an intangible admissions standard that essentially gave Harvard free reign to exclude and include according to its will. To complete the profiling process, admissions even began to require that applicants submit a personal photograph.

A GOOD MAN IS HARD TO FIND

Character, according to President Lowell, could not simply be defined as "not Jewish." Of course, the man had to meet some other standards as well. Wilbur Bender, Dean of Admissions under Lowell, touted loud and clear that the future of Harvard— its academic prestige, superiority to Princeton and Yale, and reputation for inspiring awe in outsiders —rested squarely on the shoulders of the Crimson football team. Bent on admitting "the boy with some athletic interests and abilities, the boy with physical vigor and coordination and grace," Bender dreaded athletic inferiority that would result in "no college spirit, few good fellows, and no vigorous, healthy social life... [and a] surfeit of pansies, decadent esthetes and precious sophisticates." This standard, in accordance with an unfortunate stereotype, did not bode well for Harvard's gay population, many of whom were actually singled out and expelled under President Lowell.

In 2002, the *Crimson* broke a shocking story of Harvard's previous efforts to purge itself of character detritus. Between 1920 and 1930, President Lowell played a game of cat and mouse with suspected homosexuals on campus. Following the suicide of a student expelled for academic failures, evidence of homosexual fraternization at Harvard dormitories (and in Boston apartment buildings) was uncovered in personal correspondence and caught the attention of the President. In almost complete secrecy, Lowell and a court of College administrators interrogated dozens of young men known to have been associated with the deceased student. The court exacted punishments on the young men depending on their suspected knowledge of homosexual practices. In some cases, this knowledge alone could warrant suspension, while homosexual conduct resulted in immediate expulsion from the University. Lowell's coercive questioning implicated dozens of men in alleged homosexual affiliations.

BGLTQ ON CAMPUS TODAY

Fortunately, President Lowell's views of and actions towards homosexuality have are a distant memory. Today, the Harvard College Queer Students and Allies (QSA) strives to create a community for bisexual, gay, lesbian, transgender, and queer students at the University. Aiming to provide outlets for expression, visibility, and support, the QSA hosts cultural and political events, dances, and formal talks and lectures pertaining to contemporary queer issues. The Harvard Gay and Lesbian Caucus (HGLC), now with a membership of over 5000 alumni, was formed in 1984 with the intention of including queer interests in all aspects of University administration and cultural life. Since their successful push for the inclusion of sexual orientation in the school's anti-discrimination measures, the group has seen the appointment of openly gay deans and administrators. In 1998 Professor Diana Eck and her partner Dorothy Austin were appointed as the College's first same-sex housemasters. Ironically, they now live in and oversee the residential House named after President Lowell. The Dean of Harvard College, Evelynn Hammonds, who is openly gay herself recently created a lounge and office space for BGLTQ students in Boylston Hall in Harvard Yard.

RACIAL POLICY AND CHANGE

AN OVERVIEW

There is no evidence that Harvard had a quota system in place for African Americans similar to the one it had for Jews in the late 1930s. The number of African Americans who could afford to apply to and attend Harvard remained relatively low. Between 1870 (when the first black student graduated) and 1941, only 165 African Americans graduated from the College. Once admitted, black students often received anything but a warm welcome, and segregation on campus was an established part of student life.

As World War II came to an end and the United States government issued the GI Bill, the number of applicants to Harvard surged, forcing the University to rethink its admissions standards. In a series of articles in the *Harvard Alumni Bulletin*, Provost Paul Buck and Dean of the College Wilbur Bender stated that Harvard's admissions ideology was one that "attaches much weight to character, personality, and breadth of interest…students are not accepted on the basis of scholarly attainment alone." Some argued that such language simply allowed the University to continue to favor the wealthy, athletes, and students whose parents had gone to Harvard on the basis of "character."

Harvard's discriminatory admissions policies did not go unnoticed. In October 1946, several Jewish alumni wrote to President Conant warning him that these policies would undoubtedly become problematic. That same year, the State of Massachusetts passed the Fair Employment Practice Law, which made it illegal for institutions to discriminate on the basis of religion, race,

FUN FACT

While the Ford Report was a step in the right direction, it wasn't a cure-all. One scheme used to "rate" applicants for admissions was a 12-category system that included evaluations like: "A. All-American—healthy, uncomplicated athletic strengths and style, perhaps some extracurricular participation, but not combined with top academic credentials;" or "W. Mr. School—significant extracurricular and perhaps (but not necessarily) athletic participation plus excellent academic record;" or "B. Boondocket—unsophisticated rural background." With minor modifications this system remained in place until at least 1988.

or national origin. Three years later, the Fair Education Practices Law was passed, prohibiting discrimination at educational institutions. As a result of World War II, Anti-Semitism was increasingly discouraged in American society, and although Harvard denied ever having had such an admissions policy at the time, it quietly told its admissions office that things had to change.

Another political turn of events caused Harvard to address its admissions process again: Russia's launch of Sputnik. It became increasingly important that America maintain a competitive edge in the arms and technology race during the Cold War. Government contributions to higher education increased substantially, and at Harvard, federal support increased from $36 million in 1953 to $100 million in 1964. Admissions came under even closer scrutiny; nevertheless, in 1958, 20% of entering freshmen were legacies, and athletes were still strongly favored.

The winds of change were felt most significantly in Harvard's Ford Report. Issued on April 11, 1960, this report was the first document issued by a university that wrote frankly about "the Jewish Problem" and advocated real solutions. It stated that the Harvard "philosophy of admission must preclude without qualifications, any discrimination against a boy on the basis of his ethnic background, his religion, or his family's station in life." Additionally, Harvard admissions took a decidedly more inclusive step forward: the University increased financial aid, awarding some aid to 29% of its students.

THE CIVIL RIGHTS MOVEMENT

As had often been the case in Harvard's past, real change to policy came from a social movement outside the University. The assassination of Martin Luther King, Jr. in 1968 precipitated a crisis that shook the Harvard into action. Within a month, Chase Peterson, the new Dean of Admissions, announced Harvard's commitment to enrolling a higher number of black students. The next class included 90 African Americans, 76% more than in the previous year. By 1970 Harvard's incoming class included not only African Americans but also Latinos, Native Americans, and Asian Americans.

Although Harvard was making strides to diversify its student body, it was simultaneously receiving criticism for its policy of affirmative action. In July 1988 the Office of Civil Rights began an investigation into the treatment of Asian American applicants at Harvard. The investigation found that, although Harvard evaluated white and Asian applicants through the same process, the rating system included two "tips" or "plus factors" that disfavored Asians: athletics and legacies. The Admissions Office's commitment to these two factors largely damaged Harvard's image as a university dedicated to equal opportunity. In notes on admissions office records, these biases are apparent.

Harvard justified its policy by claiming that alumni helped with recruiting, both financially and by volunteering, and that rejecting their sons and daughters might mean these resources were revoked. Harvard also pointed out that "alumni provide the bulk of scholarship funds provided for all students," an important fact for Harvard's growing endowment. As for athletes, Harvard argued that it could not run varsity level teams without robust recruiting. Preference to athletes was only given, according to Harvard, in the same way that non-athletes were given preference in other areas of strength.

DIVERSITY ON CAMPUS TODAY

The Harvard Foundation for Intercultural and Race Relations was founded in 1981 at the recommendation of a committee made up of faculty and students. The Harvard Foundation aims to foster and encourage intercultural exchange though scholarly programming and, most visibly, its annual Cultural Rhythms celebration. Every year for the past 30 years, Cultural Rhythms has invited student groups that celebrate a diversity of culture (traditional dancers, musicians, and performers, for example) to perform onstage alongside a prominent Artist of the Year. In recent years, Artists of the Year have included Will Smith, Denzel Washington, Salma Hayek, and Shakira.

Additionally, dozens of student groups celebrate racial diversity on campus. The list is exhaustive, and just about every different cultural and ethnic group is represented. Organizations range from the Black Men's Forum, which emphasizes "brotherhood, manhood, and fidelity" in Harvard's black community, to Fuerza Latina, which aims to creative visibility for Latinos on campus, to the Romanian Association, the Han Ma-Eum Korean Drum Troupe, and the Texas Club.

RADCLIFFE AND THE LADIES OF THE LEAGUE

FROM ANNEX TO ADVANCED STUDY: AN OVERVIEW

Women have always been closely associated with Harvard University—in the days of yore, they married Harvard men, cooked for them, and bore them children. More than 250 years after the founding of Harvard College on the divine principles of manliness and money, the ladies of Cambridge finally received a slice of the United States's most prized academic pie. Radcliffe, once Harvard College's sister school and now a center for interdisciplinary academic work, is the historical marker of the feminine experience at Harvard. Radcliffe's journey as an institution is exemplary of Harvard's steady (though sometimes slow) march toward all-around diversity in education.

In 1879, Elizabeth Cary Agassiz, wife of naturalist and Harvard Museum founder Louis Agassiz, took it upon herself to create an opportunity for bright young women to receive a Harvard-level collegiate education. Agassiz's intention was not to give the chosen women a Harvard experience; on the contrary, this was a move toward individual opportunity and not an attempt to force co-education upon the University. As such, Agassiz founded the Society for the Collegiate Instruction of Women (known "affectionately" as the Harvard Annex), and held courses in the home of Mr. and Mrs. James Carret at 6 Appian Way, just a few streets away from Harvard Yard. The Society quickly grew too large for its domestic boundaries, and in 1894 the Commonwealth of Massachusetts recognized Agassiz's Annex project as Radcliffe College, named for Ann Radcliffe, Lady Mowlson, Harvard's first female benefactor. The College adopted the Radcliffe coat of arms as its own.

Radcliffe continued along on its own for the early part of the 20th century. It collected its own tuition, established its own real estate holdings, and developed its own housing practices, but its educational opportunities were still explicitly linked to Harvard. To bring any kind of respect and prestige to Radcliffe must have been a frustrating undertaking—though Harvard professors taught Radcliffe courses, Harvard experienced intense internal dissent regarding the education of women. Some professors and administrators spoke out against the education of women or against the joint- and co-education programs that loomed on the horizon. To further complicate matters, the Harvard lecturers upon whom Radcliffe depended were often far from enthusiastic about teaching the same courses at both institutions. Radcliffe's leadership had to coerce disdainful professors into teaching young women, and these professors were often more than willing to call it quits between and during semesters. Negotiation and bartering marked the early days of Radcliffe, and it wasn't until the 1940s that moods began to shift.

ARCHITECTURAL SPOTLIGHT:
FAY HOUSE

Fay House was originally built in 1807 by Nathaniel Ireland, a prosperous local artisan, and named for the Fay family who had owned the house from 1835 to 1885. In 1885, the Society for the Collegiate Instruction of Women bought the house for $20,000 from Miss Maria Fay, daughter of Judge Samuel Phillips Prescott Fay, a Harvard graduate and overseer.

The Fay House of today is much larger than the house Judge Fay sold to The Society. Originally a two-story building, Fay House's third floor was added in 1890 to provide room for the Radcliffe Library. At the same time, a wing was added to the Yard side of the original structure, doubling the available space. Two years later, yet another wing was added to

ALEXANDRA DOWD

accommodate a small auditorium and several classrooms. Fay House has remained largely unchanged since then.

In the early years of Radcliffe College, Fay House constituted the entire College, except for student housing. As the College grew, however, it spilled out of Fay House, and today it is primarily devoted to the administrative offices of the Radcliffe Institute for Advanced Study.

THE PETTICOAT INVASION

During World War II, a dearth of professors and male students on campus instigated a push toward offering classes to men and women at the same time. As might be expected, concerns from the practical to the wildly presumptuous characterized the transition. Noted Harvard historian Samuel Eliot Morison, for

ARCHITECTURAL SPOTLIGHT: SCHLESINGER LIBRARY

Radcliffe's Schlesinger Library was founded in 1943. The collection's inaugural contents included the suffrage papers of Maud Park, a Boston-born and Radcliffe-educated activist for women's rights. She served in both the American Women Suffrage Association and the League of Women's Voters.

example, maintained that men and women learned differently—or, more accurately, he maintained that men learn better than women. Morison propagated the belief that men grasped ideals while women grasped only insignificant and out-of-context details. He "proved" this theory to himself when he tricked a classroom of women into taking down the line: "In 1492…Captain John Smith sailed across the ocean and set foot on the coast of Massachusetts."

Realistically, Harvard envisioned more practical problems in what was fast becoming a joint-education program. Would girls be too nervous to speak up in front of Harvard boys? Would the Harvard boys have a hard time concentrating on their coursework while surrounded by legions of bespectacled sirens? Would these ladies of learning inspire restraint, preventing professors from working themselves up into didactic tizzies? As a 1954 article in the *Saturday Evening Post* titled "They're Using Lipstick at Harvard Now" asked, "How has this petticoat invasion worked out? Is it true that girls are people, even in Cambridge?"

For the Radcliffe girls, the "invasion" worked out pretty well. By 1963, Radcliffe students began receiving Harvard-Radcliffe degrees, and by 1970 the first Harvard-Radcliffe Commencement ceremony graduated a class of jointly educated students together.

In the classroom, girls were thought to challenge and improve the conscientiousness of their male counterparts. To the claim that women would be too shy to participate in front of men in class, one Radcliffe woman replied, "Cliffites don't speak up unless they have something to say, whereas the Harvards show no such reluctance."

Now that women were educated at Harvard, Radcliffe suffered an identity crisis. In 1999, Radcliffe and Harvard officially merged, and the Radcliffe Institute for Advanced Study at Harvard was born. The Institute, now about 10 years old, supports scholars in a range of fields and offers a series of open lectures and conferences each year.

WOMEN AT HARVARD TODAY

Women at Harvard currently account for 50% of the undergraduate student body, 47% of all graduate students, and 48% of first professional degree students. Notably, 39% of the Harvard Business School Class of 2013 is made up of women. Drew Gilpin Faust is Harvard's first female President (p. 32) and currently about 27% of the university-wide Harvard faculty are female.

Harvard Undergraduate Women in Business (WIB) is the largest undergraduate business organization on campus with over 300 members. Through panels, conferences, outreach initiatives, skill-building workshops, leadership projects, and mentorship programs, WIB seeks to expose undergraduate women to a variety of business experiences, issues, and careers.

The Harvard College Women's Center, located in the basement of Canaday Hall, hosts a wide range of programs addressing women's and gender issues at Harvard and beyond. The Center provides information on a variety of issues and centralizes references to existing campus resources. It aims to support Harvard women by linking female faculty, alumnae, and current students through conferences, workshops, mentorships, meals, and networking events.

MARIANNA VERLAGE
The Seneca's crest

The Seneca, named after the Seneca Falls Convention of 1848, is a female service and social organization founded in 1999 as a response to the male-dominated social sphere of final clubs at Harvard. The group, however, was not meant to be a female version of the male final clubs; rather, it sought to provide a support network for its members while also being an active force in the un-

ARCHITECTURAL SPOTLIGHT: STRAUS HALL

Three Harvard brothers built Straus Hall to commemorate their parents, Isadore and Ida Straus, whose lives were claimed in the sinking of the *Titanic*. Standing in the southwest corner of the Old Yard, Straus was the last freshman dormitory to become co-educational, and it is one of the few freshman dorms that has never undergone renovation.

SCOTT YIM

dergraduate community through hosting social events and speakers. Because it is a single-sex organization, the Seneca remains unrecognized by the University, similar to the final clubs and Greek organizations on campus (p. 153).

RELIGION

It is a common perception that Harvard University was originally founded as a seminary, meant to train bright young scholars of the New World in the interpretation of scripture and the ways of the Lord. While the Bible may have been the only book worth reading back in 1636, Harvard's original mission was not to produce a ministry, but rather to "perpetuate a learned ministry"—to keep the clergy literate. Even so, the University's secularity evoked the concern of other institutions—a 1924 *Crimson* article reported that 13 other colleges made a habit of sending up daily prayers for the soul of "Godless Harvard." Today, Harvard maintains its secular status, but religion and religious diversity play active roles on campus.

THE DIVINITY SCHOOL

In 1811, Harvard founded its first official program for ministerial candidates, and in 1816 the Harvard Divinity School was immaculately conceived. With a general inclination toward liberal religious thought, the "Div School", which was the first non-denominational divinity school in the country, encourages ideals of religious pluralism. The core of its academic program involves the "rigorous historical and comparative study of Christian traditions in the context of other world religions and value systems." Of course, when students

JUSTIN SCHOOLMASTER

Memorial Church

and faculty bring to the table backgrounds in more than 55 religious traditions and a host of cultures and ethnicities, it is difficult to keep any voice quiet for long.

Harvard's faculty today owes a lot to the Divinity School. The oldest endowed professorship at the College and in the country, the Hollis Professorship of Divinity, wound up seating a scholar at the Divinity School. Established in 1721 and adopted by the Divinity School at the time of its founding, the Hollis Professorship set the standard for future permanent faculty positions. Until

ALUMNUS ILLUMINATED: REVEREND PETER J. GOMES, HDS CLASS OF 1968

Reverend Peter J. Gomes served as the Plummer Professor of Christian Morals and overseer of all things at Memorial Church for three and a half

decades prior to his death in February 2011. A resounding voice and learned authority on religion at Harvard and in the world, Gomes graduated from Harvard Divinity School in 1968 and received over 30 honorary degrees across the globe. In 2001, he was awarded the Phi Beta Kappa Teaching Award from Harvard, and in 2006 he was awarded the Preston N. Williams Black Alumni/ae Award from Harvard Divinity School. The *New York Times* best-selling au-

JUSTIN SCHOOLMASTER
The late Reverend Gomes in his Commencement robes

thor led prayers at the inaugurations of both Ronald Regan and George H. W. Bush. Gomes is remembered as a pioneer of tolerance and acceptance in all realms; he publicly came out as gay in 1991. A highly active and renowned figure on campus, Reverend Gomes opened up his home for a communal tea most Wednesday evenings.

recently, Harvey G. Cox, Jr., author of *The Secular City* and a 44-year veteran of the department, held the post. Shortly before his retirement in 2009, Cox, a world-renowned theologian, chose to exercise a professorial right that hadn't been observed since 1722: the right to graze a cow in Harvard Yard. Like Hollis professors before him, Cox paraded a prime piece of meat around the Yard. Yet, unlike Hollis professors centuries before him, he was serenaded by a celebratory band of tubas as he took his cow to pasture.

Ralph Waldo Emerson, Class of 1821, delivered his now famous "Divinity School Address" in July of 1838 before his graduating class, a speech that is considered today to have been one of the first explicit expressions of the ideals of Transcendentalism. Emerson said:

I look for the new Teacher, that shall follow so far those shining laws, that he shall see them come full circle; shall see their rounding complete grace; shall see the world to be the mirror of the soul; shall see the identity of the law of gravitation with purity of heart; and shall show that the Ought, that Duty, is one thing with Science, with Beauty, and with Joy.

Today, Harvard Divinity School aims to educate its students in the theory, practice, and applications of religion and religious principles in historical contexts and contemporary society.

AMELIA MULLER

Harvey Cox exercising his professorial right in
September 2009

MEMORIAL CHURCH

The epicenter of student religious life at Harvard, Memorial Church is a non-denominational place of worship. Despite a loose official affiliation with Protestantism, Memorial Church regularly opens its doors to preachers, scholars, and students of many religious backgrounds.

Dedicated on Armistice Day in 1932, Memorial Church was a gift of Harvard alumni who wished to commemorate the lives of their 413 classmates who died in World War I. The church, which seats roughly 1200, has since expanded its scope to memorialize Harvard students who died in World War II, the Korean War, and the Vietnam War.

Memorial Church's 5000 lb., 5 ft.-wide bell, a gift from President Abbott Lawrence Lowell, sits high atop the church's 197 ft. tower. The bell rings to announce church services as well as the passing hours, much to the chagrin of freshmen students who live next door in Canaday Hall. While the instrument's inscription reads, "In memory of voices that are hushed," it might as well read, in a firm yet motherly tone: "All of you get to class! Now!" Today, Memorial Church holds morning prayers at 8:45am during the week and full services at 11am on Sundays. In addition to providing lectures and group religious gatherings, the church also offers pastoral counseling services. Memorial Church is home to a group of 36 university chaplains representing 25 different religious traditions.

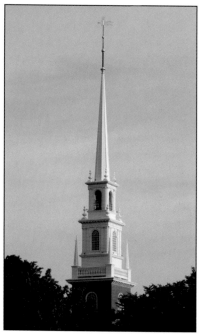

ALEXANDRA DOWD
The 197-foot high Memorial Church
tower

In 1991 the Pluralism Project was created, a two decade long research project aiming "to help Americans engage with the realities of religious diversity." Led by Diana Eck, Professor of Comparitive Religion and Indian Studies, the project demonstrates the University's commitment to creating a diverse and accepting religious atmosphere on campus.

Particularly active religious groups on campus include the Harvard Hillel, which provides Jewish Havardians with a pluralist religious and social space, services, and community programming; the Harvard *Ichthus*, a journal of Christian thought; the Interfaith Council, which hosts an annual day of discussion about religious pluralism known as the Day of Faith; the Catholic Student Association; and the Islamic Society.

CURRICULUM
AT HARVARD

PURITAN BEGINNINGS

In the earliest years of its history, Harvard adopted a curriculum that merged the traditions of the English university system with Puritan ideology. A 1643 brochure stated that the mission of the University was "to advance Learning and perpetuate it to Posterity; dreading to leave an illiterate Ministry to the Churches." Indeed, many early graduates went on to become Puritan ministers, although Harvard has never been formally affiliated with any specific religious denomination. As the University gradually broke away from its Puritan roots in the 18th and 19th centuries, it expanded beyond the strict classical studies that had previously dominated the curriculum and increased its offerings in the sciences.

HISTORY

Despite the fact that the training of ministers was never explicitly mentioned in the Charter of 1650, a strong Christian ethos pervaded the daily life of Harvard students throughout the University's first 200 years. Students began and ended their days with public prayer, the President recited a chapter of Scripture daily, and preceptors didn't hesitate to remind their pupils that the aim of their literary and scientific studies was a deeper understanding of God. In many ways, Harvard was closely modeled on British universities. As was the case in the Old World, Harvard initially emphasized the liberal arts disciplines of Logic, Rhetoric, Latin, Hebrew, Greek, Ethics, and Metaphysics over Mathematics or Natural Sciences. Entrance requirements for aspiring freshmen included proficiency in Latin and Greek and the performance of an extemporaneous translation of Cicero. The school day generally began with a lecture in which a tutor read aloud in Latin, followed by a formal meal in the College hall. Then students were faced either with recitations, in which they were tested on the morning's lecture, or, in the case of sophomores, disputations—battles of logic and wit conducted in Latin and moderated by the President. Prayers took place in the late afternoon, followed by a study hour, supper, and recre-

BY THE NUMBERS

8	Number of course categories in the General Education program
10	The maximum percentage of a graduating class that can be elected to Phi Beta Kappa
46	Fields of concentration available to undergraduates
15,000	Number of words in a typical senior thesis (around 60 pages)

ational time. Tutors, who shared their chambers with pupils, were usually recent graduates themselves and taught in all disciplines.

In the 18th century, the College's curriculum broadened to include private tutorials (with parental permission) in French and Philosophy in order to provide students with a so-called "gentleman's education." Still, Harvard Presidents still typically came from the clergy and opposed the teaching of foreign languages and the introduction of Darwinism into the sciences.

The 1869 school year saw the inauguration of chemist Charles William Eliot as President of the University. The author of a two-part series entitled "The New Education: Its Organization," published in *Atlantic Monthly* shortly before his appointment as President, Eliot helped launch a national movement toward educational reform. Entrance requirements were tightened and the elective system was formalized, allowing undergraduates to choose from a wide variety of courses in different disciplines. Restrictions were loosened outside the curricular sphere as well: under Eliot's tenure, student behavior ceased to be a factor in class rank, and mandatory class attendance was abolished, signaling a shift away from the *in loco parentis* ("in the place of a parent") model for colleges.

When University President Abbott Lawrence Lowell took office in 1909, he maintained the elective system but pushed for students to devote particular attention to a single academic discipline. Lowell famously stated in his inaugural address that "the best type of liberal education in our complex modern world aims at producing men who know a little of everything and something well." His philosophy ushered in the system of concentrations that is still in

"Charter of 1650," Harvard University Archives, UAI 15.100

FUN FACT

Even those who weren't admitted to Harvard had access to Eliot's educational philosophy in the form of The Harvard Classics. Originally dubbed Dr. Eliot's Five Foot Shelf, The Harvard Classics is a 51-volume anthology of "great books" that collectively offer readers a broad liberal arts education.

use today. Under Lowell's new system, students chose a field of concentration and were required to take a certain number of courses in their chosen department in order to graduate.

President James Bryant Conant further developed the College curriculum by introducing the General Education program in 1949. This program was conceived to ensure that every student graduating from the College would have a well-rounded, liberal background as well as thorough training in a single field. Once the student had fulfilled these two sets of requirements, he would be at liberty to take any course offered by the University, courses known as electives. Opportunities for independent coursework were expanded by the institution of the Advanced Standing and Freshman Seminar programs during the tenure of President Nathan Marsh Pusey.

President Charles W. Eliot,
Harvard University Archives, HUP Eliot, Charles W. (22)

It was President Derek Bok, however, who pioneered the creation of the Core Curriculum in 1978. Created to replace the outdated General Education program of President Conant, the Core Curriculum was designed by a committee headed by the former Dean of the Faculty of Arts and Sciences, Henry Rosovsky, and was seen as less elitist than the Great Books curriculum at Columbia and other universities. In the annual report of 1975-76, Dean Rosovsky had outlined the five educational goals of the College. According to this document, an educated person had to be able "to think and write clearly and effectively," to "have achieved depth in some field of knowledge," to "have a critical appreciation of the ways in which we gain and apply knowledge of the universe, of society, and of ourselves," to "have some understanding of, and experience in thinking about, moral and ethical problems," and to not be "ignorant of other cultures and other times." The first goal is achieved principally through the Expository Writing requirement, the second through the system of concentrations, and the third, fourth, and fifth through what became the Core program. After three decades under the Core Curriculum, the University has transitioned to a new liberal system of requirements with a familiar name: the Program in General Education (lovingly shortened by students to the title "Gen Ed").

PHI BETA KAPPA

The Harvard chapter of Phi Beta Kappa, called Phi Beta Kappa, Alpha of Massachusetts, is the oldest chapter in continuous existence. It was also one of the 25 American college chapters that made up the United Chapters, the predecessor to today's national Phi Beta Kappa Society. The Harvard chapter was founded by a graduate student, Elisha Parmele, and granted its charter on December 4, 1779, by the original chapter at the College of William and Mary, founded three years earlier. The first meeting was held on September 8, 1781, and consisted of Parmele and four newly initiated juniors.

The William and Mary chapter had adopted a Greek motto, "Philosophia Biou Kybernetes," meaning "Philosophy the Guide of Life," whose initials gave rise to the name Phi Beta Kappa. In place of the gold key awarded to initiates today, new members underwent an elaborate secret initiation which culminated in the presentation of a silver medal. In its early years, Phi Beta Kappa was primarily a social and debating club. In 1831, however, the oath of secrecy was abandoned, and the 19th century witnessed the transformation of the society from a social organization into an undergraduate honor society.

In 1914, Phi Beta Kappa, Iota of Massachusestts was founded at Radcliffe College. The two chapters merged in 1995, becoming the Alpha Iota chapter of Massachusetts.

Today, 24 juniors are elected each spring, 48 seniors each fall, and an additional pool of students in the final election prior to Commencement, yielding a total membership of no more than 10% of the graduating class. Undergraduates are elected to Alpha Iota of Massachusetts based on the rigor, merit, and originality of their academic programs.

The Phi Beta Kappa Literary Exercises have been an important part of Harvard Commencement since the 18th century, and are held annually on the Tuesday of Commencement Week. The Exercises comprise a reading by a Poet and an address by an Orator selected by the Chapter. Past Orators include Niall Ferguson, Garrison Keillor, Madeleine Albright, and Nadine Gordimer, and past Poets include Elizabeth Alexander, Robert Creeley, Allen Ginsburg, and Seamus Heaney.

ACADEMIC AWARDS AND FELLOWSHIPS

Harvard has a long tradition of awarding academic prizes, dating back to 1637, when Edward Hopkins left money to Harvard for the establishment of the Detur Prize. Prizes may be given for overall academic excellence, excellence in a particular subject, or other significant achievements. In addition, the Office of Career Services awards a number of fellowships for term-time, summer, and post-graduate study.

The Thomas Temple Hoopes Prize was founded in 1982 though a bequest by Thomas Hoopes, Class of 1919, and is considered one of the highest undergraduate academic honors. Students are generally nominated by their thesis adviser and the $3500 prizes are awarded on the basis of outstanding scholarly work or research.

The Jacob Wendell Scholarship Prize, established in 1899, is awarded annually to a Harvard sophomore in recognition of scholarship and contribution

The 1866 Phi Beta Kappa class,
Harvard University Archives, HUPSF Phi Beta Kappa (2)

FUN FACT

In 1837, Ralph Waldo Emerson delivered the Phi Beta Kappa oration at the graduation ceremonies of his disciple Henry David Thoreau.

to the College community during the freshman year. The financial award is divided into three parts: two equal disbursements of up to $5000 at the start of the summer after sophomore and junior years to fund worthwhile summer experiences, and the final disbursement in the spring of the senior year.

The Bowdoin Prizes for Undergraduates, funded initially through the 1791 bequest of Massachusetts Governor James Bowdoin, Class of 1745, and supplemented in 1901 by George Sullivan Bowdoin, are awarded to students in the following categories: English Language, Natural Sciences, Greek, and Latin. Winners are awarded a sum of money as well as a medal, a certificate, and the inclusion of his or her name in the Commencement Program.

GRADE INFLATION AND ACADEMIC HONORS

In 2001, Government professor Harvey Mansfield began his introductory lecture to his course "The History of Modern Political Philosophy" by pledging to give all of his students two grades on every assignment: the grade they deserve, and the inflated or "ironic" grade which would appear on the transcript and ensure that students are not penalized for taking his class. Shortly after Mansfield took this public stand, his photo appeared on the front page of *The Boston Globe* accompanying an article that called Harvard "the Lake Wobegon of higher education," where all the students are above average. The article pointed out the fact that over 90% of the Class of 2001 had a grade point average of at least B-minus and graduated summa, magna, or cum laude.

In 1940, C-minus was the most common grade given to Harvard undergrads, and in 1955, only 15% of students had an average of B-plus or above. By contrast, half of the grades given out in the 2000-01 academic year were A's or A-minuses, and just 6% were C-pluses or below.

One cause of the rise in college honors was a 1961 decision made by the faculty to loosen honors requirements by allowing seniors to earn cum laude distinction based on their coursework across all disciplines, without having to complete honors work in their concentration. As a result, in 1962, the incidence of honors degrees increased by 7%. Today, cum laude requires a B average overall, and one quarter of the students who receive college honors do not earn honors in their concentrations.

Grade inflation was aggravated by the Vietnam War, when the Selective Service System asked the University to help them establish rules for drafting Harvard students. Harvard responded by calculating a class rank for each student and forwarding the standings to the draft board. Should the war worsen and full-time students lose their exemption from the draft, grades and class

THE DIVISION OF CONTINUING EDUCATION

The Division of Continuing Education comprises the Harvard Extension School, the Harvard Summer School, the Institute for English Language Programs, and the Institute for Learning in Retirement. The University Extension School, founded as an experimental program in 1910 by President Lowell, enrolls nearly 14,000 students annually. Initially awarding only an Associate of Arts degree, the school now also offers a four-year Bachelor of Liberal Arts degree and a Master of Liberal Arts degree.

The Harvard Summer School is the oldest academic summer session in the United States. It has served students regularly since 1871, with only a short interruption during World War II. Students choose from among 300 courses in more than 40 disciplines, including the liberal arts, journalism, and management. The Institute for English Language Programs offers part-time and intensive summer courses to non-native English speakers in the greater Boston area. Established in 1977, the Institute for Learning in Retirement offers a variety of classes and activities to a community of 500 retired and semi-retired academics, business leaders, and professionals. With the exception of the degree programs and many Summer School programs, the Division of Continuing Education has an open enrollment policy.

rank would determine who would be drafted and who would avoid Vietnam. As a result, professors were under pressure to give higher grades to protect their students. According to former FAS Dean Henry Rosovsky, one of the most poignant traces of grade inflation can be seen above the pews in Memorial Church, where a small plaque lists the names of the 19 undergraduates who died in Vietnam. Just across from the plaque is a stone wall etched with the hundreds of names of those who lost their lives in World War II.

In 1967 and 1968, the faculty loosened foreign language requirements, pushed for the introduction of plus and minus grades, and expanded alternative pedagogical models like pass/fail courses and student-designed independent study projects.

ACADEMICS TODAY

President Lowell's doctrine of "concentration and distribution" remains the dominant academic philosophy today. A "concentration"—Harvardian for major—is a student's primary field of focus and requires between 12 and 16 semester-long courses in a particular field of study. Students seeking honors eligibility are also expected to enroll in several tutorials, which culminate in a senior thesis. Today, Harvard offers 45 different concentrations as well as the option to petition for a Special Concentration, where a student can create a unique plan of study with the help of a faculty adviser.

Two unique concentrations at Harvard are History and Literature (Hist and Lit) and Social Studies. Both Hist and Lit and Social Studies are interdisciplinary, honors-only concentrations. Hist and Lit was first proposed in the spring of 1906 by Harvard English Professor Barrett Wendell, Class of 1877, who developed the idea as an antidote to what he called the "anarchy" of President Eliot's free-elective system, which allowed students to graduate after taking any assortment of 16 courses. Introduced on April 24, 1906, Hist and Lit remained the only concentration at the College for 13 years. The concentration was designed to familiarize students with the history of Western civilization and "canonical works" such as Shakespeare's plays and the Bible. While the curriculum has evolved significantly since its creation—for instance, a Latin America track was introduced in the 1920s—Hist and Lit is still known for its academic rigor, requiring oral examinations in both sophomore and senior years, as well as a three-year series of tutorials. There is a 3000-4000 word sophomore essay, a 6000-8000 word junior essay, and a 15,000 word senior thesis. Today, concentrators specialize in the history and literature of specific regions or time periods.

Social Studies, another popular Harvard-only major, admitted its first crop of 18 students in the fall of 1960. The scholars who conceived of the program were concerned that graduating seniors in the social sciences were leaving the College as specialists in their own narrow fields, but lacked an understanding of other disciplines. In order to avoid conflicts with other departments, the committee decided that only honors candidates would be admitted to the concentration and that no formal courses would be taught

SCOTT YIM
The Expository Writing Program Office

GRADUATE SCHOOL OF EDUCATION

Created in 1920, the Graduate School of Education (HGSE) is devoted to research in educational methods and practice and to training school personnel. The Principals' Center was created in 1981 to assist principals in their personal and professional growth as school leaders, and in 1986, the school introduced a state-certified Public School Teacher Certification program for Harvard undergraduates. HGSE's Urban Superintendents Program, the nation's first comprehensive doctoral program for urban educational leaders, was launched in 1990.

The first Harvard graduate school to admit women to a degree program, HGSE now offers 13 master's programs and six doctoral concentrations in fields ranging from school leadership to arts in education to human development and psychology. In addition to about 900 degree candidates, the school hosts over 3000 educational leaders from around the world each year to participate in professional education programs.

in Social Studies, with the exception of the sophomore, junior, and senior tutorials, which would be taught by faculty from each of the social science departments. Today, Social Studies remains rooted in the belief that a theoretical perspective, a familiarity with historical context, and a grounding in the ideas of the "classic" social scientists of the past are vital to an understanding of social problems.

There is no such thing as a "double major" at Harvard, but undergraduates can choose to synthesize two disparate concentrations by pursuing a "joint concentration." Joint concentrators split their concentration requirements between two fields and integrate them into a coherent plan of study that culminates in a senior thesis relating the two subjects. In recent years, students have also gained the opportunity to pursue a "secondary field," the equivalent of what most colleges call a "minor."

Approximately 50% of Harvard students major in the social sciences, 30% in the natural sciences, and 20% in the humanities. Economics and Government are the two most popular undergraduate concentrations, followed by Social Studies and Psychology.

The other component of President Lowell's vision for curricular excellence was the "distribution" of classes among diverse fields. Rather than insist that all Harvard graduates be familiar with subjects like basic genetics or the history of the two World Wars, the Core Curriculum was replete with highly specific, somewhat esoteric topics like "The Biology of Trees and Forests" or "The Cuban Revolution: 1956-71." According to its mission statement, the Core differed from other distribution requirements in that it did not "define intellectual breadth as the mastery of a set of Great Books, or the digestion of a specific quantum of information." Rather, it sought "to introduce students to the major approaches to knowledge in areas that the faculty considers indispensable to undergraduate education." Methodology, in other words, trumps material in terms of pedagogical value. Additionally, all students are required to take an Expository Writing course during their freshman year to gain a firm foundation in academic writing before embarking on their undergraduate career.

In 2004, the Faculty of Arts and Sciences embarked on the Harvard College Curricular Review, which resulted in a vote in the 2008-2009 academic year to replace the Core Curriculum with a new Program in General Education. While the Core Curriculum aimed to expose students to a variety of approaches to knowledge, the General Education requirements attempt to "connect a student's liberal education—that is, an education conducted in

OFFICE OF CAREER SERVICES

The Office of Career Services (OCS) serves the students and alumni of Harvard College, the Graduate School of Arts and Sciences, and the Harvard Extension School. OCS organizes the visits of approximately 250 companies, representing about 25 different industries, to Cambridge each year to participate in on-campus recruiting. OCS schedules

KEVIN LIN
Entrance to the Office of Career Services

around 500 half-hour appointments each month, in addition to weekly drop-in hours in specific areas like business, medicine, or public service. A biweekly OCS online newsletter alerts students to upcoming recruiting events and fellowship deadlines. Historically the focus of these events was largely on jobs in investment banking and consulting. However, 20% of seniors entered finance and consulting in 2009, down from 39% in 2008 and 47% in 2007, according to surveys by *The Harvard Crimson*. OCS is now actively diversifying its advising services connecting students to careers in public service and global opportunities.

a spirit of free inquiry, rewarding in its own right—to life beyond college," according to the report of the Curricular Review. General Education is also intended to provide a more interdisciplinary approach, bridging not only different departments but different faculties within the University. Members of the Class of 2011 and 2012 chose whether to graduate under the Core or the General Education requirements, while the Class of 2013 will be the first class to matriculate under the new program. Unlike the Core Curriculum, under which requirements vary depending on the student's concentration, students under General Education must complete courses in all eight of the following categories: Aesthetic & Interpretive Understanding, Culture & Belief, Empirical & Mathematical Reasoning, Ethical Reasoning, Science of Living Systems, Science of the Physical Universe, Societies of the World, and United States in the World. None of the categories deals specifically with history, but one of the eight courses must "engage substantially with study of the past."

ACADEMIC CALENDAR

Another outcome of the 2004 Harvard College Curricular Review was the switch to a more generic academic calendar. In January 2008, the University approved a new calendar that would bring the University's 13 schools in sync. Beginning in the 2009-2010 academic year, students no longer had final exams looming over them during the winter vacation. The fall term now ends in December instead of mid-January, and the spring term formally begins in February. The University is still in the process of creating programming for the month of January, a period called "J-Term" by students. Currently, winter season athletes and senior thesis writers are permitted to come back to campus early to brave the harsh New England chill. Student organizations are also allowed to apply for campus housing and students can gain admittance to and obtain funding for University-sponsored programs abroad. In 2012 all students are invited to return to campus a week before classes resume to attend "Wintersession" a period comprised of "student-initiated and College-led programming."

ACADEMIC ADVISING

Academic and social advising begins the moment freshmen step into the Yard and move into their rooms. All incoming students are greeted by the proctors and Peer Advising Fellows (PAFs) of their dorm entryways. Proctors reside in dorm entryways during the year and are available to help freshmen with any problems or concerns. All proctors, as well as many non-resident faculty and administration members, serve as freshman academic advisers. These academic advisers help first-years choose their courses for the fall, give advice, and answer questions on the curriculum, concentrations, extracurricular activities, summer plans, and future career options. PAFs are Harvard upperclassmen paired with freshmen based on academic and extracurricular interests. They give a student perspective on college life and help freshmen with social, extracurricular, and academic issues as well as work with proctors to build entryway

FUN FACT

There is no pre-registration for classes at Harvard. At the beginning of each semester, students have a week-long "shopping period"—a sort of academic speed-dating—during which they can sample as many courses as they like and compare syllabi before settling on a course load for the semester. Though professors do start teaching during Shopping Week, it is customary for students to enter and exit classrooms as they please in order to attend different classes that meet at the same time.

spirit and plan social events. PAFs and academic advisers interact with their freshmen continuously throughout the year. Freshman advising culminates in mid-April with the Advising Fortnight, during which each academic department gives presentations and one-on-one advising to freshmen interested in concentrating in that field.

The Bureau of Study Counsel is designed to help students fully develop their intellectual and emotional potential. The Bureau was started in 1946 when William Perry, Jr. was asked to consolidate three services already in existence at Harvard—a tutoring service, a precursor of what is today the Writing Center, and a remedial reading course offered by the Graduate School of Education. Initially, the focus of the Bureau was tutoring and remedial study skills, but as an interest in applied psychology swept the nation in the years after the war, Perry and his colleagues began to engage in qualitative research on adolescent and early adult development. The Bureau currently provides a full range of academic and psychological services that encourage and assist students in getting the most from their Harvard educations: academic counseling through individual sessions, workshops, courses in reading strategies,

SCOTT YIM

The Freshman Dean's Office

personal counseling and individual psychotherapy, peer tutoring, and group counseling on issues affecting student lives.

SENIOR THESES

For many students, a senior thesis is the culmination of their four years at Harvard. While the senior thesis is not a graduation requirement, certain so-called "honors-only" concentrations—Social Studies, History and Literature, Folklore and Mythology, History of Science, Literature, and Studies of Women, Gender and Sexuality—require all concentrators to write a senior thesis. A significant individual project, the senior thesis allows students to immerse themselves in research on a particular area, to take part in scholarly discourse, and to work closely with a supervising faculty member. Students concentrating in English, Visual and Environmental Studies, or Folklore and Mythology have the option of a "creative thesis," such as writing a short novel or creating an art installation. Those who choose to write a senior thesis begin the process in the spring of their junior year, when they are required to come up with their topic, and often use the summer to conduct research. Theses are due sometime during senior spring, depending on the concentration, and are evaluated by two readers, usually Harvard faculty members but occasionally other experts in the field. Each reader grades the thesis individually and submits his or her grade to the tutorial committee, which determines final grades and recommendations for honors.

LIBRARIES
AT HARVARD

A WORLD OF BOOKS

Harvard was home to America's first library and currently lays claim to America's second largest library as well as the largest academic library system in the world. Harvard's expansive collection of the printed word (not to mention the recorded and the microfiched) fills stacks all over Cambridge and Boston, including Widener (p. 72), which stands four stories tall and drops four more stories underground through an underpass to a rare books collection. Harvard's collection even extends to the Hellenic/Pre-Columbian studies library at Dumbarton Oaks in Washington D.C. and the Biblioteca Berenson at Villa I Tatti just outside Florence, Italy. On top of all this, students have access to an extensive inter-library loan system—if they need a book, Harvard can get it, even if it has to hop a few planes along the way.

EARLY HISTORY

In 1638, John Harvard donated 329 titles from approximately 400 volumes of books. The College was so grateful for his gift that it changed its name to Harvard College and began constructing its first academic building that same year. A single room on the second floor of this building housed John Harvard's book collection. By 1671, the building was in need of such expensive repairs that the College decided it would be wiser to build an entirely new home for the collection of books. In 1677, the library was moved to a 30 by 40 ft. room on the second floor of the original Harvard Hall. Here the books lived comfortably, if haphazardly, for some time.

In 1723, Joshua Gee, the "library keeper," created the country's first library catalog. He arranged the books by size, subject (starting with the Bible), and author's last name.

Things remained orderly until January 24, 1764, when, during a smallpox outbreak in Boston, the General Court convened in Harvard Hall. The next morning, newspaper headlines read, "Last night Harvard College suffered the most ruinous loss it ever met with since its foundation." A heating fire in Harvard Hall had been improperly snuffed, leading to the

BY THE NUMBERS

1	Book remaining from John Harvard's original collection
2	John Singer Sargent murals in Widener Library
70+	Distinct libraries in the University library system
16.8+	Million holdings in the library system

FUN FACT

In 1828, the United States and Great Britain decided to settle their disputes over Canadian territory by arbitration. The nations were fighting over a northeastern part of Canada claimed both by the state of Maine and New Brunswick. American representatives turned to Harvard's Library for various maps and books unavailable anywhere else. The dispute ended in favor of the United States.

destruction of the building and all of the books stored inside. Luckily, 404 volumes survived, either because they were out on loan or had not yet been unpacked. Among the survivors, only one book can be definitively traced back to John Harvard's original donation: John Downame's *Christian Warfare Against the Devil, World and Flesh.* Since the fire occurred while the building was being used by the General Court, the Province of Massachusetts Bay took responsibility for the loss, and rebuilt Harvard Hall for $23,000. The new building housed not only a library but also a chapel, classrooms, a kitchen, a student dining hall, and the first experimental physics lab in America, furnished with instruments given to the University by Benjamin Franklin.

The books inside Harvard Hall had to be replaced as well. Thanks to a number of generous donors, the library contained 4350 volumes within one year of its reopening. The largest contribution came from John Hancock, who donated 1300 volumes. Not all of the books were accessible to students, though. In 1765, a list was made of prohibited books, and it remained in effect until 1789. Absolutely prohibited books were marked with a 'P,' while those prohibited to undergraduates only were marked with an asterisk.

Harvard had also kept a list of books recommended for undergraduate readers. It was 27 pages long and prefaced in Latin with the following note:

Inasmuch as the Catalogue of Books in the College Library, embracing Books in almost all Tongues and about all Sciences and Arts, most of which are above the Comprehension of Younger Students, is very long and not to be completely unrolled, when Occasion demands, save at very feat expense of time, it has seemed wise to put together a briefer Catalogue, to wit, of Books which are better adapted to their use. In the following Catalogue, then, in addition to Classical Authors, there are included Books chiefly in the vernacular and belonging to the general culture of the mind, omitting as much as possible those which are in daily use in the College, as also those which are written in foreign Languages, or which treat of specialized Disciplines, e.g., Medicine or Jurisprudence. But let no one infer from this that Students are debarred from the freer use of the Library.

COVER TO COVER:
CHRISTIAN WARFARE AGAINST THE DEVIL, WORLD AND FLESH

Included in John Harvard's donation to the College was a fourth edition of John Downame's 1634 *Christian Warfare Against the Devil, World and Flesh.* Inside the cover is a note dated May 24, 1842 and signed by John L. Sibley, who served as librarian from 1856-1877. It reads, "This book is the only one in the Library which beyond a doubt was given by John Harvard."

Although John Harvard did not sign his name into the book, the inside-cover reads "3.2.8," cryptic to an ordinary viewer, but decipherable to Peter Accardo, Houghton Library's current Program Coordinator. The numbers are a marking from the library's early cataloging system. The book resided in bookcase 3, shelf number 2, and was volume 8. Such a

OFFICE OF PUBLIC AFFAIRS
"Gift of John Harvard" inscription on Christian Warfare Against the Devil, World and Flesh

low catalog number indicates that it was likely part of the original collection. Its inclusion in the 1723 library catalog provides additional evidence that the book was in the University's possession before the 1764 fire (p. 11).

Christian Warfare is currently on display in the "Harvard" bookshelf at Houghton Library, alongside copies of other books speculated to be from John Harvard's original donation.

LIBRARY RULES

Free use of the library was not always the status quo. Only juniors and seniors were permitted to take out the books from the catalog; sophomores were not allowed to borrow books from the library until 1795, and freshmen had to wait until 1814. Even after freshmen were finally given permission to check books out, they were restricted to every third Friday and could only choose from a specific list. In addition, they were only permitted to take out a book in English if they also took out a book in Latin or Greek.

THE CREATION OF THE HARVARD LIBRARY SYSTEM

The construction of a new library for Harvard College was preceded by the creation of separate libraries at the graduate schools. The Medical School acquired its own library in 1803, followed by the Divinity School in 1812 and the Law School in 1817. As the libraries separated into factions so did the librarians. In 1828, College Librarian Benjamin Pierce asked Thomas Nuttall, the caretaker of the Botanical Garden and the Natural History Library, to take an inventory of his collection because the Corporation had requested a complete catalog of the University's holdings. It was only after a series of angry letters that Pierce was finally able to document the 303 volumes in the Natural History Library. Strangely, after 1832, the Natural History Library disappeared from the records, although a number of smaller scientific libraries appeared in the middle of the century. Frequent disputes among libraries and librarians led to the appointment of a Director of the University Library, whose office was symbolically located outside the physical library system in Wadsworth House.

GORE HALL

The College Library did not have its own building until 1841, when Gore Hall was completed. It was conceived of as a place to house and protect books, rather than a venue for independent research, and the conditions in the new library were far from ideal. The architects, seeking to reduce the risk of fire as much as possible (lesson learned, 1764!), installed only one furnace in the entire building. The ceiling and roof leaked and, because of insufficient heat, the stone building began to grow mold. Additionally, all of the books had to be read during daytime hours because there was no artificial lighting in the library until 1896. Students were prohibited from entering the stacks; instead they selected the book's catalog card and a library page memorized the entry and retrieved it for them. One library page named Frank Carney later recalled: "I fear that I was guilty sometimes of coming back and saying a book was out when I had forgotten the title or did not see anything on the shelf that looked like the title I saw on the card."

Before long, Gore Hall was filled with books. The librarian was putting books in piles on the floor until 1877, at which point six levels of iron stacks and a much-needed office for the librarian were added. The iron stacks distributed the weight of the books from the walls directly to the foundation of the building itself. This was the first time that such an addition had been made in the United States. The solution was a temporary one, however, and before long plans were put in place for an entirely new College library.

With such unappealing conditions in Gore Hall, undergraduate societies and clubs began to amass libraries of their own, though these were relatively small compared to the overall collection of the College Library. In 1849, the Harvard College Library had 56,000 books, while the books in various student society libraries totaled around 12,000. There were approximately 110 belonging to Adelphoi Theologia (a student group for religious improvement) in 1840, 750 to the Hasty Pudding in 1841, 2000 to the Institute of 1770 in 1849, 125 at the Natural History Society in 1845, and 230 in the posession of Phi Beta Kappa in 1834. The Porcellian Club amassed the largest collection, totaling around 4000 books by 1846.

HARRY ELKINS WIDENER MEMORIAL LIBRARY

Harry Elkins Widener, Class of 1907, began to ardently collect books during his junior year at Harvard, and his wealthy parents often gave him rare books as gifts. When he finally joined the family business, Harry was poised to become a leading book collector. He drafted a will, that bequeathed his books to Harvard "whenever in [his mother's] judgment Harvard University will make arrangements for properly caring for them."

Harry and his parents were on board the Titanic for its fateful 1912 voyage. Eleanor Widener survived the accident in lifeboat number 4 (alongside

JUSTIN SCHOOLMASTER

Widener Library, seen under the snow

John Jacob Astor's wife), but Harry and his father were not so lucky; they presumably drowned on that cold Northern Atlantic night.

Upon her return to Massachusetts, Mrs. Widener informed Harvard of Harry's will. She originally envisioned a small library in Harry's honor, but President Lowell and Librarian Cary Coolidge, seeing in this bequest an opportunity for expansion, embarked on the construction of the monumental Widener Library with famed architect Horace Trumbauer at the helm.

The first problem that Coolidge faced was where to store the books during the library's construction. Some were lent to other schools while others were moved to specific department libraries. Ultimately, though, most were carted off to Randall Hall, an unused student dining hall, hoisted up in dumbwaiters and stacked inside refrigerators. One refrigerator, deemed the "Inferno Case," was used to store the collections's more grisly, sinister, and salacious volumes. It also included scholarly works on sexual behavior by thinkers like Freud and Krafft-Ebing.

Meanwhile, plans for the new library were reaching completion. Eleanor Widener had the final say on all decisions; she included memorial rooms for her son and required that the Widener book collection not be merged with the general collection. Further, the deed stated that:

[Harvard] particularly agrees that it will not permit any structures of any kind to be erected in the courts around which said building is constructed, but that the same shall be kept open for light and air; and that it will not make or permit to be made any changes, additions or alterations to the exterior of the said building or to the portions of the building hereinbefore specially set apart, to wit Memorial Hall and the library room in the rear thereof, or in the entrance halls on first floor and main stairway to second floor.

Later, in 1916, Eleanor Widener wrote a letter to the Widener Collection's curator, asking:

Will you please see that at all times fresh flowers are kept on your table by the photograph of my dear son Harry, the same to be paid for out of the fund set aside for the maintenance of the Memorial Room. This is the only request I make, and I beg of you to see that it is always carried out.

On June 24, 1915, Commencement Day, Widener Library officially opened, and stacks of books were ceremoniously paraded into the library with Downame's *Christian Warfare: Against the Devil, World and Flesh* in the lead. Within 14 weeks, all 700,000 books were settled into their new marble palace.

Three years later, on Memorial Day of 1918, the Roll of Honor, which bears the names of all the Harvard men who died in World War I, was installed in the entrance hall.

In 1921, Harvard decided to install a permanent memorial for its fallen soldiers in the library. The University commissioned John Singer Sargent to paint a memorial diptych flanking the entryway to the Memorial Rooms

LEGEND HAS IT...

Harry Widener and his father had spaces reserved in a lifeboat courtesy of their first class tickets, but, upon setting foot in the lifeboat, Harry remembered that he had left his newly acquired 1598 edition of Francis Bacon's *Essays* by his nightstand. Harry ran back into the ship and his father ran after him amid the rushing water and chaos. The two were never seen again.

(which house the Widener collection, including a Gutenberg Bible). The first of the murals, *Death and Victory*, shows a soldier nearly eclipsed by the figures of winged Victory and shrouded Death. Beneath the image are the lines, "Happy those who with a glowing faith / In one embrace clasped Death and Victory."

In the second mural, *Coming of the Americans*, Sargent shows the arrival of the American soldiers in Europe as they raise the American flag and release a bald eagle. Once again, the tone is heroic, but here the single soldier

FRESHMAN DEAN'S OFFICE
The columns of Widener Library at night

is replaced by a vast army of men which seems to extend beyond the scope of the frame. The bottom of the frame contains the following inscription: "They crossed the sea crusaders keen to help / The Nations battling in a righteous cause."

HOUGHTON RARE BOOKS LIBRARY AND PUSEY TUNNEL

In 1942, the University's rare books were moved into Houghton Library, whose construction was funded by Arthur A. Houghton, Jr., Class of 1929. Prior to the move, the books were housed in special sliding, lockable, wooden closets in Gore Hall. The closets were not flawless—they were mostly made of wood which frequently swelled, preventing proper ventilation and sometimes locking the closets together—but the general idea of the shelving design was ingenious, anticipating modern compact shelving systems, in which shelves can be moved and revealed at the touch of a button.

Since 1942, Houghton has been collecting rare books and works in a variety of media and materials; it was the first-ever specialized center for the study of rare manuscripts. Its shelves were soon filled through a voracious acquisitions program, and when the plans for Lamont Library were made, Houghton was allotted one underground floor to house rare books.

The collection contains ostraca (pottery fragments reused in antiquity as writing surfaces), daguerrotypes (predecessors to the photograph), and working papers from writers and poets like Copernicus, Emily Dickinson,

FRESHMAN DEAN'S OFFICE
Houghton Rare Books Library

WOMEN? IN THE LIBRARY?

Gore: Women could only use Gore Hall with a signed permission slip from a faculty sponsor.

Widener: When Widener opened in 1915, women were only permitted in the Radcliffe Study and, unlike their male counterparts, were never allowed to stay after hours. Eventually, under Library Director Keyes Metcalf, women were allowed to work in the library after hours, but only if they had asked permission, a rule that applied not only to students but also to female faculty members.

Lamont: It wasn't until 1966 that women were allowed to study in Lamont. *The Harvard Crimson* voiced its support for the change, observing "They've been letting 'Cliffes into Lamont for close to two weeks now and lo! The hallowed walls have not fallen."

Hilles: Also in 1966, the Susan Morse and Frederick Whiley Hilles Library, designed primarily for Radcliffe undergraduates, opened in the Radcliffe Quadrangle.

Schlesinger: The Arthur and Elizabeth Schlesinger Library on the History of Women, known before 1965 as the Women's Archives, is also located in the Radcliffe Quadrangle and has awarded numerous grants dedicated to the study of women's history.

John Keats, Edward Lear, Dante Alighieri, Tennessee Williams, Johann Wolfgang von Goethe, Miguel de Cervantes, and Lewis Carroll.

Houghton's collection is organized by era. The Early Books and Manuscripts Collection contains both papyri and illuminated manuscripts dating from 3000 to 1600 BCE, and the Modern Books and Manuscripts collection has the majority of the works dating from 1800 BCE to the present. The rest of the modern works are spread among the Theodore Roosevelt Collection, which contains manuscripts, pictures, images and printed ephemera by and about the President, the George Edward Woodberry Poetry Collection of English-language contemporary poetry; the Printing and Graphic Arts Collection of illustrated books and artist books; and the Harvard Theatre Collection.

Houghton's 19th-Century American Literature Collection contains the papers of the Alcott family, Ralph Waldo Emerson, Herman Melville, Oliver Wendell Holmes, Sr. and Jr., the James family, and Henry Wadsworth Longfellow, among others. Its 20th-century holdings are equally impressive, with manuscripts from T. S. Eliot, Thomas Wolfe, Robert Frost, John Updike, John Ashbery, e.e. cummings, Gore Vidal, and many others, as well as the records of New Directions Publishing Corporation, Houghton Mifflin, Little, Brown, *Golden Book Magazine*, *The Atlantic Monthly*, and *The Nation*.

Houghton Library is currently connected to Widener Library via the Pusey Stacks. Should a student need a book housed in Pusey or even Houghton, he'll find himself winding down four flights of stairs to the depths of the Widener stacks, past a seemingly endless rows of bookshelves, to the Pusey Tunnel, which features three levels of movable (and slightly unsettling) compact shelving. Admission to the Houghton collections is granted by special appointment for research purposes only, although students can request some of the library's materials to peruse in the reading room.

LAMONT LIBRARY

Lamont Library, opened in 1949, was the first library designed primarily for undergraduates. Thomas W. Lamont, Class of 1892, donated the money for the library, which was designed by the renowned architecture firm Coolidge, Shepley, Bulfinch and Abbott. The only stipulations given to the architects were that the library had to be near the Yard, well-lit and ventilated, and able to accommodate large numbers of students.

As far as stocking the shelves went, duplicate copies of books housed in Widener were sent to Lamont. Next came books that were on undergraduate course reading lists, but not on reserve (meaning they were set aside so that students could use them in 3hr. increments within the library). In general, books were chosen based on their likelihood of being used by undergraduates rather than an attempt to create a specialized collection in a particular discipline. In 1949, when the library opened, 54,755 volumes were moved into the library.

KEVIN LIN

Lamont Library

The Lamont Library building has eight levels, including a basement, a mezzanine, and a roof. During the 1970s, the three main floors each had a reading area, an alcove area, and a smoking room. Smoking is no longer permitted, but Lamont retains its dual nature today as both a social gathering place and a venue for disciplined study.

In addition to the main reading rooms, Lamont houses two lesser known but delightful spaces. The first is the Farnsworth Room, which was designed for recreational reading. In fact, when it was originally installed in Widener Library, students were kicked out if they were caught reading course material. Its collection contains travel books and cartoons as well as contemporary and classic literature.

The second of the smaller Lamont reading rooms is the Woodberry Poetry Room, which is devoted to the enjoyment of poetry and drama. The room is equipped with listening stations meant to foster an appreciation for the spoken word. Seamus Heaney, Nobel Laureate and former Harvard professor, once called the Woodberry Poetry Room "indispensable," declaring that "it contains not only the voices—from different times of their lives—of the greatest poets, but constitutes a living history of modern poetry."

Lamont is also a bastion of modern technology, particularly in the Morse Music and Media Center and the Language Resource Center. The Music and Media Center allows students to watch or listen to assigned movies and musical compositions. The Language Resource Center helps students learn and practice over 70 languages offered in Harvard's curriculum. Students have the opportunity to watch foreign films, complete listening exercises, and familiarize themselves with different accents and dialects.

ALEXANDRE TERRIEN
The Lamont Cafe

OLD BOYS' CLUB

When it was originally decided that Lamont should be accessible to men only, the following justifications were given:

1. Radcliffe maintains an undergraduate library of its own with a collection larger than the one now installed in Lamont and as large as the Lamont collection is expected to be in the future.

2. The money available would not provide for a building large enough to care for both the Harvard and Radcliffe undergraduates.

3. Experience here and elsewhere has shown that a single-sex library only can be administered with almost no supervision in the reading rooms, though a coeducational library requires supervision if reasonable quiet is to be preserved. In order to achieve most efficiently its primary aims, Lamont has been designed in such a way that the staff would have to be doubled if adequate reading room supervision were to be provided on a coeducational basis.

The most heavily populated area of Lamont is perhaps the Cafe rather than the reading rooms or the stacks. Lamont Cafe opened in October 2006 and was funded in part by a grant from the Harvard President at the time, Larry Summers. Located on the ground floor, Lamont Cafe is a place where students catch up with friends over study breaks, refuel on caffeine, and occasionally attempt to study. Talking is allowed in the Cafe—many group projects have been assembled there, and students consider spending a night or two there each semester more or less par for the course.

Since 2005 Lamont has been the only study center open 24 hours during weekdays. Lamont is the place where you will find out the most recent gossip and maybe, if you're lucky, finish that essay more than 5min. before it's due.

OTHER LIBRARIES

For the most part, undergraduates stick to Lamont and Widener. But occasionally, specific research or overcrowding drives students to seek out one of the other libraries on campus.

Cabot Science Library was named for industrial chemist Godfrey Lowell Cabot. Located in the Science Center, Cabot specializes in—no surprise here—books relating to the sciences. It is widely known to be the place to find crazed freshman pre-meds memorizing amino acids.

The **Fine Arts Library** was originally part of the Fogg Art Museum, which remains closed for renovations. The library has since become part of the College Library and has also taken over the Harvard Film Archive, located in the Carpenter Center (p. 194).

The **Harvard Map Collection,** now housed in Pusey stacks, is one of the oldest and largest in the country and contains many rare maps of America.

Harvard-Yenching Library is the largest in the world for East Asian studies. The collection began to take shape in 1879, when the first Chinese language class was offered at Harvard, but it did not become an organized library until 1928.

Loeb Music Library was opened in 1956 to much celebratory singing. It contains books and scores from all over the world, including much of the collection of Richard Aldrich, a famous *New York Times* editor and music critic.

Tozzer Library is the oldest library in the country that specializes in ethnology and anthropology. It was once located in the Peabody Museum but now has its own building across the street.

SCIENCE

AT HARVARD

THE PROGRESS OF SCIENCE

On April 21, 1780, a student delivered a poem entitled "The Progress of Science" to the Committee of Overseers of Harvard College. The poem was prefaced, "It is humbly presumed that the Youth of the Author will be esteemed by the Candid a sufficient Apology for any juvenile Errors in the following Poem." The poem places American scholars, namely John Winthrop and John Hancock, among the great minds of Europe (where "science reigns no more") like Isaac Newton and John Locke. Science was just beginning to burgeon in America, and Harvard was its epicenter.

PRESIDENT ELIOT'S SCIENTIFIC REVOLUTION

BEFORE ELIOT

When Harvard was founded in 1636, there was no scientific curriculum. Education focused on memorization and book learning. For two centuries there was almost no change in the disciplines covered in higher education: Greek, Latin, logic, rhetoric, and philosophy. Through the 1840s, it was widely believed that the purpose of education, as summarized by a Yale Committee Report in response to curricular criticism, was to provide "discipline and furniture of the mind; expanding its powers, and storing it with knowledge." It was accepted that the best ways to expand the mind were memorization and recitation. This left practical knowledge about experimental science notably absent from the curriculum.

BY THE NUMBERS

1	Complete mounted Kronosaurus skeleton, found at the Museum of Natural History
2.3	Million dollars spent by Harvard to connect Harvard Yard to the Science Center by building an overpass above Cambridge Street
1400+	Undergraduates concentrating in the natural or social sciences each year
20,000	Artifacts in the Museum of Historic Scientific Instruments

ARCHITECTURAL SPOTLIGHT: HARVARD MUSEUM OF NATURAL HISTORY

Harvard's second most visited attraction (after the John Harvard statue) is not Widener Library (p. 72) or Memorial Hall (p. 24), but its Museum

Glass Red Maple leaves, HMNH, Photo Hillel Burger,
© *President & Fellows Harvard College*

of Natural History, which sees 180,000 visitors annually, 33,000 of which are students. Established in 1998, the museum serves as the public face of three research museums: the Museum of Comparative Zoology, the Harvard University Herbaria, and the Mineralogical and Geological Museum. Its ongoing exhibitions take place in the zoological, botanical, and mineralogical galleries. Some of the most fascinating exhibitions are the internationally acclaimed Ware Collection of Blaschka Glass Models of Plants, known as the Glass Flowers; the first triceratops ever found; the world's only mounted Kronosaurus; and a 1642 lb. amethyst geode.

MING VANDENBERG (HMNH)
The world's only mounted Kronosaurus

LAWRENCE SCIENTIFIC SCHOOL

For decades after it was introduced, Harvard's science curriculum received less attention than its liberal arts curriculum. In fact, in the late 1840s, the science curriculum did not even warrant an A.B. degree. In response to what he believed to be a major shortcoming, and with a donation of $50,000 from Abbott Lawrence, a Massachusetts entrepreneur, President Eliot created the Lawrence Scientific School in 1847 to prepare students for the practical applications of science. The school thrived in its early years, and remained the only school of its kind in the area until the Massachusetts Institute of Technology (MIT) was founded in 1861.

In 1905, the Lawrence Scientific School, which was then under the jurisdiction of the Faculty of Arts and Sciences, became the Graduate School of Engineering. In 1948, it changed again when the Graduate School merged with the Department of Engineering and Applied Sciences to become the Division of Applied Sciences. In 2007, this division became its own school.

Although Eliot received much criticism for some of his decisions, he was successful in transforming Harvard into a leading scientific institution. When he became President in 1869, he inherited a small college focused almost entirely on a moral code and strict memorization; when he resigned in 1909, he left a national institution built around laboratories, lectures, and seminars.

SCHOOL OF ENGINEERING AND APPLIED SCIENCES

Today, the School of Engineering and Applied Science (SEAS) has more than 70 faculty members, offers three undergraduate concentrations (Applied Mathematics, Computer Science, and Engineering Sciences), and has seen its graduate student population more than double in a decade. Research areas currently include Applied Mathematics, Applied Physics, Bioengineering, Computer Science, Electrical Engineering, Environmental Sciences and Engineering, and Mechanical Engineering.

EXTRACURRICULAR SCIENCE

The largest scientific clubs on campus include the Harvard Cancer Society; the Harvard Society for Mind, Brain, and Behavior; the Harvard-Radcliffe Society of Physics Students; the Harvard College Undergraduate Research Association; and the Student Astronomers at Harvard-Radcliffe.

The Harvard Cancer Society works to raise money and awareness for cancer patients and care. It also arranges many large-scale events such as a bone marrow drive, Hoops Against Cancer, and Relay for Life, in addition to weekly volunteer programs at Boston-area hospitals.

The Harvard Society for Mind, Brain, and Behavior (HSMBB) strives to "promote multidisciplinary dialogue among students involved in one of the seven MBB tracks or secondary fields (Neurobiology, Psychology, Philosophy, Computer Science, History of Science, Human Evolutionary Biology, and

ARCHITECTURAL SPOTLIGHT: THE HARVARD OBSERVATORY

The Corporation of Harvard University established the Harvard Observatory in October of 1839, and observations were underway by the end of the year. William Cranch Bond, a well known Boston clockmaker, was elected as the first "Astronomical Observer of Harvard University." This would have seemed logical, as the primary conception of the universe at that time was that it functioned like an enormous clock.

Less than a decade later, Bond and pioneer photographer John Adams Whipple began to use the Observatory's 15 in. Great Refractor telescope, the largest in the world at the time, to view and take images of the moon. Their work received an award for technical excellence in photography at the 1851 Great Exhibition in London.

While the main offices and the center for facilities for the Harvard Observatory are located at 60 Garden St., ground-based facilities exist in Hawaii, Arizona, and Chile and space-based facilities beyond planet Earth entirely. The building currently houses around 500,000 plates of images taken from these telescopes.

KEVIN LIN

ARCHITECTURAL SPOTLIGHT: MUSEUM OF HISTORICAL SCIENTIFIC INSTRUMENTS

Just across the hall from the active undergraduate laboratories in the Science Center is the Museum of Historical Scientific Instruments.

KEVIN LIN

Just one of the many histori-cal scientific instruments

Originally part of the Harvard library system, the collection consists of over 20,000 artifacts acquired by the University since 1672. The museum was opened in 1948 as a way to preserve and display the instruments, and has been a part of the History of Science department since 1987. The collection contains instruments from the fields of astronomy, navigation, horology (time-telling), surveying, geology, meteorology, mathematics, physics, biology, medicine, chemistry, experimental psychology, and communications. The instruments that Benjamin Franklin donated to the College after the fire are also housed and displayed here. The museum is free and open to the public. For more information and hours, see p. 249.

Linguistics)." Events hosted by HSMBB range from dinner discussions with faculty members to movie nights. The events are intended to create a comfortable community of scientists that encourages the flow of ideas between students and faculty.

The Harvard-Radcliffe Society of Physics Students (SPS) is one of 700 chapters of the national SPS organization, which was founded in 1968. The Harvard-Radcliffe SPS hosts lunches and dinners with professors and organizes physics talks given by undergraduates researching in the field. The society publishes the SPS Guide to Physics at Harvard, offers tutorials on topics ranging from software programs to graduate school admissions, and helps students find research opportunities.

Harvard College Undergraduate Research Association (HCURA) seeks to connect students with research opportunities and foster regular interactions

ALUMNUS ILLUMINATED:
JOHN WINTHROP

John Winthrop, great great grandson of the founder of the Massachusetts Bay Colony, graduated from Harvard in 1732. He was the second

person ever appointed to the position of Professor in Natural Philosophy and Astronomy in 1738, and he is considered one of the first American astronomers. He wrote a well-received paper entitled "Observations of the Transit of Mercury over the Sun" and, in 1761, led an expedition to watch the transit of Venus in Nova Scotia. The trip was funded by the province of Massachusetts, making it the first scientific expedition sent out and funded by the United States. Under Winthrop, Harvard's astronomy program grew significantly, though it lost ground when the fire of 1764 destroyed numerous telescopes, compasses, and dipping needles.

John Winthrop, Harvard Art Museum, Fogg Art Museum, Harvard University Portrait Collection, Gift of the executors of the Estate of John Winthrop, grandson, 1894, H113

Benjamin Franklin personally supplied new instruments, including the famous astronomical quadrant that he used to measure the heights of celestial bodies. These items are currently on display at the Harvard Museum for Historical Scientific Instruments. Winthrop served as acting President of Harvard in both 1769 and 1773 but declined offers to be the actual President.

between faculty and students through discussions and symposia. It is open to students in all science concentrations. HCURA encourages undergraduates to begin research early in their undergraduate careers and offers advice on how to find and procure research positions.

Student Astronomers at Harvard-Radcliffe (STAHR) was originally founded to watch over the Loomis-Michael Observatory, which is located at the top of the Science Center. The organization offers students a class on proper telescope use; upon completion of the class, students are given free access to the observatory. STAHR also offers classes about observing the night sky, astrophotography, and mythology of the sky. The organization occasionally co-sponsors astrophysics seminars with the Department of Astronomy.

THE SCIENCE CENTER

As the tower of Memorial Hall burned in the infamous 1956 fire (p. 24), legend has it that some faculty members stood gleefully across the street, toasting to the building's natural destruction with champagne.

As the University contemplated expanding its facilities on limited acreage during the 1950s and 1960s, the demolition of Memorial Hall was indeed a popular suggestion, especially considering President Nathan Pusey's (p. 28) contempt for Victorian architecture and commitment to modern design.

Clearly, Pusey never achieved the razing of Memorial Hall, but he certainly realized his intended modernist expansion of the University with the construction of the Science Center. Starting in the late 1950s, the faculty entertained the idea of a center dedicated to the undergraduate study of sciences. In 1964, the Harvard Corporation declared its intent to build a science center, allotting $1 million for its construction with additional funds to be raised from the government and various foundations. However, the University decided not to utilize government funds for the undergraduate-focused center, as the government was more attracted to subsidizing research and graduate studies. Ultimately, Harvard would need to fundraise $11 million from private donors, a task that delayed the project for years.

ALEXANDRA DOWD

The Science Center

An anonymous $12.6 million donation in 1968 ended this delay, and the Science Center officially opened in 1972. At a university that names nearly all of its buildings after Presidents or noteworthy donors and affiliates, the plainly named "Science Center" was an exception. And yet, when the donor was revealed shortly after the building's opening, conspiracy theorists rejoiced: the building, which does look a bit like a Polaroid camera, had been funded by Edwin Land, who studied chemistry for one year at Harvard before leaving for New York City to found the Polaroid Corporation. Architect Joseph Lluis Sert denied any intentional resemblance; he was attempting, he said, to create a physical transition from the Old Yard toward the modern structures planned for Oxford St. as well as from Old Harvard toward a technologically and architecturally advanced future. To facilitate these transitions, in 1967 the University spent $2.3 million to build an automobile underpass for Cambridge St. so that students could walk directly from the Yard to the Science Center.

In the 1970s, concerns grew over the Science Center's stability, but Harvard physics professors insisted it was sound. However, in 1977, the Center's glass roof collapsed under the weight of snow piled on it, and a plastic roof was installed to replace it. Several bomb scares in the Science Center also rattled the community—one, in 1979, stemmed from a student's personal experiments in a chemistry lab and required the building to be evacuated.

Despite these difficulties, the American Institute of Architects awarded Sert and his Science Center the prize for architectural excellence in a university setting in 1979. In 2005, the Science Center underwent construction to expand its classrooms, offices, laboratory space, and food court while also providing a more established home for the Harvard Collection of Historical Scientific Instruments and allowing more natural light to enter the building. Today, the Science Center is also home to the Freshman Mail Center, the Loomis-Michael Observatory, and the Departments of Mathematics, Statistics, and History of Science.

SCIENCE TODAY

In recent years Harvard has poured resources into the sciences with renewed energy. In 1999, the Computer Science department found a home in the Maxwell Dworkin building, donated by Microsoft magnates Bill Gates and Steven Ballmer, both Class of 1977, had Gates not cut his education short. The fall of 2008 saw the opening of the shiny doors of the new Northwest Labs on Oxford St., just north of Memorial Hall and beside the Museum of Natural History. Designed in a contemporary minimalist style by Craig Hartman of Skidmore, Owings, and Merrill, a San Francisco based architecture firm, the building is meant to encourage collaboration and innovation by assigning faculty with similar research interests to the space instead of sealing off individual departments. This includes research on neuroscience, bioengineering, particle physics, and biophysics in addition to other fields.

Harvard administrators and students alike are proud of Harvard College's Program for Research in Science and Engineering (PRISE), which was established just six years ago and has since grown tremendously. The function of

ARCHITECTURAL SPOTLIGHT:
WILLIAM JAMES HALL

William James Hall bears one of the famous psychologist's quotations above its elevators, which take visitors up to the top of the tallest building on campus. It reads, "The community stagnates without the impulse of the individual. The impulse dies away without the sympathy of the community." William James Hall houses Harvard's Departments of Psychology, Sociology, and Social Anthropology, which were grouped together and referred to collectively as the Department of Social Relations until 1972.

ALEXANDRE TERRIEN

the program is twofold. PRISE provides undergraduates the opportunity to conduct 10 weeks of research during the summer with Harvard faculty who are involved in the life sciences, physical sciences, applied sciences, mathematics, and engineering. Students either work in academic departments in the Faculty of Arts and Sciences on campus or join Harvard-affiliated principal investigators at the Harvard Medical School campus or teaching hospitals.

In the spring of 2009, Harvard added a revolutionary new undergraduate concentration, Human Developmental and Regenerative Biology. This is the first of such majors at any college in the U.S. and requires students to engage in hands-on stem-cell-focused research. Space for the Harvard Stem Cell Institute was originally intended to be included in the Allston Science Complex as part of the Allston Expansion Project (p. 33), initiated under University President Larry Summers' tenure. Since the reimagining of the expansion following the financial recession in 2008, the Stem Cell Institute has remained within existing Harvard buildings.

FROM THE ARMCHAIR TO THE LABORATORY

PSYCHOLOGY AT HARVARD

William James introduced the study of psychology to the United States at Harvard. He had originally set out to be a doctor, enrolling at Harvard Medical School in 1864, but a series of illnesses brought him to Germany in search of remedies. There he was introduced to the early inquiries into the scientific study of the human mind, in particular the work of Hermann von Helmholtz and later the work of Pierre Janet in France. Returning to the United States, William James taught his and America's first experimental psychology course at Harvard in the 1875-1876 academic term. In 1902, he reflected, "I originally studied medicine in order to be a physiologist, but I drifted into psychology and philosophy from a sort of fatality. I never had any philosophic instruction, the first lecture on psychology I ever heard being the first I ever gave."

Early in his Harvard career, which lasted from 1872-1907, James established America's first experimental psychology laboratory, which focused primarily on sensation and perception and operated under the conceit of Functionalism, a method of inquiry that focused on the causal relationship between the environment and human behavior. He was also fiercely dedicated to the relationship between the mind and the body, in particular the idea that emotions arise from physiological changes. He and another scientist, Carl Lange, converged on this idea at the same time, giving the James-Lange Theory of Emotion both of their names.

HARVARD MEDICAL SCHOOL

A SHORT STAY IN CAMBRIDGE

Harvard Medical School (HMS) was founded on September 19, 1782. In its infancy in Cambridge, the Medical School was supported by donations that amounted to less than $20,000. In 1800, Ward Nicholas Boylston donated 1100 medical books to the school that, in 1803, were incorporated into the Boylston Medical Library, named after its generous benefactor. John Nichols, whose father was a former Professor of Anatomy at Oxford, donated the majority of his collection to the library. The gift included diseased bones, copper plates, calculi, and various anatomical preparations made by Nichol's father.

The school was meager, consisting of three faculty members and a handful of students who took classes in Harvard Hall (p. 11). Admission required

FUN FACT

George Parkman, the donor of the North Grove plot, disappeared on Friday, November 23, 1849. He had been seen earlier in the day entering the Medical School. Broadcasts were sent out offering rewards for information regarding his whereabouts, but to no avail. Finally, on Sunday, Professor John W. Webster told the Parkman family that George had visited him at the Medical School the afternoon of his disappearance to pick up money that Webster owed him.

The following Friday, a pelvis, right thigh, left leg, and towel marked "W" were found in an outhouse connected to Webster's laboratory at the Medical School. A left thigh and thorax were discovered below minerals in the corner of the laboratory. In the furnace were other human bones and teeth, which were identified to be Parkman's.

Webster was arrested that night. The 12 day Webster Murder Trial, which was attended by some 60,000 people, ended on April 1, 1850, and Webster was hanged on August 30.

no previous academic experience, and students would buy tickets for each lecture instead of paying tuition. The term of study lasted three years. Those that had not graduated from college were offered courses in both Latin and natural philosophy, both prerequisites for the medical degree.

The first class graduated from the Medical School in 1788 with only "Bachelor of Medicine" degrees. It was not until 1811 that the graduating class—along with all living graduates—was awarded "Doctor of Medicine" degrees.

It wasn't long before the Medical School overseers realized that their school was missing a nearby hospital where students could obtain hands-on medical experience. Some students were able to take on apprenticeships with physician alumni during the summer, but it became clear that HMS needed a new location.

JUST ACROSS THE RIVER

In 1805, John C. Warren began to lecture on anatomy in rooms over White's Apothecary Shop at 49 Marlborough St. in Boston (now Washington St.). It was decided that the new medical school would take a temporary residence there until a different building was found. At that point, there were a total of five medical schools in the country, the most prominent of which was at the University of Pennsylvania, where 75% of all the medical students in the country were enrolled.

FROM MASON TO NORTH GROVE

In 1814, when the Medical School student population reached 120, the Faculty felt it necessary to expand further. The government of Massachusetts granted the School an annual sum of $10,000, and in 1816 the School was moved to Mason St., where it was renamed the Massachusetts Medical College. In 1858, the name was again changed to the Medical Department of Harvard University.

In 1847, as the student body continued to grow, the School moved to North Grove St. The land was donated by George Parkman, a well-known physician in the Boston area. While at North Grove, Harvard arranged for the medical students to be admitted for clinical instruction at Massachusetts General Hospital.

ELIOT TO THE RESCUE

Under the guidance of President Eliot, the Medical School established a new curriculum, raised admission standards, and required written exams, grades, and mandatory laboratory instruction in anatomy, physiology, and pathological anatomy. Twenty-four students volunteered to study under the new system, and three new rooms were built in the attic of the Medical School to accommodate laboratory facilities.

RAISING THE BAR

In 1883, a century after it was founded, the Medical School relocated to Boylston St. Boston Children's Hospital opened its doors to the school for teaching purposes and a student library was built. The school introduced entrance examinations—stipulated to be at least 1hr. long—and a systematic fourth year of clinical instruction. Sixteen physicians and surgeons who worked in nearby hospitals instructed the fourth-year students.

In 1906, HMS moved to its current location on Longwood Avenue. Although this was not the school's first location, it was the location of many firsts, including the introduction of insulin to the United States, the development of artificial skin, and the invention of the iron lung for polio patients.

Today, admission to the Medical School is based on academic records, essays, Medical College Admission Test (MCAT) scores, extracurricular activities, previous research and community work relating to medicine and health, and letters of evaluation. The acceptance rate hovers around an intimidating 3%, and tuition is about $47,500 per year.

SCHOOL OF PUBLIC HEALTH

The Harvard School of Public Health (HSPH) was founded in 1922. Instead of medicine, which focuses on the individual, students at HSPH study the population at large, focusing on topics like disease prevention in communities and patterns in global epidemics. Noteworthy graduates of HSPH include two

Nobel Prize winners and six directors of the Centers for Disease Control and Prevention since 1962.

The campus is located primarily on Huntington Ave. in Boston, next to Harvard Medical School, the Harvard School of Dental Medicine, and Countway Library. Shuttles run from HSPH's new offices in the Landmark Center Building to a number of research facilities, including the François-Xavier Bagnoud Building, the Center for Health Communications, the HSPH AIDS Initiative, and the Harvard Injury Control Research Center.

ATHLETICS
AT HARVARD

PIONEERING AMERICAN ATHLETICS

Boasting 41 Division I sports teams, the largest college varsity athletic program in the country, Harvard combines a strong commitment to academics with a top-notch athletic program.

Ever since the Harvard Athletic Association was founded in 1874, Harvard has continued to increase its dedication to athletics. The inception of the Ivy League in 1954 solidified Harvard's dual commitment to both academics and athletics.

For a full list of Harvard's Division I sports, see p. 252.

IN THE BEGINNING...

Harvard's athletics program had an unconventional start. In 1780, a group of sophomores challenged the new class of freshmen to a wrestling match. The losers had to treat the winners to dinner, and the competition quickly became an annual ritual. By the 1820s, these wrestling games were known as "football fights."

This athletic program was quite rudimentary. At the beginning of the 19th century, the only gridiron students had to play on was the delta-shaped piece of land where Memorial Hall now stands. Teams consisted of amateur players who learned the game as they went along, and games, which started at noon each day for several weeks, lasted a mere half hour.

The competitive spirit among Harvard students began to manifest itself throughout the school year as students who played football during the winter took up cricket in the spring. The competitions were a welcome addition to student life and quickly garnered support from the faculty for the health ben-

BY THE NUMBERS

2	Harvard athletic teams that still call themselves Radcliffe and wear Black and White: Women's Rugby and Crew
20	Percentage of Harvard student population active in varsity or junior varsity sports
41	Varsity teams, making Harvard's the largest Division I athletic program in the country
30,323	Maximum attendance in the Harvard Stadium, the first football stadium in the world

FUN FACT

In lieu of their banned initiation ritual, the football fights, sophomore students established a new right of passage. On the first Monday of each term, groups of sophomores visited freshmen in their rooms to haze them. Sophomores would barge into the freshmen's rooms, soak them and their belongings, force them to box, and "perform various antics." Finally, they were thrown head first into the river. According to Harvard historian Samuel Morison, "the average freshman was literally afraid for his life at the beginning of the college year."

efits they afforded the students. Indeed, in 1825, the faculty observed: "there is want of some system for bodily exercises." In response to this growing demand, in 1826 University Hall became, which featured equipment like parallel bars and flying rings. It was not until 1860, however, when Harvard constructed the Rogers Gymnasium, known as the "old gym," that sports became fully integrated into students' extracurricular lives.

The new and exciting opportunity for organized physical activity at Harvard, thanks to the Rogers Gymnasium, marked the end of the students' beloved Delta football fights. Due to increased violence, the faculty decided to ban the fights in September 1860, and students mourned by holding a symbolic burial service.

THE IVY LEAGUE

Although President Eliot attacked intercollegiate sports for promoting competition and deception and taking up time that could be spent on more intellectual pursuits, college athletics persevered during his tenure. In 1933, Caswell Adams of the *New York Herald* coined the term "Ivy League," describing Princeton's and Columbia's football teams as "only Ivy League." The league he was referring to was an informal organization of colleges on the East Coast that developed strong athletic rivalries with one another.

In 1936, the daily newspapers of seven of the eight present day Ivy League schools—the *Columbia Daily Spectator*, the *Cornell Daily Sun*, the *Dartmouth*, the *Harvard Crimson*, the *Daily Pennsylvanian*, the *Daily Princetonian*, and the *Yale Daily News*—simultaneously ran an editorial entitled "Now Is the Time," which pushed for the creation of an official league that would bring these schools together. However, it wasn't until the summer of 1954 that the Ivy League of today—uniting eight of the country's oldest and most distinguished schools, Brown, Columbia, Cornell, Dartmouth, Harvard, Pennsylvania, Princeton, and Yale—came into being. The 1954 founding document states: "Intercollegiate competition must be kept in harmony with the essential educational purposes of the institution." The key principle of the league was to keep college

ARCHITECTURAL SPOTLIGHT:
THE HARVARD STADIUM

Built in 1903, the Harvard Stadium is the oldest stadium in the United States. Inspired by Greco-Roman coliseums, the stadium is an engineering gem: it was the world's first massive reinforced concrete structure. Boasting a maximum capacity of 30,323, the stadium stands as one of only three athletic arenas recognized as National Historic Landmarks, along with the Yale Bowl and the Rose Bowl. Originally a gift of the Class of 1879, the stadium was not built until the turn of the century because many thought it would not be used or that concrete could not survive the harsh New England weather. (If the students can survive the winters here, concrete should have a fighting chance.)

In 1906, in an effort to decrease violence during football games, U.S. President Theodore Roosevelt's committee faced the choice of either introducing the forward pass to the game or widening the field by 40ft. Because the Harvard Stadium had already been built and could not be widened unless it underwent significant and costly changes, the committee adopted the forward pass, which turned out to be one of the most important innovations in football history.

In June 1906, the Classics department used the stadium to present *Agamemnon,* complete with chariots, horses, and a specially built temple. The last theatrical performance in the stadium was Euripides' *Bacchae* in 1982.

The stadium also served as the New England Patriots' home stadium from 1960-61. It was later used in the 1984 Olympics for soccer; Cameroon, Canada, Chile, France, Iraq, Norway, and Qatar all competed here.

The stadium was renovated between 2006 and 2007. Turf replaced the natural grass surface, lights were installed to allow for night games, and a removable dome-like "bubble" was added so it could be used year-round. The bubble enables Harvard varsity teams to practice in the stadium during the winter, and a number of club and intramural sports use the space as well.

FRESHMAN DEAN'S OFFICE
The Harvard Stadium, a U.S. National History Landmark

FUN FACT

Mr. John Langdon Sibley, the University Librarian at the time, described the procession in his diary: a "grand marshall with a huge bearskin cap and baton; ... two bass-drummers; the elegist or chaplain with his Oxford cap and black gown; ... four spade-bearers; six pall-bearers with a six-foot coffin on their shoulders" led the entire sophomore class as they walked across campus to the Delta. Inside the coffin was "simply a football with painted frill fastened into the head of the coffin." As the coffin was lowered into the grave, they sang, to the tune of Auld Lang Syne:

"Ah! woe betide the luckless time
When manly sports decay,
And football stigmatized as a crime
Must sadly pass away
Shall sixty-three submit to see
Such cruel murder done,
And not proclaim the deed of shame?
No! Let's unite as one!
O hapless ball, you little knew
When last upon the air
You lightly o'er the Delta flew,
Your grave was measured there.
Beneath this sod we lay you down,
This scene of glorious fight;
With dismal groans and yells we'll drown
Your mournful burial rite."

FIGHT SONGS

TEN THOUSAND MEN OF HARVARD

Ten thousand men of Harvard want vict'ry today,
For they know that o'er old Eli
Fair Harvard holds sway.
So then we'll conquer old Eli's men,
And when the game ends, we'll sing again:
Ten thousand men of Harvard gained vict'ry today!

HARVARDIANA

With Crimson in triumph flashing
'Mid the strains of victory,
Poor Eli's hopes we are dashing
Into blue obscurity.
Resistless our team sweeps goalward
With the fury of the blast;
We'll fight for the name of Harvard
'Til the last white line is passed.
Harvard! Harvard! Harvard!

For more Harvard songs, check out the Harvard University Band website at http://www.hcs.harvard.edu/~hub/.

sports unadulterated by the spirit of professionalism, specifically through a ban on athletic scholarships. It also aimed to limit acceptance of athletes to those who have proved both academic and athletic merit.

STROKE! STROKE!: ROWING

EARLY HISTORY

Rowing was a popular activity at Harvard even before the athletic program was officially established thanks to the proximity of the Charles River. In 1844, Horace Cunningham, Class of 1846, and a group of enterprising oarsmen pooled funds to purchase Harvard's first eight-oared scull, which they christened "Oneida." Thus was born Harvard's first boat club. Just two years later, the team paddled to its first victory in a 2mi. race organized on the Charles.

Other boat clubs representing different class years quickly formed at Harvard and competed against one another. Boating, however, remained largely a leisure activity until Harvard's first race against Yale in 1852. Challenged by a Yale boat club "to test the superiority of the oarsmen of the two colleges,"

Harvard triumphed in the 2mi. race on Lake Winnipesaukee, New Hampshire. This race marked America's first intercollegiate athletic event. More importantly, the race marked the beginning of the notorious rivalry between Harvard and Yale. The rivalry spread like wildfire among other athletic teams at the two schools as well as among various other groups and clubs, from debate teams to blood drives.

In 1858, Harvard rowing had a watershed season. During one of the regattas, Charles Eliot, future President of Harvard, and his captain Benjamin W. Crowninshield, too demure for "shirts and skins," bought six crimson China silk handkerchiefs to tie around their heads to distinguish members of the Harvard team from competitors. The Harvard boats won each of the subsequent races in the regatta, and the crimson costume stuck. The trend eventually spread to Harvard's other sports teams, and today all of Harvard' athletic teams proudly wear crimson uniforms.

ALUMNUS ILLUMINATED:
LEVERETT SALTONSTALL, CLASS OF 1914

Before he was elected Governor of Massachusetts and, later, U.S. Senator, Leverett Saltonstall, Class of 1914, was captain of the first ever American junior varsity crew team to win the prestigious Grand Challenge Cup at the Henley Royal Regatta.

True Boston Brahmins, the Saltonstalls trace their roots back to 1631, when Sir Richard Saltonstall's boat, the *Arbella,* sailed the Charles River. Leverett was a 10th-generation Saltonstall graduate from Harvard, where he also earned his law degree in 1917. Saltonstall served as a first lieutenant in the U.S. Army during and after World War I. Upon his return, he entered the political sphere and was elected to the Massachusetts House of Representatives in 1922, eventually becoming Speaker of the House. He served as Governor from 1939-45, and as a U.S. Senator from 1945-67. In 1944, Saltonstall reunited the crew that won the regatta on the Thames in 1914 to row together once again on the Charles.

When asked what he most believed in, Saltonstall replied, "It might sound more impressive if I said something like 'democracy' or 'the country,' but let's not be pretentious. What I believe in most is Harvard and my family."

VICTORIES AT HOME AND ABROAD

In 1869, Harvard's rowers decided to tackle a much larger body of water than the Charles River: they took to the Thames River in England. A four-oar crew from Oxford had challenged the Crimson rowers to a race. Unfortunately, the Harvard boats could not keep up, and Harvard suffered its first ever rowing loss, leading to a 45-year comeback struggle that mercifully ended in 1914, when Harvard's junior varsity crew team won the Grand Challenge Cup at the Henley Royal Regatta, Britain's most prominent rowing competition. This title was not, however, won over a competing British team, but rather over Boston's Union Boat Club, in what was called a "Yankee Grand Final." Twenty-five years later, the varsity team won the prestigious trophy at the 100th Henley Regatta, where they triumphed again in 1950 and 1959.

Harvard's outstanding rowing performances did not end at Henley. After a spectacular spring in the qualification races for the 1968 Olympic Games in Mexico City, the heavyweight team went on to represent the United States at the Games, ranking sixth in the world. Seventeen years later, in 1985, the team won the "Grand Slam," taking home the Eastern Sprints title (with a victory over Yale), the National Championship, and, once again, the Grand Challenge Cup at Henley. Andrew H. Sudduth, Class of 1985, a member of the crew in

ARCHITECTURAL SPOTLIGHT:
WELD BOATHOUSE

Situated at the intersection of John F. Kennedy St. and Memorial Dr., the Weld Boathouse is the second of two buildings in Harvard's history to bear this name. The first boathouse was a bare wooden structure that

was donated in 1890 by George Walker Weld, Class of 1860. Weld one-upped himself in 1907, donating a second time to build a newer, more modern boathouse. Today, the Weld Boathouse is home to the Radcliffe Crew team as well as the recreational sculling and intramural house crew programs.

ALEXANDRE TERRIEN
Weld Boathouse, the home of Radcliffe crew

BEN BAYLEY

Harvard Varsity lightweight eight rowing on the Charles River

that year, went on to win the silver medal at both the 1984 Olympics and at the World Sculling Championships. In 2002, the team achieved what no non-English crew had ever done before in the Henley Royal Regatta: they won three titles, the Ladies' Challenge Plate, the Britannia Cup, and the Temple Cup. Three years later, the heavyweights won their second straight national championship, crowning one of the best seasons in Harvard rowing history. The heavyweight team's most recent victory was a first place win at the Head of the Charles Regatta in the fall of 2011.

Traditionally, the lightweight crew has achieved similar success. Three years after its founding in 1921, the Crimson defeated Yale and Princeton at the first event of the Goldthwait Cup, which now occurs annually. In 1958, the lightweight team won its first of three consecutive Thames Challenge Cups at the Henley Royal Regatta, which they won again in 1966. In 1971, they captured the Thames cup in an eight-oared boat, the Wyfold Challenge Cup in a four, and made it to the Grand Finals at the Pan American Game trials. Double winners at Henley, this crew was nicknamed the "Superboat" for winning all of its races by an average of 17sec.

RADCLIFFE ROWS

In the wake of the lightweight men's success in 1971, a group of motivated Radcliffe students founded the first Harvard women's crew team. Just one year later, the team ranked third at Nationals, and the following year they won the championship. They were then chosen to represent the United States at the Moscow World Championships. The Radcliffe heavyweight rowers' success continued over the years, as they won the Eastern Sprints title three years in a row from 1973-1975. The 1987 season was particularly memorable for Radcliffe crew: the varsity heavyweights not only completed the season undefeated but also won the Eastern Championships and the Ivy League. Six of the boat's eight rowers then competed in the 1988 and 1992 Olympic games.

Of them, Anna B. Seaton, Class of 1986, and Lindsay H. Burns, Class of 1987, became the first two Radcliffe women to win Olympic medals, respectively winning the bronze in the pair without coxswain in Barcelona in 1992 and the silver in lightweight double sculls in Atlanta in 1996. The Radcliffe lightweight team, which began competing in 1974, just a few years after their heavyweight counterparts, has maintained a strong presence in the intercollegiate rowing world, including six National Championship gold medals between 1986 and 1997. Success continues into recent memory as well: Radcliffe heavyweight crew won the NCAA Team Points Trophy and the NCAA National Championship in the first varsity eight in 2003, capping their greatest season ever, and the lightweights won their most recent National Championship in 2004.

HARVARD WINS 29-29!: FOOTBALL

EARLY HISTORY

In 1871, class teams started to play each other in a new game called "Boston football." These games became so popular that the Harvard University Foot Ball Club (HUFBC) was established in the following year and found itself a rather unusual home: Holden Chapel in Harvard Yard (p. 16). Under the leadership of Charlie and Morton Prince (the latter eventually became a Professor of Abnormal Psychology at Harvard Medical School), the HUFBC proceeded to establish its own set of rules for the game, largely modeled off those of English rugby.

When McGill University in Canada challenged Harvard to a two-game series in 1874, one game followed McGill's Canadian rugby rules, in which players could run with the ball in hand and throw it, and the other followed the rules of HUFBC. On May 14th, 1874, Harvard faced McGill at Jarvis Field in Cambridge. The number of players on each side was originally going to be 15, but was lowered to 11 after four McGill players were unable to make the trip. Instead of forcing a forfeit, Harvard embraced the new team size, setting a trend that would later become regulation for Harvard football. Harvard won the first game 3-0 and tied the second.

After another game in Montreal in October of the same year, Harvard abandoned the HUFBC regulations and adopted rules that combined traditional soccer and English rugby, creating the basis for modern-day American football. Whether you're a fan of the New England Patriots, the Cincinnati Bengals, or the San Francisco 49ers, all football fans have Harvard to thank for the rules of the game. Before these games, football was mainly a kicking game, but it adopted the option to pick up the ball with one's hands from rugby. Under the new rules Harvard challenged Tufts University to the first American intercollegiate game in 1875. Harvard came fancily clad in formal

ARCHITECTURAL SPOTLIGHT: RADCLIFFE GYMNASIUM

Located next to Fay House (p. 45), the Radcliffe Gymnasium was donated by Harriet Lawrence Hemenway, whose husband donated the funds to build the Hemenway Gym, built in 1898. The building was built

KEVIN LIN

Agassiz House and the Radcliffe Gymnasium in the Radcliffe Yard

of brick to harmonize with Fay House and the other buildings in the Radcliffe Yard by the world famous architectural firm Mckim, White and Mead. However, in order to display the different functions of the two buildings, the window structuring of the Gymnasium and Fay House differ. For example, the gym has fewer windows, in an alternating scheme. In the spring of 1981, the gymnasium was renovated to house the Radcliffe Dance Center and the Henry A. Murray Research Center, which collects information and sponsors research concerning the impact of social change on women's lives. In 2006 it was renovated again and became the official headquarters of the Radcliffe Institute for Advanced Study (p. 45).

uniforms in the newly chosen school colors, crimson and white. On November 13th, 1874, Harvard wore its uniform again when facing Yale for their first rivalry game at Hamilton Field in New Haven.

THE GAME: HARVARD VS. YALE

Today's most notable manifestation of the Harvard-Yale rivalry is the annual football game between the Harvard Crimson and the Yale Elis, known to most simply as "The Game." Ever since the first game on November 13, 1875, from which Harvard emerged victorious, it has become an annual tradition for the Crimson and the Elis to face off against each other. The Game, whose location alternates between the two campuses, is traditionally the last game of the Ivy

League season. This tradition has been memorialized at Harvard in the Cambridge Queen's Head Pub, which opened in 2007 in the basement of Memorial Hall. The pub's wall proudly sports the final scores of past Games.

FOOTBALL GETS ORGANIZED

In 1876, shortly after the first Harvard-Yale game, Harvard, Princeton, and Columbia founded the Intercollegiate Football Association, the precursor to the Ivy League. Harvard also played in the first East-West intersectional football game against the Michigan Wolverines, winning 4-0, on October 13, 1881. This particularly violent game concerned the University administration. Describing football as "modified mayhem," the Athletic Committee considered banning the sport from campus in 1885. Just a year later, the ruthless Crimson scored its highest single-game total ever, beating Philips Exeter 156-0. In that same year, Harvard scored a whopping 765 points in a single season, a record that still holds today. In 1895, a strong majority of the faculty voted to abolish the game, but the Athletic Committee, composed mostly of alumni and enrolled students, voted unanimously to maintain the sport, and the Harvard Corporation followed the committee's recommendation.

A HARVARD TRADITION

The reinstatement of Harvard football saw the emergence of the "Little Red Flag," one of The Game's oldest traditions. It's as simple as it sounds: a Harvard supporter waves the emblematic flag every time Harvard scores. Originally carried by Frederick Plummer, Class of 1888, who witnessed 59 consecutive Games, the flag began to be awarded to the alumnus who had witnessed the most consecutive Games. Allen Rice, Class of 1902, was the last to hold the record, having attended 73 Games in a row. Today, the "Little Red Flag"

Harvard University Foot Ball Club in 1875,
Harvard University Archives, HUPSF Football (1)

FUN FACT

In the summer of 1890, Major Henry Lee Higginson, Class of 1855, donated 51 acres to the University for the creation of "Soldiers Field." This large piece of land was meant to commemorate six of Higginson's Harvard classmates who died fighting for the Union during the Civil War (p. 18). Twenty years earlier, Professor Henry Wadsworth Longfellow had donated 30 acres of land a short distance away from Higginson's donation. Harvard later purchased the space between the two plots to build its main athletic complex in Allston. Soldiers Field proved a versatile athletic facility, and by 1894, all of Harvard's outdoor athletics teams, with the exception of track and field, competed there.

---

has become something more of a lifetime achievement award instead of a game count. Bill Markus, Class of 1960, aptly nicknamed "Superfan" by Harvard Magazine, has held the flag since 2001.

SHAPING FOOTBALL AS WE KNOW IT

The turn of the 20th century saw the development of a fascinating contrast in the football world. The sport was becoming increasingly popular and competitive. Throughout the East Coast, colleges expanded their athletic programs and recruited a growing number of players for their athletic skills.

The football frenzy was naturally fueled by the supporters. As Craig Lambert describes, "the sport roused powerful passions and triggered primitive, atavistic celebrations." Harvard alumni felt the same enthusiasm, and in 1903 they funded the construction of a proper football stadium, the first in the nation. As more people were attending games, revenues dramatically increased. As their winning records grew and the revenue genereated by the football programs increased, colleges began to pay coaches absurd amounts of money. When Coach Bill Reid, Class of 1901, returned to Harvard in 1905, his salary was a third higher than any faculty member and approached that of University President Eliot.

On the other hand, the years following the completion of the stadium also cast a pall on the game as critics decried its inherent brutality. President Eliot was strongly opposed to violent sports and pushed to ban them on campus. Support for Eliot's position grew as death and injury tolls rose: in the 1905 football season, 18 college players were killed and 159 seriously injured. The debate raged on at the turn of the century, so much so that U.S. President Theodore Roosevelt, Class of 1880, organized a conference at the White House to discuss the future of football.

President Roosevelt's conference resulted in the creation of the Intercollegiate Athletic Association of the United States—the forerunner of the

FUN FACT

When America entered the World War II in 1941, most of Harvard's football players left to fight in Europe, and official football games were temporarily halted. Passion for the sport, however, drove remaining students to organize informal games. During one notable episode on November 20, 1943, nearly 45,000 people turned out to see Harvard confront Boston College in the first meeting between the two colleges in any athletic competition in 24 years.

NCAA—which was endorsed by 62 institutions of higher education, including Harvard, to regulate the game. Rules were altered yet again in the interest of safety, and the sport of football lived on. The new rules proved to be a boon for Harvard, and the Crimson football team saw much success over the next two decades. Coached by the legendary Percy Haughton, the team earned its record-setting 33-game winning streak in the 1910s and won four of Harvard's seven national titles, the last of which it won in 1920 with a close 7-6 victory over Oregon. Percy Haughton was inducted into the College Football Hall of Fame in 1951.

FOOTBALL IN THE IVY LEAGUE

In 1956, Harvard and Cornell competed in the first formal game of the Ivy League, which Harvard won 32-7. Since then, Harvard has won 14 Ivy League titles, the first of which was shared with Columbia on November 25, 1961, after Harvard toppled Yale 27-0 in its 27th victory over the Elis. Harvard snagged its first solo Ivy League title on November 22, 1975, with a 10-7 victory over Yale at the Yale Bowl. The most recent title was won in the fall of 2011.

Harvard victories over Yale tend to generate a great deal of excitement, and nowhere is this more tangible than in the ranks of the Harvard University Band. Two years after the Ivy League formed, after the Crimson crushed the Elis in New Haven to the tune of 28-0, it was reported that the Band made so much noise in celebration that the entire group was thrown in jail. Lucky for them, their judge was a Harvard graduate, and the Band was released with only a warning.

HARVARD BEATS YALE 29-29

In 1969, *Sports Illustrated* named that year's Game between Harvard and Yale one of the five best college football games ever played. Both teams were undefeated that season, but Yale, 16th in the nation with star players like Brian Dowling and Calvin Hill, the NFL's number one draft pick that year, kicked off as the favorite to win. After dominating the game, the Elis were ahead 29 to 13 with 42 seconds left before the end the fourth quarter. To cheers and

ALUMNUS ILLUMINATED: WILLIAM H. LEWIS HLS CLASS OF 1893

On November 30, 1893, at the Thanksgiving Day game against the University of Pennsylvania, William H. Lewis was appointed the first black captain of the Harvard football team. Lewis excelled far beyond the gridiron, however. He went on to graduate from Harvard Law School, was elected to the Cambridge City Council in 1899, to the Legislature in 1901, and then named Assistant U.S. Attorney for Boston in 1903. Finally, in 1910, U.S. President William Howard Taft appointed Lewis as Assistant Attorney General of the United States.

the singing of "Harvardiana" and "Ten Thousand Men of Harvard," Harvard miraculously got two conversions and scored two touchdowns in the last 42 seconds to tie the game 29-29. *The Harvard Crimson*'s headline the next day famously read, "Harvard Beats Yale 29-29."

THE GAME TODAY

Today, The Game remains Harvard's most anticipated athletic event of the year. Harvard hosts The Game every other year, and students, professors, alumni, and the greater Cambridge community unite to cheer for the Crimson. When The Game is held at the Yale Bowl in New Haven, thousands of Harvard students and alumni make the trip down to Connecticut to support the Crimson. Many students consider this weekend one of the highlights of the fall semester and a welcome distraction to the dismal New England November weather, which still doesn't prevented widespread tailgating at both Universities every November.

FUN FACT

On October 11, 1947, Chester Pierce, Class of 1948, a standout tackle for the Crimson, became the first black football player to play against an all-white college in the South when Harvard played against the University of Virginia in Charlottesville.

ALUMNUS ILLUMINATED:
TOMMY LEE JONES, CLASS OF 1969

You might recognize him from his film and television career—*Love Story* (1970), *Men in Black* (1997), *Rules of Engagement* (2000), and *No Country for Old Men* (2007), to name just a few—but Tommy Lee Jones, Class of 1969, commanded more than just the stage during his years at Harvard. In addition to pursuing acting and directing opportunities and joining the Signet Society of Arts & Letters, Jones was a powerhouse left guard for the Crimson football team. In 1968, he led the team to victory in an undefeated season and was honored as an All-Ivy League selection. While at the College, Jones roomed with former U.S. Vice President Al Gore in Dunster House. Since his graduation, Jones has stayed involved in the Harvard sports community in an unusual capacity. Now an avid polo player, Jones assumed the role as chief patron of the Harvard polo program and regularly invites the team to train at his ranch in San Saba, Texas. In a recent display of generosity, Jones donated three horses—Patches, Commondante, and Munyeca—to the team.

HOME RUN!:
BASEBALL AT HARVARD

The first attempts to organize baseball at Harvard took place at Lawrence Scientific School in 1858. Harvard students chose to play according to the "New York" rules, laid out by the New York Knickerbockers in 1845. These rules looked much like our rules do today, including three strikes, foul balls, and three-out innings. The rules caught on and quickly spread to Boston. In 1862, freshmen Georges A. Flagg and Frank Wright formed the Harvard University Base Ball Club, composed of "class nines" (groups of nine students, one to fill each position of the field, from the same graduating class) to play against each other. Playing and practicing in the HUBBC league paid off when Harvard won its first game against Brown in Providence in 1863. Two years later, the best players of the "class nines" came together again and won the first strictly intercollegiate game in 1865 against Williams College. That same year, the Harvard Base Ball Club won the Silver Ball, becoming New England's premier baseball team.

In the following years, the Harvard baseball team defeated Princeton, Yale, and Dartmouth. In 1872, Harvard and Yale established an annual three-game series, a tradition that mirrors that of The Game and continues today.

FUN FACT

Curve pitching was first introduced by Princeton in a game against Harvard on June 4, 1875. President Eliot, already critical of college athletics, noted that deception was not a value he wished to cultivate at Harvard, in reference to Princeton's frequent use of the sneaky technique.

One of Harvard's most significant contributions to baseball can be traced back to Frederick W. Thayer, Class of 1878. After watching teammate and starting catcher James A. Tyng, Class of 1876, suffer from game-hindering timidity in the face of blazing fastballs, Thayer engineered the first ever catcher's mask, inspired by the fencing mask, to guard him from perilous pitches. With this added security, Tyng made only two errors during his first masked game, a number exceptionally low even for a professional catcher at the time. Thayer patented the mask and it was soon sold in the 1878 Spalding catalogue and introduced to the major league, where it was quickly embraced by professionals.

After practicing all over campus, the baseball team found its home at Soldiers Field in 1898, following a donation from Major Henry L. Higginson. In 1995, the baseball field was renamed the O'Donnell Field after Joseph J. O'Donnell, Class of 1967, and MBA, Class of 1971, who endowed the baseball program with a $2.5 million gift, enabling Joe Walsh to become the first full-time head coach in the history of Harvard baseball. The O'Donnell Field, considered one of the best fields in New England, has been the home of the Harvard baseball team ever since, and it was there that the Crimson won its three consecutive Ivy League Championship titles in 1998, 1999, and 2000.

Harvard University Base Ball Club in 1866,
Harvard University Archives, HUPSF Baseball (2)

MORE SPORTS

Although President Eliot was an outspoken critic of sports, especially contact ones—he was quoted in the *New York Times* describing them as "very objectionable"—Harvard athletics blossomed during his tenure (1869-1909). New sports sprung up on campus, and track and field, boxing, and wrestling were introduced as entertainment between boat races in the 1870s and gradually developed into independent sports. In 1874, the Harvard Athletic Association was formed with Benjamin R. Curtis, class of 1875, as its president. For the next 20 years, the HAA organized sports such as running, leaping, boxing, wrestling, and gymnastics.

TRACK

It wasn't until 1880 that track began to flourish at Harvard. Evert Wendell, Class of 1882, won the 100-, 220-, and 440-yard dashes, and his success propelled Harvard to the forefront of intercollegiate track as the team won its first of seven consecutive titles. Six years later, Wendell Baker, Class of 1886, established a world record of 47.75 seconds in the 440-yard dash. His success was especially impressive given that he lost his shoe 50 yards from the finish line.

As Harvard's national athletic authority developed, so did its international competitive presence. In July of 1895, instead of playing against each other, the Crimson and the Elis united in a rare athletic partnership to organize a Crimson-Eli track team to compete against the Oxford-Cambridge team at Queens Club in London. Since that date, this competition has continued to meet biannually and is today the world's oldest continuing international intercollegiate competition.

Harvard's international track success continued in 1896, when Harvard students won eight of America's 11 silver medals at the first modern Olympic Games in Athens in 1896. This is even more impressive than it sounds: at that time, there was no such thing as a gold medal, and the silver was the Games' top prize. One member of this high-flying team, James B. Connolly, Class of 1899, made history by winning the first ever silver medal awarded at the modern Olympics in the triple jump. This historic win cost him his place at the College, as he was forced to pull out of school in order to take the time to make the trip abroad. Connolly was eventually honored by Harvard in 1949 with a varsity letter for his historic achievement.

FUN FACT

During his time as a student, Harvard President A. Lawrence Lowell, Class of 1877, set the school's records in the 880-yard dash and 1mi. race on the dirt track at Jarvis Field in November of 1875.

A couple of decades later, Edward O. Gourdin, Class of 1921, broke the world record for the long jump with his 25' 3" leap in the biannual Oxford-Cambridge match, a record that still stands today.

In 1967, Harvard's cross-country ski team embarked on an incredible string of victories, tearing through a 33-meet winning streak and claiming four Heptagonal Championships. Less than a decade later, the women's track and field and cross-country teams joined the men's as varsity programs. Among the key players on this first team was Judy Rabinowitz, Class of 1980, who later represented the United States in the 1984 Sarajevo Olympic Games as a cross-country skier. The head coach of track and field, William McCurdy, retired in 1982 after 30 years of loyal and skilled coaching at Harvard, and the McCurdy outdoor track was named in his honor.

CROSS COUNTRY

Harvard was the first American university to have a cross-country team, introducing it as a men's sport in 1880. The team started off simply as a way for track and field athletes, who compete in the spring, to stay in shape during the fall. The sport quickly spread to other colleges, and intercollegiate competition began in 1890 (though Harvard did not compete until 1902). Harvard did

DAVID A. PAINE
Harvard Track & Field

not institute a women's team until 1976, and varsity status was first given to the women's team one year later, in 1977.

Harvard's longest standing rivalries are with Yale and Princeton, against whom the men have competed in a triangular meet since 1922. The men hold a 59-39 record against Yale and a 44–22 record against Princeton. The women's teams have participated in the triangular meet as a varsity event since 1977 and hold a record of 19–15 against Yale but trail Princeton 10–24.

Harvard's men's team has won the Ivy League conference team championship seven times and has produced nine individual champions. The women's team has also won seven conference team titles and nine individual championships. Jason Saretsky, the head coach of both programs since 2006, has coached seven individual national championship qualifiers (four men and three women) as well as one individual conference champion.

TENNIS AND SQUASH

Cricket, tennis, and lacrosse originated in Harvard's Eliot era as well. In fact, tennis became an officially organized sport at Harvard a year before it was recognized by the U.S. Lawn Tennis Association, and it quickly became an important sport on campus. By 1921, Harvardians had earned 16 singles and 17 doubles championships.

Harvard tennis player Dwight Davis, Class of 1900, won several of those titles. He rose to the rank of runner-up in the U.S. men's singles championships and gained national fame as a doubles player with his partner and close friend Holcombe Ward, Class of 1900. In 1900, after winning three national championships together, Davis and Ward stepped into the international scene. They challenged a British team in a new competition called the International Lawn Challenge Trophy. Davis personally purchased the cup, designed by an Englishman named Rowland Rhodes, and the competition was named the Davis Cup. Today, the Davis Cup is the largest annual team competition in sports and one of the most prestigious competitions in international tennis.

Not surprisingly, given the popularity of its brother racket sport, squash became a hit when it arrived on campus in 1922. In its first 16 seasons, the Crimson team won five national titles. Harvard Squash remains a powerhouse today, as they have captured 17 Ivy League titles and 12 National Championships.

SWIMMING AND WATER POLO

The first athletic facility built at Harvard was a bathhouse, built in 1800 on the bank of the Charles River. In 1881, the Harvard Register argued for the need of a more "spacious water-tank, or swimming-bath" to enable students to exercise in addition to bathing. Soon after, the first athletic swimming pool was

LAUREL MCCARTHY

Women's Varsity Water Polo

installed behind the Old Gym. Harvard pumped water from the Charles River at flood tide every day in order to keep the pool filled, but swimming existed only as a recreational sport until 1929, when the competitive swimming program began to take shape. Harold S. Ulen became the first coach of the swimming team, and after 30 years as head coach he established a still-standing record of 261 victories with only 48 defeats. The University now awards a prize in his name to graduating seniors who exhibit outstanding sportsmanship and teamwork.

Ulen's impressive coaching, coupled with the natural talent and hard work of Harvard athletes, brought many Crimson swimmers to Olympic fame. Charles G. Hutter, Class of 1938, was Harvard's first Olympic swimmer, and after winning Harvard's first NCAA men's swimming title, he won the gold for the U.S. in the 800-meter relay at the Berlin games. The next Harvard American Olympian was Robert W. Hackett, Class of 1981, who not only placed second at the 1976 Montreal Olympics, but also set eight University records. He finished his college career with 12 All-America selections and 20 East Seaboard titles, and in 1978, at the first swim meet to take place in Blodgett Pool, Hackett led Harvard to a close victory over Princeton. Finally, David Berkoff, Class of 1989, won a silver medal at the 1988 Seoul Olympics, in addition to his second NCAA title during that year.

Today, the varsity acquatic programs include, traditional swimming as well as diving and water polo. Men's water polo was established in 1980, and the women's team was founded just three years later. The women's team has had incredible success both in and out of the pool: 10 of their players were recently named to the Collegiate Water Polo Association's Scholar-Athlete Team for their excellence in academics as well as athletics.

SKIING

The preceding decade has witnessed a period of tremendous growth and development for Harvard Skiing. The program is comprised of alpine and nordic squads; both follow rigorous training and conditioning schedules during the off-season, patiently awaiting the first Boston snowfall. While the teams train at separate locations, competitions occur at the same venues during the "carnival" season, which includes six weekends of intercollegiate competition from January to March.

The program has undergone an exciting transformation over the past few years. This change must be credited to both the incredible dedication of head coaches Tim Mitchell and Chris City, the increasing strength and depth of recent classes of recruits, and the passion and work ethic of each member of the team. The team has advanced from a recreational ski club to a competitive team whose members regularly post individual finishes in the top 15 on the carnival circuit.

In 2011, eleven skiers were named to the U.S. Collegiate Ski Coaches Association All-Academic Team, placing third in the league in total number of All-Academic team members despite being the smallest team on the circuit.

CLUB AND INTRAMURALS

Many students who do not participate in varsity or junior varsity sports still get involved in Harvard athletics through club sports and intramural House teams. In fact, in addition to having the nation's largest Division I Athletics Program, Harvard also boasts one of the oldest recreational athletics programs in the country.

The club program offers 48 sports, including traditional sports such as tennis and lacrosse and more unconventional ones such as aikido (Japanese martial arts), ballroom dance, and Quidditch. Its organizational structure relies on a balance of student initiative and University support. All the teams are student led and directed, while Harvard provides the facilities.

The inter-House intramural program is a three-season-long fight for the championship Straus Cup, which is awarded each year to the House that has garnered the most points (Winthrop House, p. 145); in the Yard, freshman dorms compete for the Yard Bucket. Students can participate in any number of ways, trying their hand at sports ranging from basketball to ultimate frisbee to soccer. While it is the least competitive of Harvard's sports leagues, the intramural program is certainly not taken lightly—Houses have been known to stack their basketball teams with varsity athletes and demand early morning practices for their IM crews.

ALAN KIRKPATRICK

Harvard Alpine Skiing

ARCHITECTURAL SPOTLIGHT:
THE MAC

After its renovation in 1985, the Indoor Athletic Building was renamed

ALEXANDRE TERRIEN

the Malkin Athletic Center (MAC) in honor of Peter L. Malkin, Class of 1955, who donated the funds for the renovation. Located between Kirkland and Lowell Houses, the MAC is nestled among the river Houses, making it one of the most convenient sports facilities on campus. Students can be seen dashing in and out of the building at all hours, clad in running spandex and T-shirts, regardless of the weather. The five-story Georgian-style building serves as both a mainstay for the University's recreational facilities and a satellite location for several varsity sports, including fencing, wrestling, and volleyball.

The original facility was built largely with the money of a donor known only by the pseudonym "Alumnus Aquaticus," or "Mr. Anonymous Aquaticus." These donations enabled Harvard to build its first swimming pool, which was dedicated at the 1930 NCAA championships. To Harvard's chagrin, however, no one from Harvard was eligible to participate in the championships that year, since this was the first time that the College had a pool adequate for competitive swimming.

RECRUITING

Harvard and the rest of the Ivy League schools do not award athletic scholarships but do recruit athletes for their varsity teams.

Recruitment traditionally starts in February, when coaches review databases of rising high school juniors and seniors that have expressed interest in being recruited. Coaches then mail questionnaires to a smaller pool of students selected from the database that asks for basic information such as high school GPAs and transcripts in addition to highlight videos. Student-athletes are then invited to visit campus to watch meets or games and to attend special weekends known in the Harvard athletic world as "camps." The Harvard football program, for example, invites around 600 high school students to Camp in June, and approximately 50 students are identified as top picks.

These pre-selected students are by no means, however, guaranteed admission to Harvard. They still apply to the Admissions and Financial Aid Office like the rest of their peers, but are given the added benefit of a coach's recommendation, which includes the coach's endorsement of the students' athletic and academic value.

For more information on recruiting, visit the Harvard Athletic Department website at www.gocrimson.com.

HOUSES
AT HARVARD

KEVIN LIN

Adams House

KEVIN LIN

Cabot House

KEVIN LIN

Currier House

KEVIN LIN

Dunster House

OFFICE OF PUBLIC AFFAIRS

Eliot House

KEVIN LIN

Kirkland House

ALEXANDRE TERRIEN

Lowell House

KEVIN LIN

Leverett House

121

KEVIN LIN

Mather House

KEVIN LIN

Pforzheimer House

SCOTT YIM

Quincy House

KEVIN LIN

Winthrop House

BY THE NUMBERS

1	Indoor pool turned theater: the Adams House Pool
3	Quad Houses: Residents of Cabot, Currier, and Pforzheimer Houses love the quiet suburban neighborhood feel but hate the half-mile walk from Harvard Yard, especially in the winter
13	Houses: All have their pros and all have their cons. Excepting Dudley, the House belonging to students who live off-campus, all Houses have their own dining halls, libraries, and gyms
120,000	Volumes in Hicks House, the library of Kirkland House

RESIDENTIAL HOUSES

Of all the Harry Potter analogies that can be applied to Harvard—a Hogwarts-esque Great Hall for dining, building names like "Wigglesworth" and "Pennypacker," and a regime of kindly but cryptic old wizards—the one that rings truest is the living situation. At the end of freshman year, after having spent a year in

ALEXANDRA DOWD

The Charles River

the dormitories around Harvard Yard, rising sophomores group themselves into one- to eight-person blocking groups and are sorted randomly into one of 12 upperclass residential Houses. The next fall, they leave the pastoral glory of the Yard and set up shop by the Charles River (River Houses) or in the Radcliffe Quadrangle (Quad Houses). A Potter-esque sorting hat does not come into play, although there are a few Quidditch teams floating around campus (p. 116).

Housing Day occurs each March on the last Thursday before Spring Break. Throughout the spring semester the Houses engage in friendly debate to see who can claim the title of most desirable for the freshmen to join. YouTube videos are circulated promoting individual Houses while freshmen nervously attempt to assess the merits of each. Most blocking groups gather together on Housing Day morning, anxiously awaiting the crowd of upperclassmen who knock on their doors and inform them of their House assignment for the next three years.

Each House at Harvard is unique—some feature architectural marvels, some have rooms with breathtaking views of the river, and some host notorious evenings of debauchery throughout the year—but they all share a few key characteristics that make Harvard housing special. Each has its own dining hall, athletic equipment, art and music rooms, common spaces, libraries, and series of regularly scheduled social events including community meals, formal dances, and local day trips. In the Houses, students live in any combination of single rooms and suites. Each House was built at a unique time, so housing varies across campus. Most students end up with their own bedrooms senior year, but future CEOs and Presidents sleep in bunk beds in their early twenties.

Between 300 and 500 students live in each House. The undergraduate members of the House are known as the Junior Common Room, a term borrowed from the systems in place at Oxford and Cambridge. Residential tutors and House Masters comprise the Senior Common Room, and share the House with students.

For the small percentage of students who choose not to live on campus (around 2% of undergraduates), Dudley House, which has a dining hall, study space, and a cafe in a corner of the Yard, serves as a connection to the University.

KEVIN LIN

The Quad

HOUSE SYSTEM HISTORY

The Harvard Houses took shape under President Lowell, who led the College from 1909 to 1933. In 1929, Edward S. Harkness, an alumnus of Yale University, came to President Lowell with the initiative and the funds to set Harvard up with its own residential college system, just like the residential colleges at Oxford and Cambridge across the pond. Yale, with characteristic shortsightedness, had refused Harkness's original proposition (humoring the misguided institution, Harkness generously dished out for the Yale residential colleges four years later). At Harvard, what was originally a plan to donate $3 million for the construction of seven Houses quickly ballooned to $13 million. In the 1930s, new Houses were built and existing buildings were transformed into Houses.

One of Lowell's main objectives in invigorating the House system was to bring a sense of egalitarian living to the University, by making private, more expensive housing—the "Gold Coast," as the buildings along Mt. Auburn St. were known—obsolete.

For a time, students could submit preferences for housing. This led to distinctive personalities among the Houses: Adams was the artsy house, Kirkland was packed with athletes, and so on. In the 1990s, however, the College adopted a system of randomization. Today, the stereotypes of the Dunster musician and the Lowell House poet have, for the most part, faded away.

Edward S. Harkness, Harvard Art Museum, Fogg Art Museum, Harvard University Portrait Collection, Gift of Edward S. Harkness to Harvard University for Lowell House, 1932, H424

ADAMS HOUSE

MOTTO: Alteri Seculo
"For a future generation." Cicero: "He who plants trees labors for the benefit of a future generation."

NAMESAKE
The Adams family, whence noted Harvard alums John and Elvira

IMPORTANT DATES
Oldest building from 1760; most were built or purchased between 1916 and 1932. Adams House was born in 1930.

CURRENT MASTERS
Judy Palfrey, T. Berry Brazelton Professor of Pediatrics at Harvard Medical School, and Sean Palfrey, Professor of Pediatrics and Public Health at Boston University/Boston Medical Center

NOTABLE ALUMNI
William Burroughs, Martin Feldstein, Buckminster Fuller, William Randolph Hearst Jr., Henry Kissinger, Bernard Law, Franklin Roosevelt, William Weld

ADAMS

Occupying more than two blocks of brick buildings off Massachusetts Avenue, Adams House is a bastion of luxury for its residents. Enter the main doors, walk through a gold-plated foyer, and you may well get turned away from the elegant dining hall during peak hours (see the Pforzheimer-Adams War, p. 142). The oldest in Harvard's housing system, the Adams buildings were originally "Gold Coast" dormitories that provided private, luxurious housing for students years before the official residential housing system was implemented. Made up of three main buildings—Randolph Court, Westmorly Court, and Claverly Hall—Adams is built right into the urban fabric of the city of Cambridge. At the center of this random agglomeration of buildings sits Apthorp House, built in 1760. Apthorp House has a few of its own claims to fame: during the Revolutionary War, General "Gentleman Johnny" Burgoyne was held captive here, and the building was used as a secret brew house during Prohibition. According to legend, 200 bottles of Adams-made moonshine are hidden around the House.

One of the most distinctive quirks of the Adams House experience is the Adams Pool, located in Westmorly Court. Once filled with fireplaces, sky-lights, lush ferns and lushes the Pool is now a student theater, where undergrads put on small-scale productions, including the annual 24-Hour Plays festival that takes place during reading period (p. 3). The theatrical use continues a trend set by Peter Sellars, Class of 1980. In 1978, Sellars, who would later go on to direct famous contemporary productions of operas and plays throughout the United States, brought Shakespeare's *Antony and Cleopatra* to the pool. Cleopatra floated on a raft, the audience was soaked, and actors dove in and out of the baths. Sellars contributed to Adams' former reputation as a unique house full of artists and "individuals."

Today, Adams is a House known for its history and playful snobbery. Adams has maintained many traditions over the years, including the black-tie reading of *Winnie the Pooh* at the Winter Feast, Fantasy Night, and the annual Drag Night. Concerts and lectures take place in its lavish common spaces, and students enjoy annual formal events in their secluded courtyard. The House has also preserved the college suite of Franklin Delano Roosevelt, who graduated from Harvard in 1904.

Besides being the house closest to the Yard, Adams House offers its residents a number of quirky benefits. Beneath Westmorly and Randolph Halls runs a maze of tunnels frequently painted by Adams seniors. The house main-

ARCHITECTURAL SPOTLIGHT: ADAMS HOUSE POOL

Reportedly used for less-than-wholesome (read: nude) "recreation," the Adams Pool in its heyday represented the glamour and luxury of wealth at

Harvard in the early 20th century—and by Harvard standards, skinny-dipping in a baroque bath is wild, wild, wild. A feature of the original Gold Coast dormitories, the lavish facilities were designed and built by

KEVIN LIN

Warren and Wetmore, who would later build Grand Central Terminal in New York. The famous architects and designers left no stone unturned, opting to include huge fireplaces, fountains, and leafy greenery in the plans. In the 1930s, Westmorly Court and its pool were incorporated into President Lowell's House system, and by the '60s and '70s were open for business, if you will, to all students on campus. Campus members of the Harvard-Radcliffe Christian Fellowship, who used the pool for baptisms, coexisted peacefully in this sanctuary with nude revelers. The space is remembered by Adams alum Michael Weishan '86 in a 2009 Harvard University *Gazette* article as a "romantic, fun, kind of exciting, somewhat naughty place."

HOUSING DAY

After spending a night praying to the housing gods and visiting their dream Houses, freshman blocking groups are awoken early in the morning by a mass of hundreds of upperclassmen who have gathered in the Yard to welcome new students into their respective Houses. Freshmen are forced to wait in their rooms for their assignments to be hand-delivered by a rambunctious welcome committee from their future House; often, the news arrives by a shower of champagne and whipped cream, and a student's first House t-shirt.

tains the Bow & Arrow printing press, an old-school letterpress printing workshop, and offers classes to Adams residents and friends. Adams also boasts some of the most coveted common spaces on campus, such as the Upper Common Room, decorated in Renaissance fashion, and the Lower Common Room, which features a grand organ. In these rooms, one can frequently find a plethora of events, from Tai Chi classes to a cappella group practices to thesis tutorials. In fact, John F. Kennedy, Class of 1940, used to meet with his thesis advisor in the Coolidge Room.

CABOT

Cabot House is one of the three Radcliffe Quad Houses. Made of six brick buildings surrounding a grassy green quadrangle, Cabot comprises some of the oldest residential structures on campus. Originally the Radcliffe ladies' alternative to the Yard and riverbank dormitories, Cabot was first incorporated into President Lowell's residential housing plan in 1962, when it was divided up into South House and East House. In 1970, as part of the Great Experiment in coed housing, 150 men from Harvard and 150 women from Radcliffe pulled the old switcheroo and swapped residences. By 1984, the East and South Houses, since combined into one South House, were renamed Cabot and further incorporated into the House system.

Today, a series of underground tunnels connect most of the House buildings and facilities, including one of the best-equipped House gyms and a projector room. Two buildings, known as the "islands," are not part of the tunnel system but boast some of the sunniest and largest of Cabot's suites. Cabot's refined claim to fame is that, throughout its many common living rooms, it is home to more pianos than any other House on campus. In tune with this tradition, many House dinners feature undergraduate musicians.

The Cabot Library Suite is one of the more infamous rooms on campus. A converted library, the megasuite generally hosts large parties a few times a year.

Cabot House and its grassy quad form a center for student life away from the river. Dozens of white-painted wooden Adirondack chairs now populate the grass, a precursor to the colorful chairs that now dot Harvard Yard. A popular place for reading, eating, and games, the Radcliffe Quad has also played host to Cabot House formal dances. Other favorite house events include the spring Cabot House Musical, the annual Dutch Auction, a fall apple-picking excursion, and Festivus. The Dutch auction includes a tradition known as "lambing." One lucky student is chosen each year to be smothered in spices and other marinades. Festivus, named after the non-sectarian winter "holiday" popularized by the character George Costanza on *Seinfeld*, is a time of gathering and great feasting for Cabot residents before they disperse for winter break. A cheery Festivus pole is, of course, erected in the Quad.

One of the most recent developments in Cabot House life is the opening of Cabot Cafe in the fall of 2011. Created and operated by five Cabot residents, the Cafe is open from 9pm to 1am on weeknights, and serves cookies, pie and pastries along with a full menu of coffee, tea and espresso. Cabot Cafe is a successful example of the College's commitment to supporting common social spaces on campus (p. 157).

CABOT HOUSE

MOTTO: Semper Cor
"Forever the heart," from the Cabot family motto: "Semper cor, caput, Cabot" ("Forever the heart, the head, the Cabot")

NAMESAKE
Thomas and Virginia Cabot, benefactors of Harvard and Radcliffe

IMPORTANT DATES
Construction of Cabot's six buildings completed between 1901 and 1937. From 1970 to 1984 Cabot was known as South House.

CURRENT MASTERS
Rakesh Khurana, Marvin Profsesor of Leadership Development at Harvard Business School, and Stephanie Khurana, executive director of the Tobin Project

NOTABLE ALUMNI
Stockard Channing, Rivers Cuomo, Greg Daniels, Soledad O'Brien, Bonnie Raitt, Mira Sorvino, Kerry Healy

CURRIER

Currier, the newest of the 13 Houses, is composed of four interconnected buildings: Bingham, Daniels, Gilbert, and Tuchman Halls, which surround a dining hall, a common space called the Fishbowl, and two landscaped court-yards. Currier is located in the Radcliffe Quadrangle and is the only house to be named after a woman, Audrey Bruce Currier, Radcliffe Class of 1956.

Currier's halls are named in honor of four other Radcliffe alumnae: Mary Caperton Bingham, Class of 1928, a newspaperwoman and civic leader, Mabel Daniels, Class of 1900, a composer and musician, Helen Homans Gilbert, Class of 1936, chairman of the Radcliffe Board of Trustees and the first female member of the Harvard Board of Trustees, and Barbara Wertheim Tuchman, Class of 1933, Pulitzer Prize-winning author of *The Guns of August*.

The room known as the Fishbowl is a Currier House icon. Thanks to its central location, it is almost impossible for a resident to go a day without passing through. Usually set up with comfy couches, the room functions as a forum for discussions and, with the pull of a screen, an in-house cinema. Stein Clubs, weekly informal House gatherings (the most popular of which is the annual "Curri-oke" event), take place in the Fishbowl on Thursday nights. Currier also throws the biggest campus-wide Halloween party, called Heaven and Hell, during which the Fishbowl serves as Hell, flooded in red light, while the "Ten-man" suite located above is Heaven. Currier is equipped with multiple music practice rooms, a reading room, a computer room, a dance studio, and some of the campus's largest party suites, including the three "solaria" that function as the penthouse suites of three of Currier's four towers. The House also boasts its own literary arts magazine, *The Warble*.

CURRIER HOUSE

NAMESAKE

Audrey Bruce Currier, Class of 1965, who died with her husband when their small plane was lost in a storm. Funds for the House were donated by Mrs. Mellon Bruce, Currier's mother.

IMPORTANT DATES

Currier officially opened in 1970, though many of the halls were completed a few years earlier.

CURRENT MASTERS

Richard Wrangham, Ruth Moore Professor of Anthropology, and Elizabeth Ross, founder of Ugandan development charity the Kasiisi Project

NOTABLE ALUMNI

Bill Gates, Michael Chertoff, Caroline Kennedy, Yo-Yo Ma

DUNSTER

Right along the Charles River, Dunster House is a sight to be seen. The House's distinctive clock tower, a nod to the Big Tom Tower of Christchurch College at Oxford University, is topped by a crimson dome and can be seen from Boston. More importantly, it can be seen from neighboring Mather House, which is often referred to as "The Box that Dunster Came In." Dunster cropped up in 1930 as the second House built under President Lowell's House plan.

Known today for its old-Harvard style and hearty helpings of House spirit, Dunster welcomes students with a gorgeous courtyard and a state-of-the-art dining facility, recently renovated in collaboration with the Harvard Green Campus Initiative (HGCI), where students can eat guilt-free meals thanks to reduced water and energy usage and spiffy granite countertops.

The Dunster House Opera is performed every year in the House dining hall. Founded in 1992, the Dunster House Opera Society is open to all Harvard College students.

In the spirit of bizarre Harvard traditions, Dunster hosts an annual spring goat roast. During the roast, which was initiated by anthropologist Daniel Lieberman during his time as a resident tutor in the 1980s, students skin the animal with sharp rocks before roasting it on a spit. While all Houses have

ALEXANDRA DOWD

Dunster House tower

131

DUNSTER HOUSE

NAMESAKE
Reverend Henry Dunster, first Headmaster of Harvard College

IMPORTANT DATES
Opened in 1930

CURRENT MASTERS
Roger Porter, the IBM Professor of Government and Business (White House advisor to Ford, Reagan, and George H.W. Bush), and Ann Porter

NOTABLE ALUMNI
Al Franken, Al Gore, Tommy Lee Jones, Norman Mailer, Deval Patrick

an official mascot, Dunster is particularly fond of the moose, whose head appears on its crest. Dunster residents can always be spotted sporting antlers at Housing Day each spring. The mascot also lends itself to an active House e-mail list known fondly as "Moose Droppings."

ELIOT

Eliot House is Harvard's anchor on the shores of the Charles River, coveted for its waterfront property and vibrant House spirit, not to mention its gorgeous brick building, the dark-wood dining hall, and a House library fit for a princess. Spot Eliot in the Harvard skyline with its green cupola and you'll see a huge round window. The Leonard Bernstein practice room lies behind these panes, complete with a piano played by the celebrated American conductor, a former Eliot resident (p. 190). Today, a cappella groups and other organizations use the tower practice room, but they must climb seven flights of stairs to relish in its splendor.

Eliot students enjoy well-furnished common spaces and House activities, which range from formal meals to the annual Evening with Champions, an Eliot-based figure skating exhibition that raises money for the Jimmy Fund. Most noteworthy, however, is the annual Eliot Fête, the House's lavish take on the spring formal offered by most Houses. Considered the best spring formal on campus, Fête, which is held in Eliot's inner sanctum courtyard, draws the attention of students from all across campus, who scramble to snag the few out-of-house invitations. In recent years, would-be attendees have gone so far as to climb in formalwear through kitchen servery tunnels, scale wrought-iron fences, and hide out for a full 24 hours, hoping to be on the inside when the gates are locked to outsiders. It's no wonder: elephant-shaped ice sculptures decorate the courtyard and plentiful refreshments are served. Fête features both an old-fashioned swing-dancing tent and an indoor dance floor playing popular contemporary music that attendees can drift between.

ELIOT HOUSE

MOTTO: Floreat Domus de Eliot
"May the House of Eliot Flourish"

NAMESAKE
Charles W. Eliot, President of Harvard from 1869 to 1909

IMPORTANT DATES
Opened in 1931

CURRENT MASTERS
Douglas Melton, Thomas Dudley Cabot Professor of Natural Sciences, and Gail O'Keefe, an education consultant

NOTABLE ALUMNI
David Rockefeller, Archibald Cox, Leonard Bernstein

Eliot is also the host House of the distinguished Society of Fellows at Harvard. The Society, founded in 1933 by President Lowell, supports roughly 30 up-and-coming scholars in various fields. One of the founding principles of the Society was the belief that scholars should reap the "value of informal discussions" across academic disciplines; accordingly, the Fellows have their own private wine cellar in the depths of an Eliot entryway.

ALEXANDRA DOWD
Eliot House tower

THE ELIOT HOUSE SONG

We were freshmen when we heard the news,
Mark well what I do say,
We were freshmen when we heard the news,
The lottery we didn't lose.
We packed our bags and made our way to Eliot House.
In sophomore year we made good friends,
Mark well what I do say,
In sophomore year we made good friends;
Our happy times would see no end.
On cloudy days the sun shined bright on Eliot House.
As juniors we all studied hard,
Mark well what I do say,
As juniors we all studied hard;
We lugged our books to Harvard Yard.
Old Kirkland's stars will never rise 'bove Eliot House.
As seniors we all shed a tear,
Mark well what I do say,
As seniors we all shed a tear '
Cause this would be our final year
For skating, stein club, and The Fête at Eliot House.
And then into the world we go,
Mark well what I do say,
And then into the world we go,
Our Eliot pride we'll always show.
We know our love will only grow for Eliot House.
To Eliot! To Eliot!
We raise a glass & sing a song.
By river's side our hearts are tied to Eliot House!

Andrew B. Pacelli '04, Alex M. Berenberg '04, and Alexander S. Ness '04

KIRKLAND

Built in 1914 as a set of first-year dormitories (before the House system came to Harvard) Kirkland House is nestled between neighboring Eliot House and John F. Kennedy Street. Set around an adorable courtyard, the neo-Georgian buildings probably inspired the look of the Houses that were built under President Lowell's house plan in the 1930s. Before the randomization of the upperclassman housing system, Kirkland gained a reputation as both the friendliest and the "jockiest" House. Its prime location across the Charles from Harvard's athletic facilities attracted a number of sports teams (for much of the 1970s, the entire heavyweight crew, football, and hockey teams lived in Kirkland), and the House's expansive subterranean gym and weight room attests to this legacy. Today, Kirkland fosters a cozy house com-

KIRKLAND HOUSE

NAMESAKE
Reverend Doctor John Thorton Kirkland, President of Harvard from 1810-1828

IMPORTANT DATES
Built in 1914 as freshman dormitories, long before the advent of the House system

CURRENT MASTERS
Tom Conley, Abbott Lawrence Lowell Professor of Romance Languages and Literatures and Chair of Visual and Environmental Studies, and Verena Conley, Professor of Comparative Literature and of Romance Languages and Literatures

NOTABLE ALUMNI
Jeff Bingaman, Wallace Shawn, Pat Toomey, Mark Zuckerberg

munity that prides itself on its Masters, their Bernese Mountain dogs, and a host of traditions that have only grown better with time.

Around Christmas, Kirkland invites all residents (regardless of their belief in Saint Nick) to push their spirit to the limit in their House Secret Santa month. This isn't your typical Secret Santa, though. Instead of giving pen sets, origami kits, or fruitcakes, Kirklanders aim at loftier goals: to make dreams come true.

In this Secret Santa tradition, residents complete elaborate forms for their "Santas" voicing their wildest holiday desires—and the results are fan-

KEVIN LIN

Kirkland courtyard

ARCHITECTURAL SPOTLIGHT:
HICKS HOUSE

Kirkland is one of two houses on campus to boast actual American Colonial architecture in its structures. The Hicks House Library, adjacent to Kirkland proper, was built in 1762. John Hicks, the building's original owner and namesake, lived quietly as a carpenter and tax collector in Cambridge until the onset of the Revolutionary War. Laying down his hammer and nails for a shoddy gun, Hicks participated in the Boston Tea Party and was eventually killed just down the street from Harvard Yard.

KEVIN LIN

Kirkland House Library, Hicks House

Until 1926, when Harvard purchased the white colonial structure, Hicks House was used alternately as a monastery and soldiers' lodging. In 1931, Hicks was incorporated into Kirkland House as its library, which now boasts a 12,000-volume collection. Some of the library's early jewels—today housed in Houghton Library—include early editions of *Crazy Tales* by John Hall Stevenson and *History of the World* by Sir Walter Raleigh. Hicks House is a gem of a study space, with private rooms and a windy wooden staircase.

tastic. In recent years, a dining hall full of merrymakers presented one student with a fully choreographed musical selection from the film *Sister Act*. The week culminates in a spirited Kirkland dinner and dance, with a procession featuring a stuffed-animal boar—representing the House's unofficial mascot.

With French literature professors as House Masters, it's only natural that the House also have a vibrant cultural scene. Boasting a wine seminar run by the House Master himself (which formerly counted for academic credit), a dramatic society, and an annual student art show, Kirkland distinguishes itself as a haven for relaxation and enjoyment. Hammocks dotting the courtyard complete the picture. Each year, Kirkland also acts as a host House for Cultural Rhythms, an annual celebration of diversity at Harvard as well as the Harvard Foundation's Humanitarian Award, with past awardees including Martin Luther King Jr., Elie Wiesel, Shakira and Lionel Ritchie.

In recent history, Kirkland, has gained its own ode, which students recite proudly on Housing Day and at the Holiday Dinner and Dance:

Oh Kirkland, Oh Kirkland
You are so good to me
Oh Kirkland, Oh Kirkland
You are the place to be.
Oh Kirkland, Oh Kirkland,
Damn you are so fine.
Oh Kirkland, Oh Kirkland,
Thank God that you are mine!

LEVERETT

While Leverett boasts a classic Harvard building (McKinlock Hall, 1926), many of its residents live in the two newer Leverett Towers (built in 1961), which have their own small quad. The tower rooms, almost all singles, feature enormous windows and some of the best views on campus, while McKinlock has an old-Harvard feel, with wood floors and fireplaces in the rooms.

Mather Hall, not to be confused with Mather House down the street, and six squash courts once belonged to Leverett House. In the 1960s when Quincy House needed more space, Mather Hall became a part of Quincy and the squash courts were torn down. Today, with the largest undergraduate population on campus, Leverett sprawls from the Charles River to Dunster House to Quincy, stitching the River Houses together.

When Leverett was first built (or, rather, organized—McKinlock Hall was previously used as a dormitory for freshmen), the House adopted its coat of arms and received Hudson, a stuffed rabbit that the house used as a mascot (a leveret is a one-year-old hare). The House prides itself on its monkeybread recipe: not so secret, it can be found on the Leverett House website. Its residents also exude House spirit by wearing plastic bunny ears on housing day

LEVERETT HOUSE

NAMESAKE
John Leverett, President of Harvard from 1708 to 1724

IMPORTANT DATES
McKinlock Hall built in 1926, remodeled in 1931; Leverett Towers and new Library built in 1961

CURRENT MASTERS:
Howard Georgi, professor of physics, and Ann Georgi, known affectionately as Chief and Coach

NOTABLE ALUMS
Anthony Lake, Chief Justice John G. Roberts, Peter Seeger, Cornel West

KEVIN LIN

The Leverett Library, part of New Leverett

and creating elaborate music videos set to top-40 music that put the House on full display. Popular Lev remixes include "Teach Me How to Bunny" and "I Just Got Lev."

Leverett residents also epitomize Harvard's entrepreneurial spirit. Examples of projects include LevSPN, a video site that films Leverett's intramural games for residents to view later, and CrimsonBikes, a bike-sharing program that began as a way to offer Leverett residents easy bicycle rentals and has since expanded to include all Harvard students across campus. Furthermore, like Kirkland, Leverett has a house song, which has origins in the 1960s and was revamped in 2000 and 2007:

> *It's Leverett, it's Leverett,*
> *the best of new and old.*
> *Leverett, Leverett,*
> *the home of the brave and bold.*
> *It's Leverett, it's Leverett,*
> *Harvard's noblest endeavor.*
> *Nonetheless, thank God, thank God,*
> *we won't be here forever.*

LOWELL

The Lowells, affiliated with Harvard since Papa John Lowell graduated from the College in 1721, sent an entire family tree through Harvard's gates. Their accomplishments are too fantastic and varied to list, but let it be known that

James Russell Lowell (poet), Amy Lowell (poet and rogue intellectual credited with bringing D.H. Lawrence across the pond), Percival Lowell (intuitor of the existence of Pluto), and Abbott Lawrence Lowell, President of Harvard from 1909 to 1933, can all attribute their successful careers to Harvard and Radcliffe. While President Lowell had a somewhat scandalous tenure at the University, he introduced some major structures still in existence today, including the House system, concentrations, and reading period (p. 3).

Today, Lowell House, with its pristine courtyard and close-knit community, is overseen by House Masters Diana Eck and Dorothy Austin, the first same-sex couple to serve as Masters of a Harvard House. They see to it that Lowell is run like the bastion of beautiful social tradition that it is. The most popular of the Lowell traditions is the Thursday Tea, held in the Masters Residence adjacent to the dining hall. Other events include May Day champagne toasts at dawn on the Weeks footbridge, the Lowell House Opera, performed in the yellow, chandelier-filled dining hall, the annual holiday Yule Ball and the ringing of the tower bells, which have a strange and fascinating history all their own.

The original bells were removed from St. Danilov monastery in Moscow, sold to a Harvard alumnus in the late 1920's and shipped out of the country, thus preserving them from Stalin's melting pots. They were accepted—in an inspired moment—by President Lowell just as Lowell House was being constructed. The return of the bells to their native home in Moscow occurred in 2008 after a long negotiation (p. 212)

The Lowell bells ring every Sunday at 1pm, rung by a bell-ringing club called the Klappermeisters. They ring the Harry Potter theme song, Britney Spears tunes, and Disney classics, among many others.

LOWELL HOUSE

MOTTO: Occasionem Cognosce
"Recognize Opportunity"

NAMESAKE
Abbott Lawrence Lowell, President of Harvard from 1909 to 1933, and a whole bunch of relatives

IMPORTANT DATES
Constructed in 1930

CURRENT MASTERS
Diana Eck, professor of comparative religion and Indian studies, and Dorothy Austin, professor of religion and psychology at Harvard Divinity School

NOTABLE ALUMNI
Michael Crichton, Matt Damon, Robert Lowell, Natalie Portman, David Souter, John Updike, Andrew Weil

Between 1930 and 2008, Lowell House was implicated in an international ring of smuggling and secrecy. The goods? Seventeen Russian bells, stashed away in Lowell House tower and far from silent. Around the time of Lowell House's founding, American philanthropist Charles R. Crane came to the College with a proposition. The rise of Stalin in Russia meant the destruction of churches and monasteries, and Crane saw an opportunity to save the bells of Danilov Monastery in Moscow. His plan was sound, and the bells were brought safely to Harvard.

In a new period of religious stability, Russia and the Danilov Monastery thought it apt to ask for the bells back. Eventually, Harvard and Lowell House complied. By 2008, the Vera Foundry in Voronezh had produced seventeen new bells for Lowell House, participating in the revitalization of a craft that had been essentially extinguished under Stalin—and a craft in which Lowell House maintains a personal stake. The Russian bells today ring Sundays 1-2pm and on a variety of special Harvard occasions.

MATHER

Mather positively bubbles with House spirit. To pump up potential Matherites in the run-up to Housing Day, Mather's House Council launches popular e-mail, video, and CD campaigns to publicize their House. Mather House began the current Housing Day festivities by being the first House to "dorm-storm" and release Housing Day music videos. Mather's hit singles include "Concrete Seduction," "My House (Mather House)," and "My Beautiful Dark Concrete Fantasy."

High on the list of things Matherites can be proud of is the (*New York Times*-acclaimed) "Mather Lather", a tradition since 2003. One of the most popular dances of the year, Mather Lather is held in the Mather Dining Hall, which is filled to chest height with foam. Music blasts, and dancers sometimes get lost in the giant foam pit.

Harvard Houses often wind up engaged in bitter rivalries, and Mather is no exception. In 2004, Mather instigated a large-scale inter-house war that erupted during fall finals period. According to the *Crimson*, "Mather House declared war on Kirkland during Primal Scream, Jan. 20, after concluding that Kirkland House had pilfered the Adams House gong. Mather residents organized their Department of War to combat what they call the 'Kirkland brute' and help Adams retrieve its gong." Insulted by Kirkland's audacity, a full cabinet of self-appointed Mather war officials brought Adams, Cabot, and several

MATHER HOUSE

NAMESAKE	CURRENT MASTERS
Increase Mather (AB 1656), President of Harvard from 1685 to 1692 and father of Cotton Mather (AB 1678)	Christie McDonald, Smith Professor of French Language and Literature, and Michael David Rosengarten
IMPORTANT DATES	**NOTABLE ALUMS**
Opened in 1970	Conan O'Brien, Jeffrey Zucker

other Houses into the fray. Whether it's through a stinging wall of soap suds or the sting of inter-House rivalry, Mather is never far from the Harvard action.

PFORZHEIMER

Pforzheimer House, with its blue cupola, is the visual focal point of the Radcliffe Quadrangle. Pfoho was known as North House, one of the women-only Radcliffe houses, beginning in 1961, but by 1971 men had moved in. In 1995 the House was given the name Pforzheimer for philanthropists Carol and Carl Jr.— but known as "Pfoho" to all Harvard students, a derivative of its former nickname "NoHo".

Pfoho is perhaps most well-known on campus for its insistense on placing a "pf" before most words. Pfor example, the House open email list is titled "Pfopen" and all formal events are usually advertised as "Pformals."

Pfoho's central dining hall is a communal area for residents of the House and the Quad. The room is used for meetings, talks, and informal dances, including the Pforzheimer '90s themed dance, which, in confrontational Pfoho style, was created to trump the Leverett House '80s dance.

Pforzheimer House is home to a number of large social spaces, a communal terrace often used for barbeques, and Harvard Undergraduate Television, an umbrella organization that facilitates student exploits in media and entertainment. HUTV programs, which include a comedy news broadcast, a soap opera, and a dating game show, can be found online at http://hutvnetwork. com.

Above all, Pforzheimer boasts the massive Belltower Suite. A set of 12 single bedrooms, four bathrooms, and three common rooms, the Belltower is one of the biggest and most coveted rooms on campus. The main common room, located just beneath (and with access to) the actual belltower, is traditionally the site of debaucherous late-night parties. The two Jordan apartment buildings on Walker Street are also part of Pfoho. Residents can opt to live in these spacious apartments with fully equipped kitchens instead of traditional

FUN FACT

One of the most memorable rivalries in recent residential history was a 1999 war of attrition alternately referred to as "The Adams Epic" and the "Pfoho-Adams War." It began, as many wars do, with an exclusionary practice: Adams House, a prime river destination and frequent lunch spot for Quad residents, attempted to close its dining hall to residents of other houses. To make matters worse, when a student from another house did enter the dining hall, Adams guards would ring an alarm on the large Adams House gong, a cherished House relic.

When Pforzheimer House, the most remote Quad house, attempted to ban Adams residents from its dining hall, chaos ensued. Within days, war cabinets were formed and Adams House residents composed their Articles and Declaration of War. Heavily covered by the Crimson, the war raged on. Adams stole the Pforzheimer "Pf," and for a period the houses were referred to as Pfadams and Orzheimer. Orzheimer House retaliated by securing the Adams gates with a bike lock, posing as the Freshman Dean's Office and redirecting freshmen to Adams for Sunday brunch, and, climactically, stealing the Adams gong.

KEVIN LIN

The gate in front of Pforzheimer House, with its "Pf" in place for now

As the war escalated, the campus was divided. To bring an end to the madness, a formal competition was instated. House administrators presided over a grueling afternoon of football, tug-of-war, and musical theater competition—and eventually declared Pforzheimer House the winner. The prize? Full access to Adams House dining hall.

PFORZHEIMER HOUSE

NAMESAKE
Carol K. and Carl H. Pforzheimer, major University benefactors

IMPORTANT DATES
Buildings built and acquired from 1901 to 1970; reorganized as Pforzheimer House in its current configuration in 1995

CURRENT MASTERS
Nicholas Christakis, professor at Harvard Medical School and the Faculty of Arts and Science's Department of Sociology, and Erika Christakis

NOTABLE ALUMNI
Mo Rocca, Jennifer 8. Lee, Selamawi Asgedom

suites or rooms in Comstock, Holmes, Moors, or Wolbach Halls inside the main building.

Pfoho residents continue to stay spiffy thanks to full-length "date" mirrors in residential hallways, installed once upon a time so that Radcliffe gals could primp before meeting their Harvard beaus.

QUINCY

Quincy, known colloquially as the People's House, was the first house built after the original seven from President Lowell's housing plan. When Quincy House opened in 1959, in a spot that once held (at various times) a psychological clinic and part of Leverett House, it was the most desired house among that year's freshmen: nearly one-third listed it as their first choice. Quincy's first housemaster, John M. Bullitt, interviewed each undergraduate who eventually took residence there.

Quincy became known for its free-thinking ways shortly after its founding, due to a number of student protests and an unprecedented focus on diversity. Quincy House was the first in Harvard's system to include female tutors, in 1966.

Quincy's grassy courtyard is framed by the neo-Georgian Old Quincy (once called Mather Hall) and the modern block of New Quincy. The House boasts strong spirit, a hugely popular dining hall, and two-floor student suites. In general, sophomores live in Old Quincy, while juniors and seniors graduate to the spacious suites and beautiful views of New Quincy. Additionally, the Master's Residence, perched atop New Quincy, is considered one of the finest pieces of real estate in the Boston area. Students and other guests enjoy the space when Masters Lee and Deb Gehrke hold teas, open houses, and other community events.

Quincy boasts the Quincy Qube (the eccentricly shaped house library), the ever-popular late night Quincy Grille (mozzarella sticks, anyone?), pool and ping pong tables, and the Cage, a small concert venue for rock and punk groups on campus.

Quincy's second House Master, Charles Dunn, began a longstanding Quincy tradition in 1965: the annual exorcism. Each year, Quincy's House Master (dressed in a kilt and accompanied by bagpipes) proclaims:

"We herewith exorcise, exile, expel, exterminate, and exsufflicate all evil spirits, whether banshees or bogles, warlocks or witches, from our walls and floors and ceilings, our books and briefcases, our featherbeds and waterbeds, our plumbing and pinball machines..."

Nowadays, the exorcism kicks off Quincy's newest tradition: Field Day where resident students from each year compete in a variety of outdoor activities.

Quincy also boasts the Balcony Suite—known for its immense combined common room and (surprise!) balcony access—and a functioning pottery studio and darkroom. Its ping pong table is heavily used and, beginning in 2010, home to the semesterly House Ping Pong Tournament.

New Quincy, like the Leverett Towers, introduced a new architectural aesthetic to campus. Now a major landmark, the building was a sign of modernity at the time of its construction and was favored by many students who wanted an alternative to the river houses. In line with this new vision, Quincy's dining hall features a huge sand mural by Constantino Nivola. Anxiety about this piece echoed concerns about the larger architectural choices—alums noted with disdain that Nivola's mural looked like the "doodling of inmates in a mental hospital."

QUINCY HOUSE

NAMESAKE
Josiah Quincy, President of Harvard from 1829 to 1845

ARCHITECTS
Coolidge, Shepley, Bulfinch, and Abbott

IMPORTANT DATES
Opened as a House in September 1959. Old Quincy, previously Mather Hall, was constructed in the 1930s under President Lowell. It originally belonged to Leverett House.

CURRENT MASTERS
Lee Gehrke, Hermann von Helmholtz Professor, Harvard-MIT Division of Health Sciences and Technology, and Professor of Microbiology and Molecular Genetics, and Deb Gehrke, artist and local community activist

NOTABLE ALUMNI
Lou Dobbs, Tom Ridge

WINTHROP HOUSE

NAMESAKES
John Winthrop, astronomer, scientist, and President of Harvard from 1773 to 1774, and his father, John Winthrop, Governor of the Massachusetts Bay Colony

ARCHITECTURE
Designed by Coolidge, Shepley, Bulfinch, and Abbott

IMPORTANT DATES
Buildings constructed as freshman river dormitories in 1914; incorporated into the housing system in 1931

CURRENT MASTERS
Ronald S. Sullivan Jr., Clinical Professor of Law, and Stephanie Robinson, Lecturer on Law

NOTABLE ALUMS
Ben Bernanke, Edward Kennedy, John F. Kennedy, Alan Keyes

WINTHROP

Winthrop House, occupying prime riverfront property between Eliot and Leverett, was built in 1914 as a set of dormitories for freshmen. Unlike most Harvard Houses, Winthrop has three distinct courtyards (one in each building and a third between the two), all of which were incorporated into the House when it was renovated for President Lowell's house system in 1931. These courtyards are now

NATALIE CHAPMAN

Winthrop House gate

prime locations for a sunny picnic lunch, ride on Winthrop's signature tire swing, game of corn hole during "Thropstock," the House's spring carnival, or a romantic dance during the Arabella Ball, named for the ship John Winthrop took to the New World.

Winthrop also boasts of its status as an intramural athletic powerhouse. Placing first in the past four intramural Straus Cup Tournaments, you can often hear booming chants of "The House with the Straus" echoing from Winthrop's below-ground dining hall.

Ronald S. Sullivan, Jr., and Stephanie Robinson, the Winthrop House Masters, are the first black couple to take on this role in the history of the University. Appointed in February 2009, Sullivan is a clinical professor of law at Harvard Law School. His wife, Stephanie Robinson, is a lecturer at HLS. While studying at Harvard Law, Sullivan played intramural basketball with President Barack Obama and maintains a close personal and professional relationship with the First Family. The entire Sullivan family, including their two young sons, are active members in House festivities, always placing well in the annual Halloween Costume Contest, and avidly decorating their home for every season and holiday.

President John F. Kennedy, Class of 1940, and Senator Edward Kennedy, Class of 1956, lived in Winthrop, and President Kennedy's old suite is still maintained— Harvard's Institute of Politics uses the rooms to house visiting dignitaries. Unfortunately, President Kennedy's freshman year room in Weld Hall in Harvard Yard is not as well preserved—it is currently occupied by an elevator shaft.

DUDLEY HOUSE

Located within Lehman Hall in the Old Yard, Dudley House serves as a connection to the College for those 2% of undergraduates who choose to live off campus. Founded in 1935, Dudley House was first established with the goal of maintaining a relationship between Harvard and its commuter students. While the original Dudley House was merely a collection of basement rooms in old Dudley Hall, the modern version has expanded to include a library, dining hall, game room, and cafe. Dudley House "residents" do not live in the House but they are assigned deans, tutors, and academic advisors. They are also invited to participate in a variety of community-building activities and events that help to foster a connection to the University.

For Harvard's more environmentally-conscious crowd, Dudley House sponsors a co-op near the Quad that allows students to live in a cooperative and sustainable community. Founded in 1958, the co-op houses 32 students who clean, cook, and buy food for themselves.

SOCIAL LIFE

AT HARVARD

A SOCIAL NETWORK

The social scene at Harvard, steeped in history and controversy, has blossomed in recent decades. Once centered almost exclusively around final clubs, Harvard's unique all-male societies, social life has since expanded to include the rest of the student body. Although the final clubs continue to be a presence on campus, student groups, upperclass House life, and Greek life have gained social signifance as well. With everything from mixers thrown by student groups to typical college dorm-room parties to school-wide dances, Harvard students are at no loss for social outlets. Plus, students have the distinct advantage of living in the center of lively Harvard Square and just a few T stops away from one of the most college-friendly cities in the world.

EARLY SOCIAL LIFE

SPEAKING CLUBS

Organized social life at Harvard College can be traced back to the American Revolution. Because of the precarious situation in Boston, the General Court of Massachusetts moved to Cambridge from 1770 to 1773. Prominent revolutionary orators like James Otis Jr. spoke at the meetings of the General Court, inspiring Harvard students to develop their own speaking skills.

Two students in particular, Samuel Phillips, who would become Lieutenant Governor of Massachusetts and founder of Phillips Academy, and Fisher Ames, who would become a member of the first United States Congress as well as a member of the convention that ratified the Constitution, felt insufficiently trained in the oratory arts. Inspired and determined, Phillips founded the Speaking Club, and soon after Ames founded the Mercurian Club. Four years later, the Clintonian Club, yet another oratory organization, was founded. The happenings within these three societies were kept extremely secret. Though members were not permitted to say much outside of the confines of their respective so-

BY THE NUMBERS

1	Soap-suds dance party each year: Mather Lather
13	Final clubs at Harvard College: 8 all-male and 5 all-female
25	Cents per chicken wing at Wing Night at the Cambridge Queen's Head Pub
1324	The Massachusetts Avenue address of Harvard's oldest final club, the Porcellian.

cieties, they were required to give an oral presentation in front of their fellows every two weeks, after which the group discussed the topic of their oration.

These speaking clubs no longer exist under their original names, although some were integrated into the Institute of 1770, which still exists in some capacity today.

THE INSTITUTE, THE HASTY PUDDING, AND THE DICKEY

The Institute of 1770 traces its roots back to the Speaking and Mercurian Clubs, which merged in 1773, adopting the name The Patriotic Association in 1801. In 1825, two additional organizations joined the group, and it was renamed the Institute of 1770. As it grew, the Institute merged with other clubs on campus, including the Hasty Pudding Club.

The Hasty Pudding Club was founded in 1795 in order to "cherish the feelings of friendship and patriotism." Juniors and seniors were elected each year, and the club's traditions were kept secret. The name came from club dinners usually including "an iron pot of steamy hasty-pudding," a traditional New England dish. The annual celebration of George Washington's birthday was one of the club's most popular events.

After 1800, the Hasty Pudding began organizing mock trials after dinners, a tradition that led to the creation of Hasty Pudding Theatricals (p. 191), whose annual play continues to be one of the most celebrated institutions at Harvard.

By 1878, the Institute of 1770 had abandoned any extracurricular ambitions and become a fully social entity. After election night, a rowdy procession of screaming and singing members would drag newly elected members out of their rooms. After initiation, the names of new members were printed in Boston newspapers.

Another prominent organization at the time was the D.K.E., or the Dickey. Although the club longer exists, the Dickey's legacy lives on. In the 19th century, "running for the Dickey" referred to the D.K.E. initiates' obligation to run between classes for six consecutive days. In 1880, the Pudding adopted the ritual, and today Hasty Pudding Club initiates are required to run wherever they go within Harvard Yard for an entire week.

Election to the Institute and the Dickey were considered the first steps toward "social success" at Harvard.

FINAL CLUBS

THE FOUNDING OF THE PORCELLIAN

The first true "final club" at Harvard, though it wouldn't be known as such until many years later, was the Porcellian Club. Founded in 1791, the Porcellian, also known as the "Porc" or the "PC," was established by a group of young men who would occasionally gather in a dorm room to enjoy a roast pig. The club's mem-

FUN FACT

While most social clubs emphasized some element of erudition, one club, now defunct, made its main focus a departure from intellectual pursuits. The Navy Club "consisted of all seniors who failed to receive parts at the last 'exhibition' of the class before Commencement"—those who had received no academic honors, and were likely more practiced in opening bottles than in opening books.

bership and prestige grew, and by 1800, it was believed by many Harvard undergraduates that election to the Porcellian was the pinnacle of social achievement at Harvard. 31 years later, the Porcellian merged with a similar organization, the Knights of the Square Table, founded in 1809.

GREEK TRAGEDY

The early 19th century saw a surge of notable Greek fraternities like Alpha Delta Phi and Delta Upsilon that were required to register with the University as well as with their national organizations.

In 1857, Harvard banned Greek-letter fraternities, denying them access to University buildings and voiding their rights to public functions. Most of the existing fraternities went underground or declared themselves literary societ-

ALEXANDRE TERRIEN
The McKean Gate, also known as the Porcellian Gate, donated by the club and named for its founder

ies, but many resurfaced at the end of the century, purchasing land and building their own clubhouses, unaffiliated with the college.

When they were forced to sever their affiliations with the University, many of Harvard's fraternities also separated from their national networks. Many adopted new names derived from their original Greek letters. The Alpha Delta Phi fraternity became the Haidee Club, later shortened to the A.D. Club, which still exists today; Delta Upsilon became known as D.U. and, later, the Duck.

Going private gave clubs greater control over their membership. Before the ban, a fraternity member from another undergraduate chapter who enrolled in any of Harvard's graduate programs automatically became a member of the Harvard chapter. Once the clubs renounced national membership, they no longer had this obligation.

DEFINING "FINAL CLUB"

After Alpha Delta Phi went underground, it resurfaced in 1865, under the name A.D. Club, and its laws indicated that no member could also matriculate into the Porcellian. Thus, membership in the A.D. became "final," hence the term "final club."

A student would typically join a number of freshman societies, and then attempt to make it into the Institute and the Dickey as a sophomore. In his junior year, the student would hope to join a waiting club, and finally one of the two final clubs for his senior year. Most waiting clubs, which were generally other fraternities that had broken their ties to national organizations, eventually became the remainder of the final clubs that exist today.

CLUBS ACCUMULATE WEALTH AND CRITICISM

After the Civil War, the student population grew quickly, but on-campus housing remained limited. Most undergraduates lived off-campus, while only the wealthiest students lived in the expensive dormitories along Mount Auburn Street known as the Gold Coast. Clubs vied for Gold Coast residents, hoping that they might be able to use residential space for meetings. Ultimately, thanks to expensive dues for members, clubs began buying up their own properties in Harvard Square. These clubhouses became enormous draws, particularly for students who did not live in the Square, and contributed to competition among clubs.

Not everyone at Harvard was enamored of the lavish clubhouses and the high society lifestyle that accompanied them. The behavior of overzealous clubmen was met with criticism from the faculty, and a 1913 Crimson article publicly criticized the members of the Polo Club, who had recently disrupted the annual freshman class dinner. Clubs had begun to rub many people the wrong way—as one member of the Class of 1899 put it in a personal letter, "those were the days of silver-dollar-size medals representing membership in

ALUMNUS ILLUMINATED:
ROBERT GOULD SHAW

With fellow Porcellian member N.P. Hallowell, Robert Gould Shaw led the 54th Massachusetts Regiment, the nation's first all-black military division. He orchestrated the conscription of black men into his personal regiment. Shaw died alongside his men during a charge on Fort Wagner in South Carolina in 1863. His memory is honored in Memorial Hall, where his named is inscribed on a plaque, and in a statue facing the Massachusetts State House on Beacon Hill.

Robert Gould Shaw, Harvard University Archives, HUP Shaw, Robert Gould (1-2)

undergraduate outfits"—and change was due. It came at the turn of the century, with the appointment of President Abbott Lawrence Lowell.

FOCUSING ON THE COLLEGE

President Lowell was one of the first Harvard administrators to seek borader social opportunities for students. Not only did he build a new student union; he also embarked on a mission to remedy the housing crisis by constructing affordable on-campus housing for undergraduates. The social scene was finally changing shape. The clubs made an agreement not to select members from the freshman class, to avoid segregating the class into groups in their first year. In this same spirit, the College provided housing for all incoming freshmen in Harvard Yard. These policies gave the student body more inclusive social options. Shortly thereafter, thanks to Lowell's new House system (p. 123), social life was further universalized.

By and large, final clubs survived these changes and continued to meet, mostly in secret. In fact, there was no better time to join a club than during Prohibition: as Harvard historian Richard Norton Smith points out, the clandestine nature of the clubs allowed students to enjoy illegal alcohol. "C. Douglas Dillon, later John Kennedy's Treasury Secretary, couldn't recall anyone who attended chapel regularly, but he remembered vividly a taxi stand before the Porcellian Club from which 'regular deliveries of bootleg Scotch were made to the thirsty young men inside.'"

A collection in the Harvard Archives explains that laws were written to control social organizations starting in the 1950s to little avail. One rule reads, "Women shall not enter clubhouses or the premises of undergraduate organizations without special permission of the Dean's Office. Permission will ordinarily not be granted unless chaperones are present." By all accounts, this rule was ignored just as conspicuously as the laws banning alcohol during Prohibition.

Though much has changed since women began gaining admittance to Harvard, the final club scene still remains segregated by sex. In 1984, Harvard asked all clubs to either become coeducational, in accordance with the larger mission of the University, or to sever their University ties. All of the major clubs chose to become independent, and are today entirely unaffiliated with the University. For the same reason, fraternities and sororities are also not sanctioned by Harvard and exist as independent and unaffiliated social organizations.

FINAL CLUBS TODAY

The eight male final clubs on campus today are the Porcellian, the A.D., the Spee, the Fox, the Phoenix S.K., the Owl, the Fly, and the Delphic. All of these clubs own property between the southern edge of Harvard Yard and the Charles River.

KEVIN LIN

The Fox Club

The clubhouses are some of the most beautiful and valuable properties in Cambridge, and most have a library, a dining room, a living room, a billiards room, a bar, and a garden. Clubs today are perhaps best known as party spaces—in fact, hosting parties has become central to the identity of some clubs. In addition to casual weekend parties, clubs generally host a handful of large parties each semester, often with themes and strict guest lists.

A lively debate on Harvard's campus today centers around the final clubs and their focus on exclusivity. Only a small proportion of sophomores and juniors gain membership in final clubs each fall and the clubs often restrict entrance to parties by means of either members or hired bouncers at their doors. Many students have expressed a variety of opinions ranging from a desire for the clubs to admit female members to a protest of the clubs' existence in general. Others argue that the clubs should continue to exist as their membership sees fit, as they are private entities unaffiliated with Harvard and the desires of the student body at large. Regardless of indivual opinions, the clubs continue to be a much discussed subject in Harvard's student publications, as well as in casual conversation.

FEMALE FINAL CLUBS

Though it would have been inconceivable to the old boys a century ago, there are a number of female final clubs at Harvard today. The first, the Bee, was established in 1991, and others quickly followed. Today, the Isis, the Pleiades Society, La Vie Club, and the Sabliere Society offer the final club experience to Harvard's undergraduate women. The majority of these clubs now own or rent private property in the Square, where members can gather together, share meals and (far less frequently than the male clubs) throw parties. Male and female clubs often plan events together including cocktail parties, outings, and dinners.

The Seneca (p. 47), another all-female group on campus, serves a similar social purpose but is not a final club. It selects members through an application system rather than a punch process.

PUNCHING A CLUB

The "punch" process, the Harvard equivalent of the rush process for fraternities and sororities, lasts approximately two long months, from mid-September to mid-November. While each club has its own traditions and variations within punch, the process retains a uniform structure across all clubs. Punch was described in Harvard's Alumni Bulletin in 1964:

The Season officially opens early in October, when members propose vast numbers of friends and acquaintances as punchees. The punchee first receives the eagerly awaited news when, in the middle of the night, certain club representatives steal to the candidate's door and slip under it an invitation to the upcoming Sunday Outing... The punchee is called for by a member of the club he has chosen to honor early Sunday morning, and is driven to the country home of a graduate member for luncheon and touch football.

FAMOUS CLUB BOYS

Porcellian: Theodore Roosevelt
Spee: John F. Kennedy
Fox: T.S. Eliot
Fly: Franklin D. Roosevelt
A.D.: William Randolph Hearst
Phoenix S.K.: Samuel Eliot Morison
Owl: Edward Kennedy
Delphic: J.P. Morgan

If he gets through his outing in good form, he is invited to attend a small dinner at a graduate's home. The climax of the Season centers about the final dinner, a black tie affair open only to those who have lasted through the previous weeks without faltering. The fun ends abruptly, if only temporarily, in the second week of December, when the club meets to discuss (and to vote upon) those who have lasted. This is a conclave of grave and important men.

The "punch" process is intended to facilitate interactions between members and "punches"—prospective members selected by the current membership of the club—in a variety of different environments. Around 200 sophomores and juniors are invited to the first event, which is typically a cocktail party. After deliberations, club members invite half of these original punches to the second event, traditionally an outing to a nearby alumnus's house. The real fun starts after the second event, when club members start taking punches out to lunches, dinners, and bars around Cambridge and Boston. The third event is often a formal date event, and both members and punches bring dates to an off-campus venue. The final event, called "final dinner," is a black tie affair, at which the small group of remaining punches is considerably outnumbered by a large showing of members and graduates of the club. After final dinner, the members of the club meet and elect a new membership class.

GREEK LIFE TODAY

In addition to final clubs, Harvard students have the chance to join a number of fraternities and sororities. The history of fraternities on campus is intimately linked to the history of final clubs, as most of the clubs started as chapters of national fraternities, before renouncing their national membership after Harvard banned Greek organizations. As final clubs developed and grew in popularity throughout the 20th century, fraternities came and went, but never occupied a particularly large niche on campus. In recent years, however, Harvard has seen a surge in the activity of fraternities and sororities on campus, and today students can pledge three fraternities (Sigma Chi, Sigma Alpha Epsilon, and Alpha Epsilon Pi) and three sororities (Kappa Kappa Gamma, Delta Gamma, and

FUN FACT

From 2005 until the fall of 2007, students could petition the Under-graduate Council (UC), the student governing body, for grants to throw parties. The UC allotted $1,750 a week, split up among 16 different grants, which would be used to buy food, drinks, utensils, and decorations. In October of 2007, however, Interim Dean of the College David Pilbeam wrote a letter to the UC officially ending what was known as "the party fund." Dean Pilbeam argued that the party fund caused overcrowding in spaces designed for small social gatherings and that the fund had "not made the funding of student groups a sufficiently high priority." The University's concern over underage drinking was a central factor in the termination of the party fund. In his letter, Pilbeam determined that "institutional funds can never be used to sponsor private events with alcohol that the College has no way of regulating" and blamed the UC for failing to enforce their rule that "underage students will not be reimbursed for purchasing alcohol."

Kappa Alpha Theta). Stuents can join as either freshmen or sophomores. All six organizations rent spaces within Harvard Square, host formal events each semester, and organize philanthropy events for the entire student population.

UNIVERSITY SPONSORED SOCIAL EVENTS

The College Events Board (CEB) plans many of the large student events that take place at Harvard each year. The CEB was founded in 2005 in an effort to improve social programming across campus. It is financed by the College and receives an annual budget of around $200,000 directly from the Dean of the College's discretionary fund. The CEB consists of 18 to 20 board members, who work with the Campus Life Fellow to distribute the funds for social events. Commonly referred to as the "Fun Czar," the Campus Life Fellow is a former student hired by the University one year after graduating from Harvard. Harvard selects a new Fun Czar every year. The board members are elected to their posts, with a member from each upperclass House filling the first 12 positions. Members conduct a series of interviews to fill the final spots, reserving one or two spots for freshmen.

By its own constitution, the CEB is required to put on three major events each year. These events are generally the Welcome Back carnival, the Harvard-Yale pep rally, and Yardfest. The Welcome Back Carnival occurs in the first week of school as the CEB turns Harvard Yard into a carnival with rides, games, and abundant food. The Harvard-Yale pep rally takes place in November in anticipation of the Harvard-Yale football game (p. 105), always the last game of the season. For Yardfest, one of the biggest events on campus, the CEB recruits famous musical artists to play in Harvard Yard. Kid Cudi, Patrick Park and Wale performed at Yardfest in 2009, and Far East Movement headlined in 2010. Attendance is estimated around 7,000 people, including students, staff, and guests. The CEB constitution also mandates that all events be available to the entire undergraduate population and that they be free of charge. This last stipulation has caused some backlash, as other schools who charge admission for similar events have generally been able to attract and finance more popular artists.

The First-Year Social Committee (FYSC) is advised by the CEB and is overseen by the Campus Life Fellow, but specializes in freshman social life. The FYSC attempts to foster a sense of community and social connection among the newest members of Harvard. The board consists of 14 freshmen, selected through an application and interview process. The FYSC puts on events about once a month, such as a costume catwalk for Halloween, gingerbread house decorating, and the Freshman Formal.

THE SOCIAL SPACE DEBATE

One of the debates regarding social space on campus today is that, outside of final clubs, social space really doesn't exist. For students who want to get out of their dorm rooms, who can't afford or aren't old enough for the Cambridge and Boston bar scene, and who aren't members of a club, a lack of student social space on campus is a problem.

The topic has been an integral part of many of the platforms of students running as representatives to the Undergraduate Council in recent years, including the campaigns for presidency and vice presidency which pervade the

FRESHMAN DEAN'S OFFICE
Harvard Yard, a natural social space

FUN FACT

In 2007, the Cambridge Queen's Head Pub opened in the common space beneath Annenberg Hall. Two years earlier, Dean of the College Benedict H. Gross had decided to actively seek out more social spaces for students on campus, and the Pub was a step in the right direction. Today, the Pub fills with both undergraduates and graduate students Wednesday through Saturday nights. Besides serving the cheapest beer in the Square, the Pub has special deals and events for students, like 25-Cent Wing Night, Trivia Night, and Karaoke Night.

ALEXANDRE TERRIEN
The Queen's Head seal, featuring a facedown third book

The Pub also allows student organizations to host happy hours and other events. Though students must be 21 years old to drink, students of all ages gather in the Pub to hang out and enjoy the food and atmosphere. In addition, the Pub employs five student managers and 100 students on staff; many students head to the Pub to catch up with friends who are working shifts.

student body consciousness each November. Both the UC and the Crimson voice the need for social space and a student center regularly. While University President, Drew Faust, has made it clear that she does not immediately intend to initiate plans for a student center, she is invested in the implementation and improvement of social spaces. Faust was behind the creation of the Steering Committe on Common Spaces in 2008, a group of administrators charged with the task of finding low-cost ways to promote unity within the student body. The Committee is responsible for the placement of colorful chairs within Harvard Yard beginning in the fall of 2009. The picturesque chairs remain in the Yard throughout the non-snowy months of the school year and are always occupied by both students balancing laptops on their knees while soaking up the sun and families of tourists gawking at the squirrels. Students agree that things like the Yard chairs and the construction of the Queen's Head Pub are steps in the right direction, but most believe that there is quite a bit of work left to do if Harvard wants to reduce its social dependency on final clubs and city establishments and create a more diverse social scene.

PUBLICATIONS
<u>AT HARVARD</u>

THE REIGNING TRIFECTA

Harvard's student publications run the gamut from newspapers and political reviews to literary journals and humor magazines. The three most famous undergraduate publications *The Harvard Crimson*, the *Harvard Lampoon*, and the *Harvard Advocate* boast a wide range of distinguished alumni. The *Advocate* emerged first on the scene in 1866, seven years before the founding of the *Crimson*. In 1876, some *Advocate* members defected to form the *Lampoon*, the humor magazine which later spun off the magazine and associated comedy brand *National Lampoon*. Each organizations owns its own building and is a prominent presence on campus.

THE HARVARD CRIMSON

The Harvard Crimson, founded in 1873, is one of the oldest student newspapers in the country and the only daily newspaper in Cambridge, Massachusetts. Overseen entirely by undergraduates, the newspaper is a non-profit organization that is independent of Harvard and receives no funding from the University.

The *Crimson*, which bills itself as "Cambridge's only breakfast table daily," is one of only four college newspapers in the country that owns and operates its own printing presses. The presses, located in the basement, are run by two full-time non-student employees. The *Crimson* also hires a full-time bookkeeper and maintains its own independent legal counsel. Early in 2004, the *Crimson* unveiled a major redesign, including the introduction of full color on the front and back pages. The *Crimson* currently publishes three weekly pullout sections in addition to its regular daily paper: a Sports section on Mondays, the magazine *Fifteen Minutes* on Thursdays, and an

BY THE NUMBERS

1	Dollar per year paid to Harvard by the *Advocate* to lease their building on South Street
3	Widely-read and enduring undergraduate publications
5	Different addresses claimed by the *Harvard Lampoon*'s Castle
15	Hottest freshmen chosen by *FM* Magazine each spring

Arts section on Fridays. The *Crimson* also prints 15 other publications on its presses for other Harvard organizations, as well as for local high schools and colleges.

HISTORY

The Harvard Crimson was one of many college newspapers founded shortly after the Civil War. Initially called *The Magenta* (for Harvard's original school color*)*, the newspaper was first published on January 24, 1873, despite opposition from the Dean of the University. In the late 19th century, publications on campus faced tremendous opposition from the University; by 1873 the faculty of the College had already suspended the existence of several previous student newspapers, including *The Collegian*, whose motto "Dulce est periculum" ("Danger is sweet," later adopted by the *Advocate)* spoke to the environment of student journalism at the time. The publication lived up to its "dangerous" mantra, publishing an attack on mandatory chapel attendance that scandalized the faculty, who promptly shut down the publication.

The Magenta's determined editors ignored the Dean's warnings and put out a twice-weekly paper—"a thin layer of editorial content surrounded by an even thinner wrapper of advertising," according to a history of the *Crimson* published on the occasion of its 125th anniversary entitled "Keep the Old Sheet Flying." The paper was originally based in the dorm room of founder Henry Alden Clark, Class of 1874, in Stoughton 22.

The Magenta's first staff editorial exemplifies what distinguished it from the preeminent publication at the time, the *Advocate:* "Our work, as a whole, is meant to show no affectation of fine writing, nor does it lay claim to literary excellence. The *Advocate* has this ground by right of possession; we do not attempt to rival it in *jeux d'esprit*, or in cunningness of speculation, or otherwise poach upon its preserves." The mission of the paper articulated here— "satisfying the curiosity of our readers about what is going on in Cambridge, and at other colleges, and of giving them an opportunity to express their ideas upon practical questions"—remains largely unchanged today. The editorial ends with the paper's motto: "I won't philosophize, and I will be read," a loose approximation of a quotation from Canto X of Lord Byron's *Don Juan.*

Editorials continued to be published on the front page of each issue, in the form of short paragraphs on a variety of issues relating to student life. The biweekly also featured one or two poems, a news column entitled "Brevities," and various stories and essays.

The paper changed its name to *The Harvard Crimson* after the University, at a meeting of all departments on May 6, 1875, voted to change its official color. A fortnight later, on May 21st, 1875, a full-page editorial announced that "Magenta is not now, and…never has been, the right color of Harvard." The issue also called for local shopkeepers to stock the proper shade of crimson ribbon, to avoid "startling variations in the colors worn by Harvard men at the races."

Although the *Advocate* mocked the fledgling newspaper, referring to it as "Crime's Own," the two papers considered merging in the spring of 1882, when the *Crimson* was experiencing financial difficulties. The merger agreement stated that "the publication of the *Crimson* should be stopped, that its editors should be elected to the *Advocate* Board and that the *Crimson*'s debt, amounting to several hundred dollars, should be assumed by the *Advocate*." The proposed agreement was defeated at the last minute by an editorial vote of the *Advocate* staff. After the *Advocate* declined the merger, the *Crimson* moved to publish just once a week.

In 1879, a publication called the *Echo* became the first Harvard daily. On January 3, 1882, a new daily, twice the size of the *Echo*, called *The Harvard Daily Herald*, emerged, complete with advertising revenue. The competition between the two dailies bankrupted the *Echo* and threatened the *Herald*. On October 1, 1883, the *Herald* and the *Crimson* decided to merge. Four days later, the merger went through, and the President of the *Crimson* became the President of the new *Herald-Crimson*. The new paper consisted of four pages of four columns each, with the left column of the front page set aside for advertising and the other three reserved for news and communications. The paper was renamed *The Harvard Crimson* in 1884, and in 1885 the editors moved from their Yard office to spacious new quarters on Holyoke Street.

Over the course of the 1880s, the *Crimson* became a more substantive newspaper, as the editors aspired to the kind of muckraking journalism that was being conducted at big-city newspapers. The six officers, elected in February of their sophomore year, would often skip class and miss meals to put out the daily newspaper (still the case today!). One officer from the Class of 1875, quoted in "Keep the Old Sheet Flying," remembered "very vividly certain days on which I went to the Riverside Press immediately after Chapel and stayed there without tasting a mouthful of food, correcting proofs and so forth, until, grimy and inkstained and ravenously hungry, I carried up the first numbers, still damp from the press, as the printing office closed and deposited them in the news office in Harvard Square. It was a most thrilling experience." *Crimson* editors also took their duties seriously, and were required to sign a "dummy" onto which their assignments were written vowing to cover the story. Editors who failed to turn in an assigned article were fined two dollars. The President and writers took pride in their hard work, though, as evidenced by the lyrics of the *Crimson* song, written in 1887:

> *This is the Daily Crimson,*
> *That now is at the head*
> *Of all the College Publications because it's always re[a]d.*

In April 1917, the day after the House of Representatives passed the War Resolution that officially involved the United States in World War I, the *Crimson* attracted national attention for publishing a two-column, three-inch headline announcing "WAR," a bold statement in an era of smaller, more modest headlines.

The *Crimson* continued to publish for the remainder of the year, but with future enrollment down 40% because of the number of enlisted students, the paper ceased publication on June 7. Publication didn't resume until January 2, 1919, when *Crimson* President George C. Barclay, Class of 1919, returned from the war. Today, a plaque in the *Crimson*'s headquarters' main gathering space commemorates the editors who gave their lives in World War I.

On May 3, 1920, the *Crimson* installed a new printing press, which allowed the paper to print five columns instead of four. The *Crimson* also bought out *Harvard Illustrated Magazine*, whose editors became the first members of the *Crimson*'s photography board.

In a tribute to the *Crimson* on its 50th anniversary, in 1923, the *Advocate* wrote: "Mother *Advocate* has, indeed, changed very slightly… The Gentleman [the *Crimson*], on the other hand, has been content to forget the romantic tendencies of his youth and to plunge into the whirl of business, with the result that he now has a mansion, a gold watch-fob and a bank account of his own. But he has something more valuable—a reputation that none can respect and honor more than Mother *Advocate*."

Sobered by World War I, the *Crimson* of the 1920s was a serious organization. *Crimson* editors defied the mood of the roaring 20s, shunning stories about the Jazz Age or the budding movie culture and focusing exclusively on news events. The design mirrored the conservative tenor of the paper, with few pictures, long articles, and straightforward headlines. As the stock market boomed, *Crimson* advertising revenue followed suit, and the paper became driven by the desire to make money. Business editors were rumored to regularly sneak in at night to replace news stories with last-minute ads.

The effects of the Depression were felt quickly enough, as advertising revenue plummeted in 1931. In 1932, *Crimson* editors, who had always been paid, had to forgo their salaries. They also took up the role of proofing the paper, a job that had previously been outsourced to employees.

A group of news editors, frustrated by the quality of a paper that now rarely reached six pages, broke off from the *Crimson* to form their own publication, the *Harvard Journal*. Those who remained at the *Crimson* pressured the business board to allot more editorial funding, and pushed for more pictures, more national and international news coverage, and longer issues. After a brief but fierce competition, the *Journal* ultimately folded in June of 1936, leaving the *Crimson* as the College's only daily.

The onset of World War II immediately affected life at the *Crimson*. The iron fence outside 14 Plympton St., the building where the paper still resides, was donated to a scrap drive as part of the war effort. Meanwhile, the staff fought to stay in print, despite widespread opposition from those who thought academic life should not continue as normal while others were risking their lives for their country. Nonetheless, the *Crimson* voiced strong support for academic programs at Harvard, and penned editorials condemning Yale's policy of funneling students into reserve programs. The *Crimson* also expressed its support for the New Deal policies of U.S. President, and former *Crimson* President, Franklin D. Roosevelt, Class of 1904, who reciprocated with a letter stating that "I voice the sentiments of all that company of happy men when I say that none of them would exchange his *Crimson* training for any other experience of association in his college days."

Despite the best efforts of the staff, the paper fell under the direction of a board of University administrators, *Crimson* alumni, and undergraduates in 1943. The banner on the now semi-weekly paper read *Harvard Service News*, the stories focused almost exclusively on Harvard's contributions to the war effort, and alumni discouraged the *Service News* from editorializing. The paper did not return to its civilian incarnation until 1946.

The major issue of the 1950s at the *Crimson* was the debate over whether women could be elected as editors. Because Radcliffe women were subject to a curfew, they could not put in the late hours required of *Crimson* editors, and therefore could contribute articles but could not be editors. *Crimson* editors pushed the administration to allow later curfews for women working at the

PRESIDENTIAL SCOOPS

In 1983, *Crimson* news editor Paul M. Barrett '83 wrote to the White House requesting an interview with President Ronald Reagan and was granted a press interview. Since then, however, coverage has shifted from a focus on national political issues that dominated in the 1960s and 70s to more campus-centered stories. Indeed, editors today continue to place major emphasis on "the Harvard angle."

After being scooped with the news of Derek Bok's selection as University President in 1971 by the weekly *Harvard Independent*, *Crimson* editors were especially determined to break the story of Bok's successor, former Princeton Provost Neil Rudenstine, in 1991. For seven months, *Crimson* reporters tracked candidates from Loeb House, where the Harvard Corporation was headquartered, to Boston's Logan Airport and even to New York City, where *Crimson* reporters took to the streets of Rudenstine's Manhattan neighborhood with photos of the new President to learn more about him, from his magazine of choice (*Time*) to his laundry preferences (a little starch). The reporters then took the same flight back to Boston as Rudenstine, who, in his surprise, confirmed his appointment. *Crimson* editors filed the story with the dateline "30,000 feet over New England." The news ran on a Friday, a full three days before the official announcement was made, scooping both *The New York Times* and the *Boston Globe*. The *Crimson* scooped national news outlets again with the news of President Lawrence Summers' appointment in 2001 and Drew Gilpin Faust's appointment in 2007.

Crimson, and under *Crimson* President Phillip Cronin, Class of 1953, women were elected as staff writers rather than mere Radcliffe correspondents. It wasn't until the late 1950s, under the leadership of *Crimson* President Adam Clymer, Class of 1958, that women were allowed to become full-fledged executives. The first female President of the *Crimson*, Gay W. Seidman, Class of 1978, was elected in 1976, and five other women have been elected since.

RECENT HISTORY

In February 1992, the *Crimson* introduced *Fifteen Minutes*, a magazine devoted largely to popular culture, which took its name from Andy Warhol's adage, "In the future everyone will be world-famous for fifteen minutes." The magazine's most popular issue is the highly anticipated "Fifteen Hottest Freshmen" spread, published every spring semester.

The 1990s also witnessed a particular emphasis on diversifying the *Crimson*'s staff. A financial aid program was introduced, allowing students to receive work-study money for time spent working at the *Crimson*.

In 2004, the *Crimson* printed its first color edition thanks to the installation of a new color press. That same year, in an effort to glean information regarding several noteworthy incidents, the *Crimson* filed a lawsuit against Harvard in an attempt to force the Harvard University Police Department to

NOTABLE ALUMNI

Notable alumni of the *Crimson* include Franklin D. Roosevelt, Class of 1904, who served as President of the newspaper; Caspar Weinburger, U.S. Defense Secretary under Ronald Reagan, '38; John F. Kennedy '40, who served as a Business Editor; author David Halberstam '55; *New York Times* Company President Jack Rosenthal '56; *New York Times* journalist Adam Clymer '58; alternative medicine advocate Andrew Weil '63; author Michael Crichton '64; *Washington Post* CEOs Donald Graham '66 and Boisfeuillet Jones '68; *New York Times* Supreme Court reporter Linda Greenhouse '68; *New York Times* columnist Frank Rich '71; *Washington Post* columnist E.J. Dionne '73; Dean of Columbia School of Journalism Nicholas Lemann '76; Microsoft CEO Steve Ballmer '77; host of CNBC's *Mad Money* Jim Cramer '77; Caroline Kennedy '79; Senior Vice President of NBC News Mark Whitaker '79; *New York Times* columnist Nicholas Kristof '82; environmentalist Bill McKibben '82; CNN legal analyst Jeffrey Toobin '82; *New Republic* editor Charles Lane '83; NBC Universal President and CEO Jeffrey Zucker '86; and *New Republic* journalist Jonathan Cohn '91.

make its records public. Though the Massachusetts Supreme Judicial Court ruled in favor of the University in January 2006, the case was an important testament to the *Crimson*'s role as a watchdog for the University.

In April 2006, acting on an anonymous tip, a *Crimson* reporter broke the story of the plagiarism charge against Harvard student Kaavya Viswanathan, Class of 2008, for her book *How Opal Mehta Got Kissed, Got Wild, and Got a Life*. After the *Crimson* identified over a dozen passages that appeared to be lifted from novels by Megan McCafferty, the plagiarism controversy was picked up by the national and international press, making the front page of *The New York Times* and appearing in newspapers from India to England. In March 2009, the *Crimson* launched FlyByBlog.com, which offers students brief, pertinent posts about campus happenings.

Despite all the changes the *Crimson* has undergone throughout its storied history, the dedication of its undergraduate staff to producing the paper day after day—to the occasional exclusion of homework, laundry, and social lives—has remained constant.

THE CRIMSON TODAY

The *Crimson* is currently divided into 11 boards: News, Business, Arts, Sports, Fifteen Minutes (FM), Editorial, Photography, Design, Blog, Video, and Information Technology. Beginning in the late 1990s, the *Crimson*'s news board has organized itself around a beat system whereby coverage is divided into

KEVIN LIN

The Crimson

distinct genres, allowing beat reporters to specialize in a particular issue or sector. *Crimson* beats are currently divided among four teams: University, College, Faculty, and City.

Students may choose to "comp" any of the boards, each of which has its own series of comp requirements (p. 1). Any student who decides to join the *Crimson* and completes all of the comp requirements is elected an "editor" of the newspaper, known as a "Crimed," in a ceremony held at the end of each semester called "Grand Elections." All staff members, including business staff, photographers, and designers, are technically considered "editors."

Garry Trudeau, creator of the comic strip *Doonesbury*, ridiculed this policy in his 1983 Commencement speech. "What other university would have an eight-page newspaper which boasts 100 editors and no reporters?" he asked, calling it "a flagrant example of resume padding," according to the *Crimson*'s anniversary book.

All of the elected members of a particular class are referred to as a "guard," and the guard number is determined by the number of years that will have elapsed between the founding of the *Crimson* and the class's Commencement. Executives are chosen for one-year terms each November by the outgoing executives in a process known as the the "turkey shoot" or "shoot." During the shoot process, as the executives are busy conducting one-on-one interviews with those shooting, *Crimson* alumni, called "dinos," return to the building to edit stories and proof the paper.

The president of the *Crimson* may be elected from any board, though historically the President has been most likely to come from the news board. When writer Cleveland Amory, Class of 1939, a former President of the *Crimson*, was asked by Katherine Hepburn's mother what he planned to do after college, he apparently quipped that "once you had been President of *The Harvard Crimson* in your senior year at Harvard there was very little, in afterlife, for you."

THE HARVARD LAMPOON

From honoring Paris Hilton with the *Harvard Lampoon*'s Woman of the Year Award, a spoof on the Hasty Pudding Theatricals' award of the same name, to sending fake e-mails on behalf of University Health Services soliciting stool samples from Harvard freshmen, *Lampoon* editors have long been the pranksters-in-residence on campus. Housed in a mock-Flemish castle, the *Harvard Lampoon* is known for its bacchanalian parties and penchant for secrecy. For all its pranks and rituals, distinguished guests, and architectural eccentricity, the *Lampoon* remains, first and foremost, a humor magazine. As John Updike put it in his introduction to *The Harvard Lampoon* Centennial Celebration, "The *Lampoon* is saved from mere sociable fatuity by being also the *Lampoon*."

ARCHITECTURAL SPOTLIGHT:
THE LAMPOON CASTLE

The Lampoon Castle, which stands at the intersection of Mount Auburn Street and Bow Street, is one of the most peculiar, idiosyncratic, and

ALEXANDRE TERRIEN

mysterious buildings on Harvard's campus. The building parodies 16th-century Dutch and Flemish architecture, with the proportions of certain elements, like the tower, noticeably exaggerated. A face, made up of two round windows, a red lantern for a nose, and a grinning mouth, faces up Mount Auburn Street. A copper statue of an Egyptian ibis bird stands perched on the roof. The building's first floor interior contains rooms of varying styles, including a study replicating a Dutch fisherman's cottage and a circular humor library. Only *Lampoon* members are allowed in the upper stories of the castle, generating much speculation and mystery. The building was constructed in 1909 by Edmund Wheelwright, with funding from former *Lampoon* staffer and leading newspaper publisher, William Randolph Hearst, who had been booted from Harvard in the mid-1880s after pulling too many pranks. The building was added to the National Historic Register in 1978. The castle technically has five addresses, all of which have been mentioned on the TV show *The Simpsons*.

HISTORY

The *Harvard Lampoon,* founded in 1876, is America's oldest humor magazine and the world's longest-running humor magazine still in publication. It is now published five times a year. Ask for an authoratative history, however, and you might be out of luck: even the *Lampoon*'s own record, detailed in *The Harvard Lampoon Centennial Celebration*, is suspect: its preface proudly proclaims itself:

> *"far from accurate. One could even go so far as to say that the number of distortions, gross misrepresentations, and downright lies nestling between this volume's cover is positively mind-boggling. Exaggerations and over-statements crouch in ambush on every page. Historical inaccuracy is affronted at every turn. Truth is sacrificed incessantly in the eternal search for the quick yuk."*

From its early years, the *Lampoon* has entertained a fierce rivalry with the *Crimson*, but the victims of *Lampoon* pranks are not limited to other student organizations. In 1933, members of the *Lampoon* stole the Sacred Cod of Massachusetts, in what became known as the "Cod-napping."

Despite its antics, the *Lampoon* is known nationally, above all, for its famed parodies. The *Lampoon* started out spoofing local magazines like the Boston-based *Popular Mechanics*, but by the middle of the 20th century, it had begun parodying major national publications. The first time the *Lampoon* successfully replicated the full format of a magazine, including the advertising layout, was in 1939 with a parody of *The New Yorker*. The last small, locally produced parody was that of *The Saturday Review* in 1960. The following year, in what marked a decisive shift toward the lampooning of national publications, *Mademoiselle* approached the *Lampoon* about having the humorists create their July issue. Like all the national parodies to come, this *Mademoiselle* issue and a second *Mademoiselle* parody, commissioned in 1962, included both real and bogus advertising. The July 1963 parody of *Esquire* appeared inside a special issue of *Mademoiselle*, leaving people wondering who exactly was behind the lampoon and who was being lampooned.

FUN FACT

The *Lampoon* took its inspiration from the now-defunct British satire magazine *Punch*. In 1897, *Punch* contributing writer R.C. Lehmann was made an Honorary Editor of the *Lampoon*. "I cannot offer you terrapin or soft shell crab," Lehmann wrote in a letter of thanks, reproduced in the Centennial book, in which he offered to welcome the *Lampoon* Board to his home if it should ever cross the Atlantic. "But our white bait is not without merit and we take some pride in our raspberry and currant tarts."

FUN FACT

In *Babar Comes to America,* Babar the Elephant describes his visit to the Lampoon and provides an illustration of the castle's Dutch fisherman's room.

It wasn't until 1966 that the *Lampoon* parodied a nationally distributed magazine and distributed the issue on its own. The *Playboy* parody of that year, called *Pl*yb*y,* sold 450,000 copies in just three weeks.

Lampoon branched out from magazines to newspapers with its 1968 parody of *The New York Times.* The issue was substituted locally for real copies of the March 7 *Times* early in the morning, before local subscribers—mostly Harvard undergraduates—woke up. One particularly memorable headline read, "Ancient Parthenon Topples As Quake Rocks Greece," in response to which a classics professor canceled class as a memorial.

In 1956, the *Lampoon* issued a parody of *Newsweek,* which asserted in one article that "Adolph Hitler has resided in a Cambridge, Massachusetts apartment since 1946."

The *Lampoon*'s best-known parody of a book came in 1969 with *Bored of the Rings,* a parody of the J.R.R. Tolkien classic written by *Lampoon* editors Douglas Kenney, Class of 1968, and Henry Beard, Class of 1967. In 1970, Kenney and Beard came together again to form the magazine *National Lampoon,* which later yielded a live show called *Lemmings* and a radio show, *The National Lampoon Radio Hour.* Writers for these shows were later hired to help create *Saturday Night Live,* which debuted on October 11, 1975. In 1978, Kenney was among the screenwriters for *National Lampoon's Animal House,* which remains one of the highest-grossing comedies in movie history. Licensing rights to the *Lampoon* name remain a major source of funding for the student organization.

THE LAMPOON TODAY

Despite its notorious history, the *Lampoon* today is the object of general disappointment on campus. Its parties are well-attended and rigidly exclusive, and its pranks are anticipated eagerly, but its actual publication is the victim of inside jokes and insufficient copyediting, and it enjoys its most consistent attention from visiting alums and confused tourists.

John Updike wrote in the introduction to the *Centennial Celebration* that: "The *Lampoon* is a club and, as do all clubs, feeds on the delicious immensity of the excluded." This is reflected in the organization's semester-long comps—for the Business, Arts, and Literature boards—which are particularly competitive and involve three rounds of cuts.

CRIMSON-LAMPOON RIVALRY

The *Crimson* and the *Lampoon*, located less than a block away from one another, have long harbored a fierce rivalry. Since May 30, 1901, the *Lampoon* has published an annual *Crimson* parody, replete with typos and mocking headlines like "Bacteria at Large" and "The Cricket Game a Tie: Score 107 to 18." In 1925, the *Crimson* published a six-page special section before the annual *Crimson-Lampoon* softball game even began, declaring its traditional 23-2 victory over "Lampy." The next year, a front-page *Crimson* story trumpeted the "financial failure" of the humor magazine. In 1929, a group of *Lampoon* editors led by President Alan Blackburn, Class of 1929, snuck into the *Crimson*, replacing the copies of the next day's paper with 1,400 fake issues. In 1941, the *Crimson* stole the Ibis, a large copper bird that perches atop the Lampoon castle. Lampy retaliated by kidnapping five *Crimson* editors, binding them to chairs, and burying them in their own newspapers. A few years later, in 1944, the *Lampoon* extended a fake honorary *Crimson* editorship to U.S. President Harry S Truman. When Truman wrote to *Crimson* President Robert S. Sturgis, Class of 1944, Sturgis was forced to reply that no such honor existed and the invitation was nothing more than a *Lampoon* prank. Truman good-naturedly replied that "I am greatly relieved for I was very certain it would not be possible for me to acquire a Harvard accent at this late date." In 1946, *Crimson* editors stole the Ibis once again, and the bird wound up that same night on the stage of Blackstone the magician and at the Opera House with Orson Welles. *Lampoon* editors proved equal to the task of thievery when, in 1949, 16 members broke into 14 Plympton St. to steal the *Crimson*'s antique punch bowl. A week later, the *Lampoon*, calling itself the Boston College for Curley Club, presented Bos-

ALEXANDRE TERRIEN
The Lampoon Ibis

SPIGOT-BIGOT

In 1924, the Lampoon held a contest with a $25 prize to come up with the best epithet critiquing the so-called "drys" who upheld Prohibition. Of 3,280 entrants, "Spigot-Bigot" was selected as the winner.

ton Mayor James Curley with the bowl. *Crimson* editors were forced to go to Curley's office the following day to retrieve the bowl.

The pranks of the 1940s, however, were quickly outshined by the famous prank of the 1950s, which reached an international audience. One night in 1953, *Crimson* cartoonist David Royce, Class of 1956, scaled the wall of the castle and seized the Ibis. *Lampoon* President John Updike, Class of 1954, demanded that the bird be returned. When his request went unanswered, *Crimson* President Michael Maccoby, Class of 1954, and Managing Editor George Abrams, Class of 1954, were kidnapped by the *Lampoon*. Updike apparently went on the radio to announce that: "No *Crimson* Editor can rest safe in his bed. We promise, within a week, to depopulate Cambridge totally of this unfortunate element." Maccoby and Abrams escaped, however, and were not seen or heard from for a whole weekend. Eventually, the pair wound up at the Russian Delegation Headquarters in New York City, accompanied by a *Crimson* photographer. Abrams presented the Ibis in the name of the *Lampoon* to Deputy United Nations Representative Semyon Tsarapkin, expressing his desire that the bird be placed atop a spire on Russia's new Moscow University. Magazines across the country picked up the story and the photograph of Abrams, standing in front of a giant picture of Stalin, presenting the Ibis to a puzzled Tsarapkin. One major news magazine ran a caption next that read "*Crimson* Gives Russia the Bird." Updike was forced to arrange for a group of *Lampoon* editors to go to New York to recover the Ibis. After *Lampoon* editors attempted to explain college humor to the Russian U.N. representative, reporters asked the diplomat to smile for a photograph. Tsarapkin responded coolly, "I am unsmiling." The battle had ended, but the war between the two organizations was far from over.

In the 1970s, the *Lampoon* stole the *Crimson*'s President's chair, with the names of all the past *Crimson* Presidents inscribed on the back, while *Crimson* Editors made a failed attempt to steal the Ibis again. In 1985, the *Lampoon* was inspired by a *Crimson* article that called the town of Duluth, Minnesota a "cultural wasteland." In order to enhance the town's culture, members of the *Lampoon* removed drawings and paintings of past Presidents of the *Crimson* from the *Crimson* building and crated them off to Duluth.

Today, *Crimson* guidelines demand that writers refer to the *Lampoon* for the first time in an article as "a semi-secret Sorrento Square social organization that used to occasionally publish a so-called humor magazine." Meanwhile, the *Lampoon* continues to publish its annual parody of the *Crimson*. It has also become a sporadic tradition in recent years for Poonsters to pour lobster juice into the ventilation system of the *Crimson* on the night of the *Crimson*'s Grand Elections ceremony, making the whole building reek of seafood.

The *Lampoon* does not limit its trickery to the *Crimson*, however. It celebrated its centennial in 1976 by seceding from the United States, declaring "Poona" the only free and independent state surrounded entirely by U.S. territory, demanding a seat in the United Nations, and threatening a display of its "nuclear capabilities." (The U.S. government has yet to respond to Poona's demands for a corridor to the sea.) In 1994, the *Lampoon* president claimed that Aerosmith guitarist Joe Perry was going to purchase the Lampoon castle to turn it into a summer home and recording studio. Boston radio station KISS 108 fell for the hoax and reported news of the sale on air.

The *Lampoon* has also been known to prank the final clubs (p. 153), posing as club alumni to send unsuspecting punches and initiates on bogus tasks, and even hosting their own punch process: in the spring of 2009, about 30 freshman received letters inviting them to a "punch" event for a Lampoon Final Club. Half of the group was invited back to a second round event, and a few more were cut before the final dinner. It wasn't until later, when no one was accepted, that the freshmen realized that no such final club exists. In 2011, the Lampoon sent forged punch invitations on behalf of an actual final club to a group of (soon dissapointed) freshmen.

NOTABLE ALUMNI AND MEMBERS

Famous alumni of the *Harvard Lampoon* include William Randolph Hearst, Class of 1885, John Updike '54, Andy Borowitz '80, Conan O'Brien '85, Cass Sunstein '75, and B.J. Novak '01, as well as writers for *The Simpsons, Futurama, Saturday Night Live, Late Night with David Letterman, NewsRadio, The Office,* and *30 Rock.*

Famous guests and honorary members of the *Lampoon* include Winston Churchill, Kurt Vonnegut Jr., Robin Williams, Billy Crystal, John Cleese, Bill Cosby, Jon Stewart, The Strokes, Aerosmith, Zac Braff, Dan Aykroyd, and Paris Hilton. It is also an annual tradition for the cast of *Saturday Night Live* to pay homage to the castle.

THE ADVOCATE

The oldest continuously published college literary magazine in the country, the *Advocate* predates both the *Crimson* and the *Lampoon*. It currently publishes student-produced art, poetry, fiction, and features.

HISTORY

Originally published in newspaper format, the *Advocate* was founded by Charles S. Gage and William G. Peckham, both Class of 1867. Its first issue, published on May 11, 1866, represented a major risk: the *Collegian*, a predecessor to the *Advocate* that Gage and Peckham had edited, had attacked compulsory chapel services and was shut down by the faculty on threat of expulsion. F.P. Sterns, a friend of Gage and Peckham, proposed the *Advocate* as a substitute. Sterns waited nervously for the faculty to decide the fate of the new publication, but apparently the faculty approved of the less-controversial *Advocate*. While the *Advocate* of today, a literature and arts magazine, has evolved considerably since its early days as a campus newspaper, it has been published continuously since 1866 with the exception of a short hiatus at the end of World War II.

For the first few years, the fortnightly *Advocate* was a mixed bag, reporting football and baseball scores, printing student poetry, and publishing editorials criticizing College policy. When the *Crimson* came along to publish football scores, and the *Lampoon* to make jokes, the *Advocate* was left to devote itself exclusively to essays, fiction, art, and poetry.

As at the *Crimson* and *Lampoon*, headquarters facilitated not only meetings, readings, and discussions, but also social events. However, for the more formal reunions the *Advocate* would seek out other venues, and after one particularly lavish decennial celebration in 1876, the magazine found itself so far in debt to the Parker House Hotel that boards several years later were still paying off the cost of the affair. In 1916, in celebration of the *Advocate*'s 50th anniversary, a dinner was held, at which Harvard's President Abbot Lawrence Lowell addressed over 100 editors. The evening continued with songs, mock speeches, and even an impersonation of Theodore Roosevelt.

The *Advocate* was the only campus publication to continue publishing throughout World War I (albeit in a smaller format to save paper). The years between the two wars were a kind of golden age. For the first time, famous professional writers began submitting to the magazine, alongside the usual Harvard undergraduates. The *Advocate* also began to publish reviews of the fine arts accompanied by plates of the images.

The first special issue was published in December 1938 and was devoted to T.S. Eliot, Class of 1910. The installment included short critical articles, personal recollections, tributes to Eliot by other writers, and a reprinting of Eliot's undergraduate work. Two years later, another special issue was published, devoted to Wallace Stevens. The tradition, which earned the *Advocate* national recognition, continued with issues including the 1951 William

Faulkner issue, the 1952 British Novelists issue, and the 1961 Robert Lowell issue.

On May 1, 1956, the *Advocate* completed construction on their headquarters, a Georgian wood-framed building located at 21 South Street The property is owned by the University and leased to the *Advocate* for $1 per year.

In 1981, rumors circulated that the *Advocate* would have to shut its doors due to financial problems. Overwhelmed by publishing debts, the *Advocate* even had its phone service cut off several times. Trustee bailouts, however, helped the organization recover.

In December 1996, the *Advocate* once again faced financial difficulties: it owed thousands of dollars to its printer, its building was crumbling, and the University was considering using the property to build additional undergraduate housing. Once again, however, alumni and trustees rallied behind the *Advocate* to pay off the printing debts and fund building renovations.

The *Advocate*, more so than any other publication on campus, has reimagined itself countless times over the course of its history before evolving into the organization it is today. As one *Advocate* board member wrote in the magazine's centenary edition, "The *Advocate* has been a record of football scores; a caterer to old, impecunious Cambridge ladies; a monitor of intramural scandal; a register of literary tastes which have often lagged twenty years behind the fact; a club; a wet-nurse and house-marm for febrile poets; a victim of Comstockery; a proponent of literary freedom; an organ of responsible criticism; a ghost; a myth; a great organic zilch…."

KEVIN LIN

The Advocate

ORGANIZATION AND THE COMP

The *Advocate* comprises seven boards: Art, Poetry, Fiction, Features, Design, Technology, and Business. All of the comp requirements are board-specific. With the exception of the Business board, all boards have subjective comps, meaning that there is no formula for admission and not everyone who completes the requirements is elected. The comps for the Poetry, Fiction, and Art boards consist primarily of soliciting and evaluating submissions. The Design and Tech comps entail a series of task-specific assignments. The comp for the Features board, which produces the essays in the magazine, involves critiquing features that have already run in the magazine, brainstorming feature ideas, and writing an original feature. Business board compers must generate $1200 in revenue in order to be elected.

In addition to the president, publisher, and board heads, the *Advocate* executive board comprises four Pegasi and two Dionysi. Pegasi, named for the winged beasts found in Greek mythology, are responsible for setting up events. Two *Advocate* Pegasi are charged with organizing literary events such as student readings and guest speakers, and the other two with organizing artistic events like film screenings and small shows. The Dionysi, whose name pays homage to the Greek god of wine, are responsible for taking care of the building and planning parties.

ALUMNI AND CONTRIBUTORS

The *Advocate* boasts a long list of distinguished alumni, many of whom went on to pursue careers as writers. Theodore Roosevelt, Class of 1880, edited the magazine in his senior year. T.S. Eliot, Class of 1910, e.e. cummings, Class of 1915, Richard Wilbur '47, John Ashbery '49, Frank O'Hara '50, Robert Bly '50, Donald Hall '51, Harold Brodkey '52, Jonathan Kozol '58 and James Atlas '71 all published poetry in the *Advocate* as undergraduates. Malcolm Cowley '20, James Agee '32, Robert Fitzgerald '33, Leonard Bernstein '38, James Laughlin '39, and Norman Mailer '43 all worked for the publication.

The magazine also solicits contributions from non-students, and Ezra Pound, William Carlos Williams, and Archibald MacLeish have all published work in the *Advocate*. Other contributors from outside Harvard have included Adrienne Rich (the first woman whose work appeared regularly in the *Advocate*), John Hawkes, Howard Nemerov, Marianne Moore, Robert Lowell, and Tom Wolfe.

LET'S GO TRAVEL GUIDES

In 1960, Oliver Koppell came to Harvard as a young man with a big idea: to create a travel guide for those who thought travel was beyond their reach. The 18-year-old entrepreneur found the perfect partner to put his plan into action: Harvard Student Agencies (HSA). On the floor of his freshman dorm room, Koppell crafted 25 pages of travel tips for touring Europe, including brochures and advertisements. With the 1960 European Guide in hand, three planeloads of customers blasted off for Europe on jets chartered through HSA. The enterprising Koppell assembled a staff of fellow students and convinced HSA to turn the 1960 European Guide into an annual title, called *Let's Go: The Student Guide to Europe.*

Let's Go prided itself on combining budget tips—such as letting travelers know that a ferry ride from Europe to Asia across the Bosphorus in Istanbul cost a mere four cents—with wit and irreverence. Young travelers appreciated this new breed of travel guide, and it showed: *Let's Go: Europe* grew from 64 pages and 6,500 copies of the 1961 edition to 321 pages and 65,000 copies of the 1968 edition.

The Let's Go universe kept expanding when its business manager, Andrew Tobias '68, was interviewed on the *Today Show* in 1966. Sales immediately skyrocketed, and glowing reviews flooded in from *Newsweek, Time,* the *New York Times,* and others. Before long, the students at Let's Go had become the pilots of a professional company, and in 1971 Let's Go partnered with its first professional publisher, EP Dutton.

In 1968, the team introduced *Let's Go II: The Student Guide to Adventure,* and the next year they released *Let's Go: USA.* Shortly thereafter, Let's Go introduced a permanent line of regional guides, starting with *Let's Go: Britain & Ireland* in 1976, followed by *Let's Go: France* in 1978 and *Let's Go: Italy* in

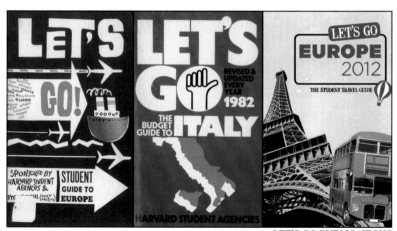

LET'S GO PUBLICATIONS

Let's Go *travel guides in 1961, 1982 and 2012*

1979—series mainstays to this day. In 1982, Let's Go enlisted St. Martin's Press as its new publisher.

In the following decades, Let's Go's title line and popularity grew exponentially. Let's Go published six titles in 1981, growing to 10 by 1985. That year, the first edition of *Let's Go: Mexico* sold more copies than any previous debut guide. By 1986, almost 500,000 Let's Go books were being produced, hitting the shelves just three months after being researched—light-years ahead of the competition. By 1988, readership was up to 1,600,000, and five years later it hit 3,500,000. By 1998, Let's Go had planted flags in over a hundred countries on six continents. Let's Go now publishes with Avalon Travel and Publisher's Group West, which also publishes the *Rick Steves* guides and the *Moon Handbook* series.

Let's Go continues to employ hundreds of Harvard students each year, as both editors in the office and researchers on the road. In addition to over 50 titles, the company now offers exclusive content and interactive features on www.letsgo.com, and remains the only travel guide in the world written and operated entirely by—and, in large measure, for—students.

OTHER PUBLICATIONS

The weekly *Independent*, founded in 1969 as an alternative to the *Crimson*, was once a major news outlet on campus, but is now less widely read. The tabloid-style newspaper contains sections on News, Sports, Arts, and Forum (Op-Ed).

The *Harvard Salient*, founded in 1981 and advised by government professor Harvey Mansfield, is a conservative biweekly magazine known for its right-wing viewpoints. The *Salient* is known for its "Back Page" section, which parodies what *Salient* editors view as the politically correct culture on campus.

Perspective, founded in 1985 as a reaction to conservative campus media and the Reagan era, offers a liberal slant on global, national, and campus issues. The magazine, which publishes seven times a year, was the first publication to have a yearly women's issue, and also called for Drew Faust's appointment as president before the announcement was made. *Perspective* editors pride themselves on being "the only explicitly anti-final club media outlet on campus," and organized the "Swat the Fly" protest against the Fly Club in 1989 for gender discrimination. The magazine, advised by renowned progressive academic and activist Timothy McCarthy, is best known today for its coverage of student activism and Harvard community news.

Other campus publications include the *Harvard Undergraduate Research Journal, Harvard Political Review, Harvard International Review, Harvard Book Review, Harvard Asia Pacific Review, Harvard College Investment Magazine, Harvard College Economics Review, Satire V, Harvard Ichthus* (a journal of Christian thought featuring contributions by both students and notable theologians), *Harvard Voice* (covering issues of student life), and *Tuesday Magazine* (a literary magazine). *Freeze College Magazine*, a lifestyle and fashion magazine at Harvard, is published exclusively online.

TELEVISION

Harvard Undergraduate Television (HUTV), formerly Harvard-Radcliffe Television (HRTV), is the student-run television network at Harvard. Since its creation in 1993, HUTV has produced a variety of programs, ranging from game shows, sitcoms, and sketch comedy shows to news programs and computer animations. HUTV alumni now work for major media outlets such as ABC, NBC, MTV, and Comedy Central. Harvard graduates Jim Cramer, Class of 1976, and Conan O'Brien, Class of 1985, as well as Harvard dropout, Matt Damon, Class of 1992, sit on HUTV's honorary board.

HUTV's most popular current programs include the satire news show On Harvard Time (OHT) and Ivory Tower. OHT, named after the Harvard policy of starting classes seven minutes past the hour, releases new episodes Sunday evenings that spoof both Harvard happenings and real-world news.

"Ivory Tower," a college soap opera, premiered in 1994 and ran for five years with screenings across the campus. By 1999, however, interest had waned, and producers scaled back production, renamed the show "Tales from the Ivory Tower," and eventually ended the program altogether. The show returned to regular production in 2003, and in 2004 "Ivory Tower" began streaming on the internet.

EXTERNAL PUBLICATIONS

The weekly *Harvard University Gazette* is the official newspaper of the University. Published by the Harvard University Office of Public Affairs and Communications, the Gazette contains news stories and features about current students, faculty, and staff, as well as photo essays, job listings, and a calendar of upcoming events.

Harvard Magazine, founded by Harvard alumni in 1898, is designed to keep alumni connected to the University and to one another. The only University-wide publication that is regularly distributed to all graduates, faculty and staff, the bimonthly magazine is independently edited and has a circulation of 240,000.

In 1986, Stratis Haviaras, Curator of the Woodberry Poetry Room in Lamont Library, founded a quarterly publication called *Erato* as a forum for literary discussion and as a means of publicizing events at the Poetry Room. The first issue of *Erato* contained a Seamus Heaney poem, an article on Louis Simpson, and a news bulletin from the Harvard University Press, as well as a three-page insert of book reviews. Those three loose-leaf pages of book reviews expanded to over 30 pages within three years, and the publication was renamed the *Harvard Book Review*. In 1992, Haviaras replaced the *Harvard Book Review* with the *Harvard Review*, a bound journal published semi-annually to nurture the voices of young writers, showcase the best new poetry and short fiction, and promote literary criticism. The *Review*, operated through Houghton Library since 2000, is now a significant American literary journal whose contributors include David Mamet, Arthur Miller, Joyce Carol Oates, John Ashbery, and John Updike.

Many leading publications are also edited through the graduate schools, including the famous *Harvard Law Review* (p. 222), *Harvard Business Review*, and *Harvard Design Magazine*.

THE ARTS

AT HARVARD

THE HARVARD CANVAS

To the untrained eye, a glance at one of the poster kiosks in Harvard Yard is dizzying. Plastered with notices announcing everything from senior art shows to a cappella jams to artist panels, the poster kiosks offer a glimpse of the energy that Harvard students pour into their artistic pursuits.

These pursuits are not limited to the extracurricular: undergraduates concentrate in fields like Visual and Environmental Studies (which includes studio art), Music, and History of Art and Architecture, while students at the Graduate School of Design study architecture and urban planning.

The tempo picks up during Arts First, a campus-wide celebration of the arts at Harvard founded by actor John Lithgow, Class of 1967. During this weekend in May, the campus is enlivened by the sounds of student musical and dance groups like Kuumba and Gumboots, by the brush strokes of student artists, and by the excitement of hundreds of other artistic events.

Harvard artists have always found ways to turn their own campus into a canvas for their work. In the "Report from the Task Force on the Arts," University President Drew Gilpin Faust identifies some of these canvases: "A disused swimming pool, a dungeon-like basement chamber, an oak-lined common room, a grassy courtyard with an overhanging balcony—Harvard artists routinely make ingenious use of every space they can find." She continues, "Moreover, the arts have the power to bring us together as a community in the present, but also to provide powerful connections to those who have come before us and to those who will follow us."

BY THE NUMBERS

1	Number of buildings in North America designed by renowned Swiss modern architect Le Corbusier: the Carpenter Center, on Quincy Street
3	Days of student-led performances and exhibitions held in early May during Arts First weekend
556	Seats from which to watch Harvard's dramatic talents at the Mainstage Theater at the Loeb Drama Center
4,898	Miles between Harvard Yard and Sardis, Turkey, where the Harvard Art Museum has conducted an ongoing excavation since 1917
265,000	Pieces in the holdings of the Harvard Art Museums

ARCHITECTURAL SPOTLIGHT:
SEVER HALL

Sever Hall was designed in 1880 by American architect Henry Hobson Richardson, who also designed Trinity Church in Boston. Ann Sever bequeathed $115,000 for the building in honor of her husband, James

KEVIN LIN
Sever Hall, designed by H.H. Richardson

Warren Sever, Class of 1817. Though a notorious figure during his time at Harvard, Sever served as the class secretary of 1817.

Joseph Hudnut, Professor Emeritus of Architecture, called Sever Hall "the most American of our buildings—and our most important one...a turning point in the course of American architecture." German art historian Ettlinger Leopole elaborates: "With this building, the period of Richardson's mature work begins. Here is no Romanesque revivalism but a highly essential individualized design incorporating many of the essential qualities of 18th-century buildings in Harvard Yard with real freshness in detail and composition."

Sever contains classrooms and lecture halls for College courses by day and Extension School courses at night. The top floor is home to the Visual and Environmental Studies department (p. 185). On the interior color scheme, University President Derek Bok (1971-1991) reportedly remarked, "At least they didn't do it in polka dots."

After a 14-month, $6.3 million renovation directed by architect Marjorie Hoog, Sever reopened in 1983. A large portion of the renovation was funded by the Harvard Extension School, and the remainder was paid for by the Faculty of Arts and Sciences.

THE BEGINNING

The arts have long been an integral part of Harvard life, and longstanding artistic traditions stand testament to this commitment. The Hasty Pudding Theatricals is the nation's oldest sustained theatrical company, dating back to 1844, the year of their first musical production. The *Harvard Advocate*, a student literature and arts magazine and the nation's oldest continuously published college magazine, was founded in 1866. Harvard's first art museum, the William Hayes Fogg Art Museum, opened in 1895, displaying world-class art across the street from Harvard Yard. Professor Charles Eliot Norton began to incorporate architectural history into his courses in 1874.

It was not, however, until the appointment of University President Nathan Marsh Pusey in 1953 that the University made real strides to invigorate programming for the arts. Pusey's fundraising genius enabled the construction of two new facilities devoted to the arts: the Loeb Drama Center, in 1960, and the Carpenter Center for the Visual Arts, in 1963.

THE TASK FORCE
ON THE ARTS

In recent years, Harvard has continued to strengthen its programming for the arts, most notably with the "Report of the Task Force on the Arts," issued by President Faust in 2008. The report emphasizes arts programming at Harvard equal to that of humanities and sciences. Faust explained: "The report calls for Harvard to end the 'curricular banishment' of the arts and recognize that they belong at the core of the University's educational mission."

The 19 members of the task force, who began the project in November of 2007, included faculty, students, and professional artists. Their primary proposals include a new Dramatic Arts undergraduate concentration, fully funded graduate programs, and construction and renovation projects for arts facilities in Cambridge and Allston. Though the report was met with enthusiasm, the 2008 economic crisis has halted many of the more ambitious expansion projects. In a statement to the *Harvard Crimson*, President Faust remained confident in the Task Force's proposals, noting that funding for the arts still exists, including a recent $100 million gift from benefactor David Rockefeller, Class of 1936, of which $5 million is reserved for arts initiatives.

ACADEMICS AND THE ARTS UNDERGRADUATE PROGRAMS

VISUAL AND ENVIRONMENTAL STUDIES

Visual and Environmental Studies (VES) concentrators, conspicuous in paint-speckled jeans and Converse sneakers, congregate in Sever Hall and the Carpenter Center, the two departmental hubs and bastions of studio art on campus. Studio courses focus on painting, drawing, sculpture, printmaking, design, film, video, animation, and photography. Sawdust flies from the second floor of the Carpenter Center, which houses a wood workshop that is used both for three-dimensional creations and for painting students who need wood stretchers for their canvases. All art materials are included in VES courses, at no additional cost to students. VES also offers lecture courses and seminars in film history and theory, design and urbanism, and contemporary arts.

HISTORY OF ART AND ARCHITECTURE

Students who get a thrill out of dark classrooms and the click of a slide projector are drawn to the History of Art and Architecture (HAA) Department. Formerly known as the Department of Fine Arts, HAA concentrators focus in one of thirteen fields: African, Medieval, Byzantine, Chinese, Renaissance, Japanese, Baroque and Rococo, Indian, Modern and Contemporary, Islamic, Architectural History and Theory, Ancient, and Latin American/Pre-Columbian. With classes held in the Arthur M. Sackler building, part of the Harvard Art Museums, students have the luxury of frequenting the galleries. Housed within HAA, and in conjunction with the Massachusetts Institute of Technology, the Aga Khan Program for Islamic Architecture (AKPIA) is a center for the study of Islamic art and architecture, urbanism, landscape design, and conservation, with the aim of application to contemporary design projects. Established in 1979, AKPIA is supported by an endowment from His Highness the Aga Khan, Prince Karim al Hussayni, Class of 1959.

FINE ARTS LIBRARY

Art and art history students buzz in and out of the bright, airy reading room of the Fine Arts Library, currently housed in the Littauer Building near the Law School while the Harvard Art Museums undergo renovations. The walls of the room are lined with recent issues of glossy art journals, and the stacks below hold the volumes, folios, slides, and photographs of Harvard's third largest library (after Widener and the Law School library).

ARCHITECTURAL SPOTLIGHT: GUND HALL, GRADUATE SCHOOL OF DESIGN

The Graduate School of Design (GSD), the hub of spatial thought at Harvard, is based in Gund Hall. Designed by architect John H. Andrews '58 and

built in 1972, Gund Hall has seven levels, two of which are below ground. The central studio space is arranged on five terraced levels under a stepped, clear-span roof that offers plenty of natural light and spectacular views

SCOTT YIM

The distinct terraced design the GSD's Gund Hall

of Boston. It features an auditorium, lecture and seminar rooms, computer facilities, workshops, a darkroom, and a cafeteria dubbed "Chauhaus."

Gund Hall won both the American Institute of Architects Honor Award and the Bartlett Award in 1973. The Frances Loeb Library, which occupies two levels at the center of the building, was the gift of John L. Loeb, Class of 1924, in honor of his wife. The library's current holdings include over 250,000 volumes, 130,000 audiovisual materials, over 1,650 periodicals, and more than 50 special collections.

The GSD offers: professional degrees in Architecture, Landscape Architecture, and Urban Planning; post-professional degrees in Architecture, Architecture in Urban Design, Landscape Architecture, Landscape Architecture in Urban Design, and Design Studies; and PhDs in Architecture, Landscape Architecture, and Urban Planning. Graduates of the school (including I.M. Pei, Phillip Johnson, and Frank Gehry) pepper the list of Pritzker Prize laureates. Notable faculty who have taught at the GSD include Walter Gropius (founder of the Bauhaus movement and architect of the Law School's Harkness Commons), Marcel Breuer, Josep Lluís Sert (Dean of the GSD, '53-'69), Sigfried Giedion, Zaha Hadid, and Rem Koolhaas.

The printed collection of the library includes the Rübel Asiatic Research Collection of more than 12,000 volumes in Chinese, Japanese, and Korean. In addition, there are 2,602 individual East Asian rubbings, most of them from China.

Meanwhile, the Photography Collection, which includes approximately 30,000 images, emphasizes the social history of America as recorded by documentary and studio photographers. The secondary emphasis is on art photography, with over 1,000 photographs, sampling from the major figures in this field.

The Harvard Film Archive, located in the Carpenter Center, is also part of the Fine Arts Library. The collection contains over 1,000 classic and experimental films from around the world, selections of which are made available to the public through the Archive's award-winning film series.

ALUMNUS ILLUMINATED: I.M. PEI

Ieoh Ming Pei, M.Arch '46, founded Pei Cobb Freed & Partners, a New York-based architecture firm that has completed more than 200 major projects across the globe. Pei is best known for his addition to the National Gallery in Washington, DC, the pyramid at the Louvre in Paris, the 71-story tower for the Bank of China in Hong Kong, and the John Hancock tower in Boston. His clients have ranged from the Kennedy family to the government of France.

Pei was born in Canton, China in 1917 into a prominent family from Suzhou. He left China in 1935 at 17 to study architecture at the University of Pennsylvania, where he became so discouraged about the emphasis on drawing that he transferred to the Massachusetts Institute of Technology to study engineering. At MIT, however, his dean urged him to switch back to architecture, and Pei did. In 1942 he enrolled at Harvard's Graduate School of Design (GSD) and received a Masters in Architecture in 1946.

Pei's many tributes and awards include the prestigious Pritzker Prize, which he won in 1983, and whose inscription reads: "Ieoh Ming Pei has given this century some of its most beautiful interior spaces and exterior forms."

THE MUSIC DEPARTMENT

Leonard Bernstein, Class of 1939 (p. 190), world-renowned conductor, composer, author, music lecturer, and pianist, once said, "music can name the unnameable and communicate the unknowable," an ethos that continues to resonate within the Harvard Music Department. Located in the Fanny Peabody Mason Music Building, the department houses classrooms, practice rooms, the Eda Kuhn Loeb Music Library, the John Knowles Paine Concert Hall and the Harvard University Studio for Electroacoustic Composition (HUSEAC) and opened in 1914. In the 1970s, the Department broadened its approach to music education, introducing courses on oral tradition and folk music. In addition, departments across the University began to collaborate, yielding courses in music and drama, as well as music and VES. The Department sponsors numerous concerts, colloquia and lectures each month, free to students and the public. A professorship in music was first proposed in 1832, but it wasn't until 1855 that Harvard's catalogue listed its first music course, "Vocal Music." The College now offers an undergraduate concentration in music, PhD programs in musicology, ethnomusicology, theory, and composition, and an A.M. program in historical performance practice. Since 2006, Harvard College and the New England Conservatory have offered a five-year joint degree program (Bachelor's of Arts and Masters in Music).

EXTRACURRICULAR ART

The Student Activities Office supervises and coordinates more than 300 officially recognized student organizations, many of which are entirely student-operated and financed. The others often receive funding from the Office for the Arts at Harvard (OFA).

MUSICAL ARTS

Harvard's first instrumental music organization was the Pierian Sodality, founded in 1808 and now known as the Harvard-Radcliffe Orchestra. It proudly holds the distinction as the oldest musical organization in continuous existence in the United States. The Harvard-Radcliffe Orchestra, as well as the smaller Bach and Mozart Society orchestras, cater to classical tastes. The Harvard Band, which comprises two active Jazz Bands and a Wind Ensemble, plays more contemporary hits and supports the University's athletic teams. The all-male Harvard Glee Club, the all-female Radcliffe Choral Society, and the co-ed Collegium Musicum are three of the largest choral groups.

The Harvard Krokodiloes were founded at the Hasty Pudding Club in 1946 and are Harvard's oldest a cappella singing group. The group's twelve tuxedo-clad men perform music from the 1920s, 30s, 40s, 50s, and 60s, with jokes and antics thrown into every show. Performing over 200 concerts every year, the group is well known at Harvard and beyond; each summer the Krokodiloes take an 11-week, six-continent world tour to share their music. They have performed for Ella Fitzgerald, Yo-Yo Ma, Class of 1976, Princesses Grace and Carolina of Monaco, King Bhumibol of Thailand, Elizabeth Taylor, Julia Roberts, and Leonard Bernstein, who has also composed music for the group.

The Harvard Din and Tonics are another well known male a cappella group, famous for performing in bow ties, tails, and lime green socks. Originally dubbed The Dunster Dunces in 1946, the group stayed together until the 1960s, when it disbanded. In 1979, a new group was formed as a public service activity at the Phillips Brooks House in Harvard Yard. The group became the Din and Tonics as we know them today, and they began to perform at Harvard and for local charitable organizations.

The Opportunes, the Veritones, the Pitches, the Call Backs, the Low Keys, and the Fallen Angles are other popular Harvard a capella groups. Ask at the Harvard Box Office (☎617 496 2222; boxoffice.harvard.edu), located in the Holyoke Center, about upcoming shows.

Other music groups include Kuumba, a gospel choir founded in 1970 and dedicated to the musical expressions of the African diaspora, and the percussion group THUD (The Harvard University Drummers).

SAM GALLER

The Din and Tonics performing in Sanders Theatre

ALUMNUS ILLUMINATED:
LEONARD BERNSTEIN, CLASS OF 1939

"One didn't know from which springboard he would dive, but one knew there would be a hell of a splash," wrote Marc Blitzstein about Leonard Bernstein in the *New York Post.*

Bernstein earned good grades in his courses at Harvard, but, like many a brilliant student, never appeared to be working very hard. He was a part of the Glee Club, played squash, rowed a one-man skiff, and edited the music section of the *Harvard Advocate.* In January 1937, at a Harvard tea party, Bernstein met Dimitri Mitropoulos, the conductor whose flamboyant podium style strongly influenced his own.

Throughout his life, Bernstein entertained a close relationship with the Harvard Krokodiloes. "The Harvard Krokodiloes have the gift of warming one's soul and enriching one's day," wrote Bernstein. Kroks alumnus George E. Overholser '82 described a visit to "Emperor Bernstein": "He sat there in his satin robe, flanked by two 'pretty boys,' whom he ignored entirely, except for when he reached his hand out to the left (without looking at it) so a cigarette would be lit and, three minutes later, reached his other hand to the right (again still looking straight at me) to receive a small flask."

After working as a conducting assistant for the Boston Symphony Orchestra, Bernstein became a star overnight when he stepped in as a last-minute substitute in the New York Philharmonic in 1943, to much critical acclaim. In 1953 Bernstein became the first American to conduct an opera at Milan's Teatro alla Scala, and was appointed Music Director of the New York Philharmonic in 1958. He also earned great success on Broadway, particularly with *West Side Story.* Bernstein died in 1990.

© *The Leonard Bernstein Office, Inc. Used with permission*

DRAMATIC ARTS

Harvard does not currently offer degree programs in musical or dramatic performance, but there is no shortage of opportunities for extracurricular involvement on campus.

Founded in 1908, the Harvard-Radcliffe Dramatic Club (HRDC) is an umbrella organization for Harvard's theater scene, and its membership is composed of students who participated in theater on campus during the previous year. The HRDC board heads student productions in the Loeb Drama Center; these productions include two residencies per semester on the Loeb Mainstage, including the annual Visiting Director's Project in the fall, as well as five to seven shows per semester in the Loeb Experimental Theater.

The HRDC shares the Loeb Drama Center with the American Repertory Theater (ART), founded in 1980. ART has garnered, among other awards, the Tony Award and the Pulitzer Prize, and was named one of the top three theaters in the country by *Time* magazine in 2003. The ART's repertoire includes new American plays, reinterpretations of classical texts, and new musical theater productions. The ART staff teaches non-credit undergraduate classes at Harvard in acting, directing, dramatic literature, dramaturgy, design, and playwriting. In 1987, ART founded the Institute for Advanced Theater Training at Harvard, which operates in conjunction with the Moscow Art Theater School.

PETER SHIELDS

The Hasty Pudding Theatricals performing their 2009 show,
Acropolis Now

Distinct from other theatrical groups on campus, the Hasty Pudding Theatricals (HPT) puts on a pun-filled musical every year. The group, founded in 1844, evolved out of the Hasty Pudding Club (p. 15), a social group that dates back to 1795. A tradition of mock trials had developed in the HPC, and when HPC member Lemuel Hayward secretly arranged the production of an opera, entitled *Bomabastes Furioso*, HPT was born. The first productions were adapted and satirized shows from the professional theater of the era; by the 1860s, HPT was producing student-written shows. Harvard granted theater space to HPT in 1876, opening the performances to a general audience. Today, the HPT's shows remain "no-holds-barred burlesques," with men cast in both the male and female roles. Women do, however, participate in all other elements of the shows, including the technical staff, the band, and the authorship and production of the show. HPT began annual Woman of the Year (1951) and Man of the Year (1967) celebrations, during which awards are presented to performers who have made a "lasting and impressive contribution to the world of entertainment." Past Woman of the Year honorees include Meryl Streep, Katharine Hepburn, Julia Roberts, Jodie Foster, Elizabeth Taylor, Charlize Theron, and Anne Hathaway, and past Man of the Year winners include Clint Eastwood, Tom Cruise, Robert De Niro, Steven Spielberg, Harrison Ford, Anthony Hopkins, Bruce Willis, Christopher Walken, and Justin Timberlake. Every year, the show runs for one month in Cambridge in Farkas Hall (formerly the New College Theater) and then goes on tour to New York and Bermuda. The group donates portions of their profits to the arts programs of Cambridge Public Schools.

Other campus theatrical groups include Black C.A.S.T., an African-American theatrical organization, and the Gilbert and Sullivan Players, who have performed comedic operas since 1956. Additional productions, including the Lowell House Opera, the Dunster House Opera, and the Cabot House Musical, are organized by individual undergraduate Houses.

VISUAL ARTS

The Harvard Art Museum Undergraduate Connection (HAMUC) is sponsored by the Harvard Art Museum and encourages undergraduates to explore the University's remarkable museum collections, most notably through its "Nights at the Museum" series, which features student-led tours and entertainment by other student groups.

Figure drawing, ceramics, and public art non-credit courses are offered through the OFA. Various other arts spaces are scattered throughout the Houses, including Bow & Arrow Press in Adams House, pottery studios in Quincy, Mather, and Dunster Houses, and *The Warble*, a literary magazine operated out of Currier House.

FASHION DESIGN

Various campus groups are devoted to showcasing student models and fashion designers. The Harvard Vestis Council is best known for producing

ARCHITECTURAL SPOTLIGHT:
THE LOEB DRAMA CENTER

The Loeb Drama Center, at the corner of Brattle and Hilliard streets, was designed in 1960 by Hugh Stubbins and Associates and funded primarily through a $2 million donation by John Langecloth Loeb, Class of 1924. In 1979, the American Repertory Theater (ART) moved to Cambridge from its home in New Haven, CT (wouldn't you?) and took up residence at the Loeb, with Robert Brustein continuing as artistic director.

ANNA SANTOLERI

The Loeb Drama Center has a costume and properties workshop, a set workshop, practice rooms, dressing rooms, executive offices, and two performance spaces. The Mainstage, which seats 556, was the world's first "convertible" theater and can be transformed into three types of stage: the standard proscenium arch with stadium seating, the Elizabethan thrust stage, and the theater-in-the-round. The stage can be changed in minutes, thanks to an ingenious device designed by George C. Izenour of the Electro-Mechanical Research Laboratory at the Yale School of Drama. Another exceptional feature of the theater is its synchronous winch system—a series of thirty winches, operated and synchronized through a computer console, controls the movement of the curtain and stage props. Even with all of this state-of-the-art technology, the Loeb Drama Center had a rather precarious start: during its first production, the curtain caught on fire.

The Experimental Theater, known to students as the "Loeb Ex," is a black box facility that seats over 100 and offers tremendous flexibility in terms of seating and stage placement. The Loeb Ex, the mainstage, and the costume area are separated by soundproofing that allows for simultaneous activity in all three areas without noisy interference.

ARCHITECTURAL SPOTLIGHT:
CARPENTER CENTER FOR THE VISUAL ARTS

It was on a piece of stationary from San Francisco's Mark Hopkins Hotel that the Carpenters finalized their pledge of $1.5 million to Harvard for a new Visual Arts Center.

The Carpenter Center for the Visual Arts is Swiss architect Le Corbusier's only building in North America. A stunning departure from Harvard Yard's red-brick colonial architecture that characterizes Harvard Yard, the Carpenter Center is a concrete bulwark of a building that challenges the architectural character of the University. Connoisseurs of Le Corbusier will recognize the Center's characteristic columns, sunbreakers, curving ramp, dramatic glass walls, and disregard for the surrounding architecture or urban fabric.

From Quincy Street, the exterior of the building comprises four elements: a tall tower, a central square dissected by sunbreakers, a curving mass moving out toward the Yard, and a dramatic, winding ramp, entering the building at the third story. The ramp and the cantilevered curving mass are supported by freestanding concrete columns, beneath which stretches a cavernous outdoor lobby. Legend has it that Le Corbusier sent the plans for the Carpenter Center to the contractor and had not seen the building until he arrived for its dedication in 1963. When he finally arrived, he took one look at the building and exclaimed to the builder, "You've built it upside down!"

Unlike its exterior, the walls inside are not cold, grey concrete, but rather floor-to-ceiling panels of glass, allowing ample direct sunlight and views between different areas of the building. At night, recessed lighting casts the stairwell, which stretches from the basement to the fifth story, as a column of light.

Le Corbusier's idea of a building dedicated to the conception and creation of art called for a space that would trigger both mental and physical creativity in the students who would work there. As an article from *Architectural Forum* put it: "To him, the notion of a conformist building for the visual arts must have seemed a contradiction in terms."

Exhibitions are showcased in the Lobby Gallery at the entrance level, as well as, at times, in the landscape surrounding the building.

"Haute," a fashion show featuring the designs of undergraduate students. Eleganza, an annual charity fashion show started in the spring of 1994, is one of the best-attended events on campus. The consistently sold-out show donates proceeds to Teen Empowerment, a Boston-area organization that works for youth-led community organizing. As much a dance performance as a showcase of fashion, Eleganza uses clothing, often from local stores, in an innovative show featuring the work of both student choreographers and models.

DANCE

The OFA promotes dance on campus through a number of non-credit courses in modern jazz and ballet. Harvard also hosts a multitude of organized dance groups, including Ballet Folklórico de Aztlán, Harvard Ballet Company, Mainly Jazz Dance Company, Dance Theater Project, Expressions Dance Company, and the Modern Dance Company.

Founded at Harvard in 1983, CityStep is a mentoring program for under-privileged Cambridge public school students, the program aims to increase self-esteem, creativity, and confidence through dance. The inaugural end-of-the-year event brought over 100 local kids together with Harvard students in the performance of an original dance theater production in Sanders Theater. The mayor of Cambridge was in attendance on opening night, and an official

SCOTT YIM

The Carpenter Center, Le Corbusier's only building in North America

195

ANDREAS RANDOW

Harvard-Radcliffe Modern Dance Company

"City Step Day" was declared in Cambridge. In 2004, the program was extended to the University of Pennsylvania and the city of Philadelphia, and it thrives in both locations.

Another dance group, the Harvard College Gumboots Dance Troupe, pays tribute to the struggle against the apartheid in South Africa and commemorates South African history by employing a dance tradition that evolved in South African goldmines. Other dance groups include the Asian-American Dance Troupe, Harvard Ghungroo (South Asian dance) and the Harvard Breakers Organization.

SIGNET SOCIETY

The Dining Room inside the Signet Society

ARCHITECTURAL SPOTLIGHT: CALDER AND MOORE STATUES

Two of the most recognizable pieces of art in Harvard Yard are Alexander Calder's "Onion" and Henry Moore's "Four Piece Reclining Figure."

Proudly standing outside the sunken entrance to Pusey Library, Calder's light steel sculpture was completed in 1965. Following the Second World War, Calder went from sculpting moveable mobiles, of which he was the inventor, to larger "stabiles"—static, self-supporting sculptures. "Onion," on loan from a Radcliffe trustee, is emblematic of this shift.

Henry Moore's "Four Piece Reclining Figure" is the bronze abstraction that faces Lamont Library and is one of the best kept secrets of Harvard Yard. The piece was donated by Sandra and David Bakalar, who earned both his B.S. from Harvard College in 1947 and an M.S. in Physics from Harvard Graduate School in 1948. According to legend, if you count the rungs of the iron gate along Quincy Street from the portal nearest the sculpture to the 37th rung, then view the Moore's sculpture from between the 37th and 38th rungs, the likeness of the figure becomes clear. Not long after the dedication of the sculpture, in the winter of 1981, a heavy snowfall allowed sculptors of another kind to pay homage to Moore's work. After covering the sculpture's four pieces with snow, students carved out the four faces of Mount Rushmore.

LITERARY ARTS

In addition to taking creative writing courses offered through the English Department, young fiction writers can submit their work for publication in the *The Harvard Advocate* (p. 174), Harvard's storied literary magazine, *Tuesday Magazine*, Advo's much younger sibling, and the satirical *Harvard Lampoon* (p. 167). For the more critically inclined, *The Harvard Crimson* (p. 160), *The Harvard Independent*, and *The Harvard Book Review* all feature student reviews of recently published books.

THE SIGNET

Founded in 1870, the Signet Society is an organization of undergraduates dedicated to fostering artistic production. Members are selected based on criteria of literary and artistic talent, character, and intellectual achievement.

Through lunches, dinners, and teas, the Society aims to foster intergenerational conversation among students and faculty. It hosts special events like readings, shows, and screenings, and houses a new artist in residence each year. The Signet Society helps its members live up to its motto "Mousiken Poiei Kai Ergazou," which in Greek means "create art and practice it."

HARVARD ART MUSEUMS

Housing masterpieces from across the globe, the Harvard Art Museums serve as a portal of aesthetic appreciation for both the Harvard community and visitors. Harvard boasts three distinct collections at the Fogg, Busch-Reisinger, and Arthur M. Sackler museums. Together, the Harvard Art Museums' holdings total 265,000 works of art. In addition to the permanent collection, the museums regularly show travelling exhibitions and major exhibitions organized by distinguished scholars. The museums also oversee an archeological excavation in Sardis, Turkey, which has been in progress since 1917.

The Harvard Art Museums are currently undergoing a five-year renovation designed by world-renowned Italian architect Renzo Piano. Since the renovation began in 2008, highlights from the museums' collections have remained on display in the Sackler building. Soon all three collections will be displayed under one roof.

ALEXANDRE TERRIEN

The Fogg Museum

THE FOGG

The William Hayes Fogg Art Museum opened in 1895 with funding from a bequest by Mrs. William Hayes Fogg. Originally designed by architects Coolidge, Shepley, Bulfinch, and Abbott, the Fogg will serve as the main entrance to the Harvard Art Museums after the renovation is complete. The main entrance of the Fogg leads to a two-story central court, copied from a façade designed by Antonio da Sangallo for the canons of the Church of Madonna di San Biagio in Montepulciano, Italy. The Fogg holds primarily Western art from the Medieval period to the present. Highlights include a collection of pre-Raphaelite works, a Jean-Auguste-Dominique Ingres collection, Claude Monet's masterpiece *Gare St-Lazare*, and several other Impressionist works, including canvases by Edgar Degas and Pierre-Auguste Renoir. Special collections include the Archibald A. Hutchinson Collection of English Silver, the magnificent Grenville Winthrop Bequest of European painting, and the Wertheim collection of 19th- and 20th-Century Painting and Drawing.

THE BUSCH-REISINGER

The Busch-Reisinger Museum became affiliated with the Fogg after Charles Kuhn was named curator in 1930. Kuhn actively collected original works of art and, by the time he retired in 1968, had assembled one of the finest collections of German Expressionist art in the world. The museum acquired modern art purged from major German museums by the Nazis. The Busch-Reisinger was later enriched by gifts from artists and designers associated with the famous Bauhaus School, including the archives of the artist Lyonel Feininger and Professor Walter Gropius, the celebrated architect at the Graduate School of Design. The museum collection also contains important collections of late medieval, Renaissance, and Baroque sculpture, 16th-century painting, 18th-century porcelain, and post-1945 art, including one of the largest collections of works by Joseph Beuys.

The Busch-Reisinger collection is devoted to the work in all media of Central and Northern European artists, particularly the early 20th-century masters. Its collections of German Expressionism, Vienna Secession art, and 1920s Constructivism rank among the finest in America.

THE SACKLER MUSEUM

A push for additional display space in 1977, coupled with a generous donation from research physician Dr. Arthur M. Sackler, resulted in the 1985 construction of the Arthur M. Sackler Buidling across the street from the Fogg. The Sackler building, designed by renowned British architect James Stirling, originally held collections of Ancient, Asian, Islamic, and Indian Art. Today, the facility also houses the Rübel Library (a research center for Asian Art), the offices of the Department of History of Art and Architecture, and the highlights of the Harvard Art Museums' collection for the duration of the renovation.

OTHER CENTERS

The Harvard Art Museums also include the Straus Center for Conservation and Technical Studies, the Center for the Technical Study of Modern Art (part of the Straus Center), and the Mongan Center for the Study of Prints, Drawings, and Photographs. The Straus Center preserves the works of art from the Museum collections and also restores objects from outside the University. It is home to the Alan Burroughs Archive: between 1925 and 1944 Burroughs produced X-ray images of approximately 3,200 paintings from the great collections of America and Europe. As a source of technical information for studying the working methods of artists, the Burroughs archive is among the largest and most important of its kind in the world. The Straus Center also houses the Edward Waldo Forbes Collection of Materials of the Artist, which contains hundreds of pigment samples and other painting materials from across the globe. It also includes palettes, brushes, and paints used by artists like John Singer Sargent, John Singleton Copley, and José Clemente Orozco. The Gettens Collection of Aged Pigments and Media, established in the 1930s, contains several hundred carefully documented samples of aged pigments in a variety of media, including oil, egg, resins, and varnishes.

BUSINESS
AT HARVARD

THE ENDOWMENT

THE HARVARD MANAGEMENT COMPANY

Harvard University, a privately endowed institution, has serious money. Estimated at $32 billion in June 2011, Harvard's endowment is the largest in higher education, on par with the Gross Domestic Products of Lesotho, Haiti, and Laos—combined. How did it get so large? Good question.

Although John Harvard was the University's first major benefactor, his donation was immediately spent to build Harvard Hall, leaving Harvard's endowment barren. The bankroll started to take form 11 years later, when four recent graduates donated a cow yard at the site where Widener Library currently stands. Upon acquiring the land, Harvard spruced it up with apple trees (not spruces) and renamed the space "Fellows' Orchard." Shortly thereafter, Harvard took a cue from its English brethren and began to keep and manage an endowment in the form of actual money, rather than just grass and trees. In 1654, a number of Harvard graduates living in Concord, Massachusetts signed a document promising a donation to the College of £7 each year for seven years.

Gradually, the endowment grew. By the time Thomas Jefferson drafted the Declaration of Independence, Harvard's endowment had reached £17,000; by the time President Lincoln accepted Confederate General Lee's surrender in Appomattox Court House, Harvard's endowment had topped $4 million. This tremendous growth was largely the result of private donations. Between 1865 and 1868, Harvard raised $370,000 to build Memorial Hall and Sanders Theater; this amount represented one-twelfth of the total endowment.

BY THE NUMBERS	
1	Undergraduate course offered by the Harvard Business School
14	Students founded Harvard Student Agencies in 1957, the largest student-run business in the U.S.
36	Billion dollars, the largest the Harvard Endowment has ever been, in 2008
300+	Members of HUWIB: Harvard University Women in Business, the largest student organization on campus

In the 20th century, Harvard's endowment continued to grow slowly but steadily. Harvard's strategy was simple—invest in areas like fixed income securities including municipal, railroad, and industrial bonds. As the rest of the United States was going bankrupt during the Great Depression, Harvard's endowment strategy ensured continued moderate growth. It was also monumentally boring. From 1948 to 1974, Harvard's money was managed by State Street Research and Management Company, which subscribed to an investment strategy that shunned aggression and risk. State Street managed to grow Harvard's fortunes to $1.4 billion, making it the largest endowment in higher education.

When George Putnam, Class of 1949, became Harvard's treasurer in 1973, he launched a thorough investigation of how Harvard could improve its financial prospects. Ultimately, he embraced an ethos that had guided Harvard students for centuries: if you want something done right, do it yourself. Thus was born the Harvard Management Company (HMC), an in-house team of investors that assumed control of the majority of Harvard's finances. Changes in investment philosophy were made immediately following the creation of HMC in 1974. Initially, members of HMC were each given a piece of the endowment and were driven by competition among themselves to see who could generate the best returns. Compensation was directly linked to each investor's yields. However, both Putnam and HMC's first president, Walter Cabot, Class of 1955, soon realized that this created incentives for investors to focus on short-term returns, which would harm Harvard's finances in the long-term. Thus, HMC's strategies were revised to focus on teamwork among the investors, in hopes that they would complement each other's investing strategies. Under Cabot's 26-year reign, HMC grew Harvard's endowment to $4.7 billion.

The endowment flourished under Cabot, but it was under HMC President Jack Meyer, who arrived in 1990, that Harvard's finances really flew off the charts. In just twelve years, Meyer increased Harvard's endowment by nearly 500% to $22.6 billion. The trick, Meyer claims, was diversification. Before, traditional stocks and bonds had sustained Harvard's financial growth. Under Meyer, though, Harvard was soon investing in exotic hedge funds and an even more exotic $600 million forest in New Zealand. Through the work of Meyer and his successors, Harvard's endowment grew to a high of $37.2 billion in the 2008 fiscal year.

That same year, when Harvard's endowment value was at its all-time high, the University named Jane Mendillo, formerly the chief investment officer of Wellesley College, as the first female head of HMC.

COLLEGE EXPENSES

If undergraduate tuition had to cover all of Harvard College's expenses, it would need to be four times as large—about $200,000 per year. Luckily, the endowment is large enough to cover 52% of Harvard College's budget, with an additional 28% coming from outside sources, including private and corporate donations and federal funding. When Harvard parents complain about having to pay an arm and a leg for college tuition, they should keep in mind that the true cost of a Harvard education is four arms and four legs.

As the endowment has grown, so has the College's annual budget. For example, Harvard's average salary for professors is one of the highest in the nation at $192,600 in 2008-09 compared to the national average of $108,749. For Harvard's approximately 18,000 total students, there are 18,000 employees who teach, clean, cook, counsel, and carry out the various services upon which students depend.

ENDOWMENT DROP

Harvard's heavy dependence on its large endowment meant exacerbated problems when the global financial crisis began to affect the University in fall 2008. Following a nation-wide trend in poor endowment performance and budget cutting, though, Harvard estimated that it would lose $11 billion by September 2009. Some proposed cost-cutting measures, ranging from increasing the average class size to limiting shuttle service to the Quad, have become the subject of significant controversy as Harvard grapples with upholding its educational mission while dealing with financial obstacles. Despite all the controversy and uncertainty surrounding budget cuts, Harvard upheld its commitment to its expanded financial aid program. Indeed,

BRAHMIN BULLS

"I dwell 'neath the shades of Harvard
In the State of the Sacred Cod,
Where the Lowells speak only to Cabots
And the Cabots speak only to God"

True Boston Brahmins, the Cabots arrived on the Mayflower and, once here, made a killing in commerce (read: slaves, rum, and opium). Harvard graduates from this well-to-do family include early shipping magnate George Cabot, Massachusetts Senator Henry Cabot Lodge, HMC founder Walter Cabot, and founding member of Harvard's Porcellian Club Francis Cabot Lowell, who went on introduce the power loom to America and modern corporate finance to the world. More important than the Cabots' ability to make money has been their fondness for giving it away—consider Cabot Hall, Cabot Science Library (p. 79), and Cabot House (p. 128) as testaments to the family's philanthropy.

because many families' incomes suffered as a consequence of the financial crisis, Harvard's spending on undergraduate financial aid increased substantially, from approximately $120 million in 2008-09 to $166 million in 2010-11. Overall, a true crisis was averted for Harvard in the aftermath of the global finanical meltdown. In the 2011 fiscal year, Harvard's endowment grew at a rate of 21.4% to $32 billion, exceeding HMC's growth goals by 1.2% and raising the endowment close to its pre-recession level.

CONTROVERSY

The ongoing controversies surrounding the Harvard Management Company started in the 90s and heated up in 2004 when the salaries of HMC's top money managers came under harsh public scrutiny and criticism. Under Jack Meyer, HMC's compensation system for its in-house money managers was largely based on performance. In addition to a salary of approximately $400,000, money managers also received bonuses based on how well they outperformed the general market, using the common benchmark of the Standard & Poors 500 index, a standard used by many in the private sector. If the S&P 500 went up 5%, for example, Harvard's money managers would have to generate returns of above 5% to receive a bonus, with larger bonuses going to those who beat the index by larger margins. From 1995 to 2005, HMC's average annual rate of return was 16%, outperforming its peers by 50% and at times outperforming the overall market by 300%. And so, as Harvard's money managers beat the market by such significant margins, their own wallets fattened along with the University's coffers.

Controversy began to erupt when alumni, students, and other third party groups compared the earnings of Harvard's money managers to the compensation of Harvard's other employees. While Maurice Samuels, Harvard's top money manager, earned an astonishing $35.1 million in fiscal year 2003, Larry Summers, Harvard's President at the time, was earning just over $500,000, and the average salary for full professors was $157,000. In November of 2003, seven members of the Class of 1969 began writing letters to Summers concerning the compensation of HMC's money managers, attracting national press attention and making the topic a hot-button issue on campus. As a result of the negative publicity and a decrease in alumni donations during the 2004 reunion, the maximum money manager salary was drastically reduced. When Mohamed El-Erian became CEO of HMC in 2006, his money managers were paid between $2.1 and $6 million. Unfortunately for Harvard, this salary policy change meant the loss of its top money managers, who were offered significantly higher compensation for their talents elsewhere.

Jack Meyer, the former CEO of HMC who increased the endowment by 500%, and Jeffrey Larson were some of Harvard's greatest losses after the salary cuts; they left to found their own new hedge funds, Convexity Capital and Sowood Capital. HMC's decision to invest in these hedge funds started by its former managers became another topic of debate. Harvard invested $500 million with Sowood Capital, which collapsed in 2007, costing Harvard an estimated $350 million. Harvard also invested about $500 million with Convexity Capital. The next year, Convexity Capital failed to outperform the market benchmarks. While both fund managers had track records of success while at Harvard, critics argued that Harvard should not have used its money to invest in funds that were new, untested, and operated by individuals closely tied to Harvard's own money managers.

Finally, Harvard has been subject to a great deal of criticism recently over its general investment strategy leading up to the market crash of 2007. Under President Summers, Harvard started leveraging its endowment by 105%, meaning that Harvard was investing 105% of the money it actually had. On top of this, Harvard's endowment portfolio was largely illiquid. Liquid equity, such as stocks, can be converted into cash or traded easily. Illiquid assets, such as acres of rainforest or investments with hedge funds (which mandate that their clients give them money at fixed intervals to invest over time), cannot be so easily or rapidly accessed. When the market crashed, although Harvard's endowment was still considered the largest in the world, it could not convert its endowment investments into cash to pay off its expenses.

To make matters worse, Summers introduced a long-term deal with Goldman Sachs in 2004 to put in place $3.52 billion in interest rate swaps: Harvard would pay Goldman Sachs a fixed rate, and Goldman Sachs would pay Harvard the Federal Reserve rate. The logic behind this deal was that the Federal Reserve rate was expected to stay stable or rise (but never fall), hedging the University's investments against rising interest rates on the money it had borrowed. This, however, was not what happened when the market crashed and the Federal Reserve cut interest rates to record lows. Harvard lost $570 million.

As if Harvard wasn't in enough of a bind, its expenses had ballooned during the same period, for two reasons. First, Harvard was making huge returns off of its investments in the early 2000s, and confidence that these returns would continue was prevalent among Harvard's decision-makers. Second, Harvard was under a great deal of pressure from outside groups, including the federal government, to increase its spending. There was growing resentment against universities "hoarding" their endowments despite rising tuition costs, and legislation was proposed to mandate that universities spend at least 5% of their endowments annually as other non-profits are mandated to do. Harvard was accustomed to spending between 4% and 5% of its endowment annually, exceeding 5% only once between 1997 and 2007.

In response to these concerns, Harvard's Faculty of Arts and Sciences, which encompasses Harvard College and the Graduate School of Arts and Sciences, increased its budget by 50% from 2005 to 2008, mostly through the appointment of 126 new professors (a 22% increase in Harvard's professorial ranks) and a new science lab construction project. These expenses only added to Harvard's debt, which increased from $538 million in 2005 to $1.1 billion in 2008. According to *Boston Magazine*, interest on its debt costs

Harvard $85 million a year. In the period of economic recession that began in 2008, many proposals introduced during the boom years, including, most notably, the massive construction project in Allston (p. 33), were cut or put on hold.

DONATIONS

Harvard's endowment has been bolstered in recent years by generous donations by alumni and philanthropists. Before 2008, the biggest donation Harvard had ever received was of $75.5 million, from a financial securities investor in 1982. That record was shattered in 2008, when David Rockefeller, Class of 1936, gave $100 million to fund international travel and arts initiatives for undergraduates.

Also in 2008, Hansjorg Wyss, a 1965 graduate of the Business School, gave $125 million to found the Hansjorg Medical Center for Biologically Inspired Engineering.

Finally, in 2008, Eli and Edyth Broad gave $400 million in a shared donation to both Harvard and MIT to support biomedical research at the Broad Institute. The Institute, founded in 2003 with an original grant of $100 million, currently supports over a dozen biomedical projects, including research into psychiatric disorders like autism and schizophrenia and the molecular description of human cancers.

THE UNDERGRADUATE BUSINESS EXPERIENCE

The proximity of Harvard College to Harvard Business School (HBS) makes it easy for undergraduates to attend seminars and training programs with HBS professors and students. In fall 2011 HBS professors offered the first exclusively undergraduate course, entitled "Innovation and Entrepreneurship: American Experience in Comparative Perspective." Unfortunately for the students, they are still required to trek over Anderson Bridge to HBS for class twice a week. A variety of undergraduate student groups on the Cambridge side of the river also strive to introduce students to the worlds of finance, consulting, management, and business.

BUSINESS CLUBS AT HARVARD

The largest undergraduate business organization at Harvard, with more than 300 members, is Harvard University Women in Business (WIB; p. 47). As its mission statement explains, WIB "seeks to empower a dynamic group of enterprising young women by uniting them through business education and experience." After a rigorous "comp" (try-out process), WIB offers its "associates" opportunities to participate in workshops and panel discussions, learn about careers in business, and meet recruiters.

Another prominent business organization on campus is the Harvard Investment Agency (HIA). Of the six major finance organizations on campus—the African Business and Investment Club, the Harvard Financial Analysts Club (HFAC), HIA, the Veritas Financial Group, the Harvard College Venture Capital and Private Equity Club, and the Harvard College Investment Magazine—HIA is perhaps the most widely known. All of the above aim to educate students about finance and prepare them for careers in the field. Specifically, HIA seeks to augment the existing economics and government curriculum by giving students a better understanding of financial markets. Members of HIA can gain hands-on investment experience by helping to invest the organization's $15,000 fund.

Other major business-focused organizations include the Leadership Institute, the Harvard International Business Club, the Harvard College Consulting Group, and the Harvard College Economics Review.

HARVARD STUDENT AGENCIES (HSA)

In 1957, 14 entrepreneurial students started a group of small-scale businesses out of their dorm rooms. Their revenues helped them pay Harvard's rising tuition, which had doubled in the previous ten years; however, by turning a profit within Harvard buildings, they placed Harvard's real estate tax exemption in jeopardy. To put these student initiatives to good use, the Dean of Financial Aid, John Monro '35, suggested regrouping these student businesses into a larger corporation: Harvard Student Agencies (HSA). HSA would provide opportunities for students to start and develop student-led businesses

TITUS JAHNG

The HSA Team for the Fiscal Year 2013

FUN FACT

The initial capital for the establishment of HSA came from the sales of linen to incoming freshmen. After a first summer mailing, an overwhelming 90% of freshmen purchased linens.

while offering a wide range of services to the University community. For instance, the House Painting Agency provided employment for students in Cambridge during the summer to paint local houses.

Europe-by-Air was created in 1959, selling $200 charter round-trip flights to Europe on several jet-propelled, British Overseas Airways Corporation planes. For $545, students could take a full seven-week tour of the continent, room and board included. The success of Europe-by-Air led to the creation of Europe-by-Car, which allowed students to buy a car in Europe, take a road trip there, and then have it shipped back to the U.S. to be resold. HSA's forays into European travel were bolstered by its partnership with the budding *Let's Go* travel guide series (p. 177).

In 1969, with the civil rights movement sweeping the nation, HSA produced a movie highlighting the difficulties for African Americans seeking employment, and promoted the movie nationwide to potential employers. They also published a 36-page book entitled *College and the Black Student* to inform "black people of the expanding opportunities available for higher education."

HSA's national recognition was exemplified in 1982 when its first female president, Lynn Liakos, was featured in *Glamour* magazine for her accomplishments.

Today, HSA has a major presence on campus, employing more than 500 students. HSA continues to provide creative services for students including bartending courses and unique Harvard insignia clothing. HSA's 11 agencies have combined revenue of approximately $5 million, making it the largest university-affiliated student-run business in the country.

STUDENT START-UPS

There must be something in the Cambridge water, judging by the student start-ups that continually crop up on Harvard's campus. So impressive are the ideas brought to life by Harvard entrepreneurs that Harvard Student Agencies and the Technology and Entrepreneurship Center at Harvard (TECH) created the Harvard College Innovation Challenge to award over $50,000 each year to promising student businesses, and in the summer of 2009, they established an "incubator space" for students to use as office space in which to develop and grow student businesses.

Among the most famous businesses started by students at Harvard College are Bill Gates's Microsoft Corporation and Mark Zuckerberg's Facebook. Incidentally, both Gates and Zuckerberg dropped out of Harvard before graduating in order to oversee their companies, challenging the idea that a Harvard degree is necessary for success. However, Gates was awarded an honorary degree when he was chosen as the commencement speaker for the class of 2007.

In the building which once housed the public broadcasting company WGBH, the Harvard Innovation Lab (i-Lab) opened in November 2011. Across the Charles River from Harvard Square and adjacent to the Business School campus, the i-Lab is part of Harvard's expansion into the Allston area (p. 33). Parts of the i-Lab are open to the public: the building is meant to encourage innovation and entrepreneurship between Harvard students across the undergraduate and graduate schools, as well as with the Cambridge and Allston communities.

FUN FACT

Facebook, the global social networking phenomenon, started as a media platform used exclusively by Harvard students. As it gained popularity, the website was opened to other Ivy League universities, before spreading to other colleges and, finally, to anyone with a valid email address. In protest of the rapid spread of Facebook beyond Harvard's borders, a small body of Harvard students organized an (apparently unsuccessful) boycott of the online network, pushing for its reinstitution as a Harvard-only website. Facebook is now the largest social networking site in the world. Its Kirkland House (p. 134) beginnings and meteoric rise is chronicled in the 2010 Oscar-winning film *The Social Network,* starring Jesse Eisenberg as Mark Zuckerberg and Justin Timberlake as Napster founder, Sean Parker.

HARVARD BUSINESS SCHOOL

Sometimes referred to as "The West Point of Capitalism," Harvard Business School (HBS) is often regarded by many as the best business school in the world. Unsurprisingly, an invitation to join this institution is not easy to come by: each year, over 9,000 talented men and women apply to HBS for around 900 coveted spots in the incoming class. Notable HBS alumni include New York City Mayor Michael Bloomberg, legendary General Electric CEO Jeffrey Immelt, and U.S. President George W. Bush, as well as current and former CEOs of Boeing, Burger King, Continental Airlines, Johnson &

ARCHITECTURAL SPOTLIGHT: CLASS OF 1959 CHAPEL

One of the most interesting buildings on the HBS campus is the Class of 1959 Chapel, which is comprised of three distinct architectural elements.

ALEXANDRE TERRIEN

The first is a clock tower engraved with the names of the members of the MBA Class of 1959. A large bronze ball within the tower moves up and down on a glass scale to indicate the time of day. The second element of the chapel is a glass prism, reminiscent of the pyramid at the Louvre in Paris, which juts out of the ground and serves as an entrance to the building. Inside this structure is a greenhouse with a fountain and plants from "biblical lands." After walking through the entrance, visitors enter the third and largest element of the building: a circular chapel, built with no corners so as to "leave the Devil with no place to hide." The chapel, which is non-denominational, is simply furnished, with chairs, a piano, and a harpsichord.

ARCHITECTURAL SPOTLIGHT:
BAKER LIBRARY AND THE BAKER BELLS

Baker Library, which faces the river and the rest of Harvard, is the focal point of the Harvard Business School campus and one of its most recognizable buildings. Originally used for classes, Baker Library now houses many of the school's books and archives. Baker's collection has grown so large that a significant portion of it is now housed in underground "stacks," much like the collections of Widener Library across the river. In addition to housing the world's largest collection of business literature, Baker is the home of Robert Nerton's Nobel Prize, which is on display for visitors.

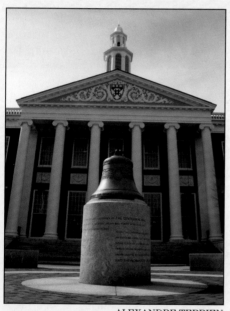

ALEXANDRE TERRIEN
The one remaining Baker Bell

Baker's reading room is a popular spot for MBA students to study. The skylights that now provide much of the lighting for the reading room were only recently rediscovered after having been covered for 50 years—a result of the air raid blackouts during World War II.

For much of Baker Library's 80-year existence, a bell from Russia's Danilov monastery occupied its bell tower. This bell, along with its sisters in Lowell House (p. 138), was rescued by American businessman Thomas Crane from Stalin's attempts to purge religion from Russia in the mid-20th century. After years of ringing for HBS students, the bell, along with those from Lowell, was recently returned to the Danilov monastery in exchange for a cast replacement. A half-scale version of the new Baker bell now sits in the lawn in front of the Library, along with a plaque commemorating the old bell and its return to Russia.

Johnson, JP Morgan, General Motors, Proctor & Gamble, Sony Pictures Entertainment, and many other Fortune 500 companies.

HUMBLE BEGINNINGS

On March 29, 1900, Harvard alum and MIT professor Robert G. Valentine asked Harvard President Charles Eliot, "Can Harvard do anything of a systematic sort to provide from year to year a few good men who can grow into the leaders wanted?" In 1908, the University responded to this request by launching "The Delicate Experiment," in which it dedicated 15 faculty members and 75 students to become members of a branch of the Graduate School of Arts and Sciences dedicated to the study of business education. Thus, HBS was born. In 1920, President Lowell announced that HBS had "proved its value," and the budding moguls and future tycoons of the Harvard Business School relocated across the Charles.

Just three short years after New York banker George F. Baker gave $5 million for the construction of a new campus in Allston, the move was complete, and on June 4, 1927, GE President Owen Young gave the keynote speech at the dedication ceremony for the new campus. In honor of Baker's contributions, the new Business School library was named after him.

NEW FACES ON CAMPUS

Since the completion of the new campus in 1927, little has changed on the surface of the HBS campus. Much has changed, however, among the students and professors in its classrooms. It wasn't until 1960 that HBS conferred its first MBAs to three Radcliffe women. One year later, Henrietta Larson became the first female full professor at HBS. In 1969, HBS named its first female valedictorian. Today, over one third of each class is made up of women (p. 46).

THE FEARFUL FIRST YEAR

In her book *Toughing it out at Harvard: The Making of a Woman MBA*, Fran Worden Henry describes the anxiety facing a first-year student at HBS: "It was Saturday morning. I had finished one week at Harvard Business School, and I was in shock. That very morning I had jumped out of bed at six, forgetting it wasn't a school day. I heated water for my coffee but forgot to put the grounds in a Melitta filter; I tasted a mouthful of grit and was too numb to care. Terror had hold of me."

First-years enter HBS fearing the worst about their upcoming workloads, and they are rarely disappointed: Dean Light once likened the experience to "drinking from a fire hose." Small student "sections" and "learning teams" offer some relief from this onslaught: classes are broken into 10 sections of 80-90 students, and students are also separately grouped into assigned learning teams of 5-6 students from differing sections, which serve as study groups. Along with the famous case method, the sections are one of the key aspects of the HBS education. Since first year students take the entirety of their classes with the same classmates in the same classroom, the section becomes like a second home, and many students end up making their closest friends within their sections.

THE CASE METHOD

The case method plays an enormous part in both an HBS student's life and in the history of HBS itself. It was first conceived of in 1922 by Dean Donham, who wanted business cases to be designed like those he had studied in law school (p. 222). Later that year, HBS Professor Melvin T. Copeland wrote *Marketing Problems* and created the first of a long line of cases written by HBS professors. Today, the average student will read, analyze, and discuss around 600 cases over the course of two years at HBS.

For each case, students are given a relatively short (8-12 pages plus exhibits) description of a problem faced by a particular company at a particular time in its corporate history. These cases are often written from the perspective of a protagonist (usually the CEO of the company) and are tailored for the specific class in which they are being taught. The cases provide background information on the company and then leave students with a problem to solve.

The whole process is designed with the purpose of preparing students for the problems they will face when they enter the business world. Cases are often left open-ended, and students are always expected to come to their own conclusions. As one student put it, "the point is, you're on the last page of the book, you can't flip the page."

KEVIN LIN

Baker Library on the HBS campus

HBS VERNACULAR

From the school that fathered the case method also comes a unique vocabulary, which includes the following key terms:

Chip Shot — A flimsy attempt at class participation by a student who hasn't read the case being discussed.

Pit Diver — Someone who attacks the professor at the front of the classroom with questions after each class ends; also known as "that guy." One type of student you probably don't want to be.

Loops — Low grades given to students in the bottom of each class. Another type of student you probably don't want to be.

Dinged — Rejected by a prospective employer after an interview. A type of student you definitely don't want to be.

After (presumably) spending hours picking apart and analyzing each case, one student will be called on at the beginning of class in what is known as the "cold call." The professor chooses someone to give a 10-15 minute explanation of the case at hand and present his or her suggestions for the protagonist. Because the faculty are familiar with the students' backgrounds and career goals, they are able to cold call students with unique and well-informed perspectives on each individual case. For instance, a student with an investment banking background might be called upon to introduce a recent case involving the collapse of Bear Stearns. After the case has been introduced, students engage in a lively conversation about the merits of each option.

At the end of each class, the professor will often tell the students what the protagonist of the case actually did in real life, but the emphasis is rarely on the resolution. Sometimes, the protagonist will actually be present for the discussion of the case. HBS student Tom Long describes one such encounter: "Gene Harms, CEO of Henry Manufacturing, has decided to fire a key employee. The class is discussing the merits of the decision, and I get a chance at some quality 'airtime.' In the middle of my vituperative attack on the decision, into the classroom walks Gene Harms himself. With a cold stare he walks directly over to me and says, 'Suppose you tell me just exactly what you would have done?'"

Many of the cases used in the classrooms at HBS are taught at business schools around the world. The business of selling Business School cases is a profit-maker of its own accord: over 6% of HBS's yearly revenue is attributed to case sales.

CRISIS AND CRITICISMS

While a degree from HBS is considered a stamp of approval in many corporate circles, the school has not escaped its fair share of criticism. In light of the recent economic crisis, and with HBS alums like former Merrill Lynch CEO John Thain, ousted GM CEO Rick Wagoner, and former Treasury Secretary Hank Paulson coming under public scrutiny, critics have questioned not only the business acumen of HBS grads but also the soundness of their ethical reasoning. In a particularly characteristic response, an HBS faculty panel recently wrote a case exploring the role of HBS in the economic crisis.

LAW, GOVERNMENT, AND SERVICE

AT HARVARD

SERVING THE WORLD

Turn on your TV and flip through a few channels: chances are you won't have to wait long to see an alum of Harvard Law School (HLS), the Harvard Kennedy School of Government (HKS), or the Phillips Brooks House Association (PBHA). These three—two graduate schools, and one undergraduate-staffed service umbrella—provide training and hands-on experience to Harvard students interested in public service or law.

HARVARD LAW SCHOOL

Whether witnessed through John Osborn's *The Paper Chase*, Richard Kahlenberg's memoir *A Broken Contract*, the film adaptation of *Legally Blonde*, or in real life, Harvard Law School has a reputation that precedes it. In these depictions, it is a cruel arena in which young lawyers-to-be fight one another for the highest grades, the best *Harvard Law Review* positions, and the most impressive internships.

This is, at best, an incomplete picture, and one that does little justice to such figures as Christopher Langdell, the father of the case method, and Derrick Bell, the first African American tenured professor of the school; or to the countless eager students who have graced the corridors of Austin Hall.

IN THE BEGINNING

In 1778, Isaac Royall, a wealthy citizen of Massachusetts, stipulated as part of his will the provision for "a Professor of Law in [Harvard] College or a Professor of Physick [sic] and Anatomy, whichever the said Overseers and Corporation shall judge to be best for the benefit of the College." Harvard quickly decided Law would be more lucrative.

Royall's money was not enough to yield a professorship right away: it took the Corporation more than 30 years after his death in 1781 to fulfill his

BY THE NUMBERS

44	The percentage of international students at the Harvard Kennedy School
550	Open spots in an incoming Law School class
86	Student-led community servce programs organized through PBHA
10,000	Members of the Boston community served by student volunteers in PBHA organizations

ARCHITECTURAL SPOTLIGHT:
LANGDELL HALL

Named after Christopher Columbus Langdell, Langdell Hall is the center of Law School life. Built in 1905 during an expansion of the School, the building was designed to contain classrooms, faculty offices, and the library.

During a 1996 renovation of the School, the library's 300,000 rare books were sealed into their two-story permanent home in Langdell while construction took place around them. The renovation produced one of the most beautiful buildings on campus. The library seats 700 students in its carrels, sofas, chairs, and beanbags.

Langdell Hall, the Law School's library,
Harvard University Archives, HUV 179 (3-4)

Langdell's collection includes more than 1.5 million bound volumes, making it the world's leading resource for legal scholars. Beyond that, is a place where students come to study, write, debate, lounge, and get their caffeine fixes: the "coffee room" on the 4th floor of the building provides students with free coffee after 9pm. Even undergraduates have been known to venture past the safety of Harvard Yard to make use of the 4th floor reading room, a cup of joe in hand.

FUN FACT

At the north end of Langdell Library is a room called the Casperson Room, once known as the Treasure Room.

The Treasure Room, which currently holds valuable artwork and memorabilia of past alumni, was designed during World War II to protect research surrounding the atomic bomb. The room is self-enclosed within the library (the Library windows surrounding the room look in on solid walls), and it offered researchers access to tunnels connecting the Law School to the Harvard physics labs.

wish. Finally, on August 18, 1815, the Corporation established the Royall Professorship of Law, electing the Chief Justice of Massachusetts, Isaac Parker, to the position.

The job description of the Royall Professor did not in the least resemble those of modern-day professors. Rather than teach law to professional students, the Royall Professor gave a small number of lectures a year, mainly to College seniors, resident graduates, and Boston lawyers. Nonetheless, the teaching of Law was deemed important enough to establish its own faculty separate from the College, and on May 17, 1817, Harvard Law School was officially founded.

STORY'S STORY

There was no honeymoon period for the Law School. It quickly proved unable to compete with better-known and more practice-oriented law schools in the area: between 1817 and 1829, HLS managed to graduate only 25 students, and in 1829 the School was down to its last student. In the nick of time, Nathan Dane, a distinguished Massachusetts lawyer, came to the rescue, devoting $10,000 for the creation of the Dane Professorship of Law. Upon Dane's request, a young man named Joseph Story was appointed its first professor.

When Story agreed to the Dane Professorship he was already a busy man: he was an accomplished law scholar, and at age 32 he became the youngest ever Justice of the Supreme Court. Harvard had brought a celebrity to its Law School, and with him came a fundamental change in its philosophy. When the School opened in September 1829 under the leadership of Story, it attracted twice as many students as it had ever had before.

Story's personal dedication toward the school and the students earned him great respect, and the school grew rapidly in size and fame. English lawyers testified that the school's methodology and legal education were "deeper and fuller" than those of Oxford. In addition, Story ran the school with three goals that would help define its future course: to make the Law School national, rather than local; to become an achievement-based school in which students were chosen on merit rather than status; and, finally, to cultivate leaders for the nation.

ARCHITECTURAL SPOTLIGHT: AUSTIN HALL

Increased enrollment, fueled by Langdell's popular policies, required an expansion of HLS facilities. Austin Hall was constructed in 1883 with a $135,000 donation from Edwin Austin, a Boston merchant. The Hall was designed by Henry Hobson Richardson in the Romanesque Revival style (also known by the eponymous term "Richardsonian") and replaced Dane Hall, the original building dedicated to the Law School. It is now one of the oldest buildings in the country continuously used for the instruction of law. The building was designed for core classes employing the case method, and, just as the case method has been reproduced around the country, so has the design of this building.

Every year the building houses the Ames Moot Court Competition, usually presided over by a justice of the United States Supreme Court. Success in the competition is one of the Law School's most coveted achievements. Previous winners of the competition include Deval Patrick, Governor of Massachussetts, and Professor Cass Sunstein, former head of the Office of Information and Regulatory Affairs for the Obama administration.

ALEXANDRA DOWD

Austin Hall, designed by H.H. Richardson

THE "CASE" OF CHRISTOPHER LANGDELL

Christopher Langdell's appointment as the next Dean of the Law School in 1870 proved another turning point for the institution. Langdell created a new curriculum, extending the course of study to three years and requiring that every student obtain a Bachelor of Arts degree before being allowed to attend the Law School. In addition, a scholarship program was instituted, in which tuition fees were covered for men of high ranking who could not support themselves. New faculty members were appointed to assist Langdell and his two professors.

Also under Langdell, HLS moved from Dane Hall to Austin Hall, a new building north of the Yard, and the *Harvard Law Review* was founded.

Langdell's time as Dean of the Law School is best remembered, however, for his introduction of the casebook method, or the case method. Langdell was the first professor to institute a system of teaching in which professors directly challenged students and students learned to analyze cases by themselves. He would collect actual cases that best represented a particular area of law, and students read the cases before being questioned about them in class. Within a decade of its introduction the case method had received enormous acclaim, and today it has been adopted by an overwhelming majority of law schools in the United States.

HARVARD LAW REVIEW

On the edge of campus, surrounded by large, ornate buildings overflowing with professors and budding lawyers, stands the Gannett House, an unassuming building wedged between a parking lot and the law school gymnasium. This austere Greek Revival house, built in 1838 and now the oldest surviving building on the HLS campus, is home to one of the most influential student groups in the country: the *Harvard Law Review.*

The *Review* has gained prominence and publicity for its notable alumni, among them President Barack Obama. Now widely regarded as one of the

FUN FACT

President Barack Obama's tenure as the first black President of the *Harvard Law Review* has been widely publicized. Through a process that has been described as "a fussy affair, part intellectual debate, part frat house ritual," Barack Obama beat out 18 other candidates to earn his historic post. He was not the first member in the *Review*'s history to defy social norms, however. One of the *Review*'s first female editors was Supreme Court Justice Ruth Bader Ginsberg.

FUN FACT

Harvard Law School didn't graduate its first female student until 1950, when other leading law schools had been graduating women for years. The idea of educating women in law at Harvard, however, had been around for a while.

In the 1920s and 1930s, a handful of professors decided to take matters into their own hands, and in the basement of the Harvard-Epworth United Methodist Church they began to teach the exact same classes they taught to HLS men during the day to women at night.

most influential legal journals in the United States, the *Harvard Law Review* has been published for over 100 years.

In 1886, inspired by the 250th anniversary of Harvard College, a group of eight third-year law students started a new student organization at the Law School called the Langdell Society. The Langdell Society, like many other contemporary student groups at the Law School, was likely founded to encourage informal thought and debate about contemporary legal issues. However, after reviewing a copy of the *Columbia Jurist*, these enterprising students created a law journal of their own. In 1887, the *Harvard Law Review* was born.

The eight editors who started the *Harvard Law Review* have been replaced by the more than 80 editors currently listed on the publication's masthead. Little else, however, has changed since the journal's inception.

Currently, prospective first-year editors are given a week to complete a mock editorial piece in need of revision (the "subcite") and a writing sample (the "case comment")—an application process that has been known to keep students up for days at a time. Once on the *Review*, editors are given the chance to write a published piece in each of their two years of membership.

TIMES A-CHANGIN'

As a result of increased enrollment after World War II, HLS had more qualified candidates than it could possibly accept. Admissions rates were cut in half and cut in half again. By 1974 applicants had only a one in nine shot at getting accepted.

It was during these years that the school developed the cut-throat reputation popularized in contemporary novels and films. One Professor would famously welcome nervous first years with his prediction that one in three of them would fail by the end of the year, and one psychiatrist on the Law School faculty described inter-student relations in terms of "enmity, friction, hostility, distaste, contempt and the lack of group cohesiveness and morale."

ARCHITECTURAL SPOTLIGHT: GANNETT HALL

Designed by Samuel William Pomeroy in 1838, Gannett Hall is the oldest surviving building on the Law School campus. Both the *Harvard Law Review* and the Harvard Legal Aid Bureau have made Gannett Hall their home since 1925. Originally, Gannett Hall faced Harvard Square, but it was rotated 90 degrees as part of a proposed mall project that was never completed.

ANNA SANTOLERI

As HLS became more competitive, it also became more diverse. Between 1967 and 1975, the enrollment of women jumped from under 4% to 21%; the number of African American students was up to 53 from 3 in 1963, and the first waves of Latino, Asian American, and Native American students were enrolling at the Law School. Women won the right to shower in Hemenway Gym, and men stopped wearing coats and ties to class.

Students' attitudes were also changing around what to do with their Harvard Law degrees after graduation, and increasing numbers of graduates were turning to legal aid.

KEVIN LIN

The recently constructed Wasserstein Hall on the HLS campus

FUN FACT

In 1953, two second-year law school students, twins Jonathan and David Lubell, were subpoenaed to testify before the Senate Subcommittee on Internal Security. The McCarthy-style hearing would investigate the twins' political activities: both had been organizers for radical parties during their undergraduate careers at Cornell University, even though they had not been politically active since coming to Harvard. Although the Law School and Dean Griswold had been outspokenly hostile toward McCarthyism and the Red Scare, Dean Griswold urged the twins to cooperate.

At the hearing, the twins were accused of engaging in Communist activities. In the aftermath of the hearing, some professors wanted the Lubell brothers expelled. Although a divided faculty voted against this, one professor went so far as to recommend that the twins be immediately indicted. The head of the New York City Selective Service publicly refused. Within a week of their appearance before the subcommittee, the twins were forced by the *Harvard Law Review* to resign their editorial positions. Jonathan Lubell was also forced to quit the Legal Aid Bureau. Students refused to sit next to the brothers in the classroom, and former friends ignored them or kept their distance. When Jonathan Lubell's grades entitled him to serve on the *Review* again in the fall of 1953, the third-year members of the *Review* voted 18-6 not to elect him.

HLS TODAY

After a decade of turmoil surrounding the diversity of the HLS faculty, and terrifying statistics about student satisfaction, the Law School has experienced a meteoric rise in recent years. Under Dean Elena Kagan, appointed in 2002, students became much happier. In 2008 the faculty voted to transition from a letter grading system to a pass-fail system, and even little things have improved the quality of life at HLS: Langdell Library began serving free coffee after 9pm, and Dean Kagan distributed her personal email address to students as a first step toward increasing faculty-student interactions.

On January 26, 2009, President Barack Obama appointed Kagan as the Solicitor General of the United States, making her the first woman to hold this position. She was subsequently confirmed as a United States Supreme Court Justice. Although her Deanship had been brief, Kagan was admired and respected by both faculty and students for the positive changes she had brought about at HLS.

On July 1, 2009, Professor Martha Minow was appointed to succeed Kagan as Dean. Today, the Law School welcomes approximately 550 new students each year into three different degree programs, and they are able to choose from over 400 different courses, seminars, and reading groups. The Law School also features in-house clinics through which students can practice law instead of just reading about it.

THE HARVARD KENNEDY SCHOOL

The red-brick buildings known as the Harvard Kennedy School of Government are unassuming, nothing like Langdell Hall at the Law School or Baker Library at the Business School. Much more interesting than its design is what happens within its walls, as HKS regularly welcomes some of the most interesting, controversial, and powerful men and women in the world.

IN THE BEGINNING

The Harvard Kennedy School was born out of a shift in American politics, as the Great Depression and the dawn of World War II shocked the country into a newfound awareness of the complexities and importance of government. In 1933, Lucius N. Littauer donated $2 million to Harvard, in what was at that point the largest ever single gift from an individual donor to a university. His donation led to the construction of the Graduate School of Public Administration three years later, in 1936, and yet another graduate school joined Harvard's already impressive ranks.

The first decades of the school's existence were dedicated to establishing a niche for itself in the academic world. A year after its founding, the school created the Littauer fellowship program, which would be the precursor to the mid-career Masters Degree in public administration. The school was originally situated on Kirkland Street and would remain there for the next 40 years.

When Edward S. Mason assumed the deanship in 1948, change was imminent. The school began to diversify. In 1956, women began to be judged on the same grounds as men for admission to the school, and two years later the Mason Fellowship was established to allow emerging leaders from third world countries to attend the mid-career program. The school was starting to make a name for itself, and it was time to expand.

THE INSTITUTE OF POLITICS

The opportunity for expansion presented itself in June of 1961, when Harvard President Nathan Pusey met with President John F. Kennedy about building a library on the Harvard campus. Kennedy was quite enthusiastic about building a library and museum that would be more than just a space for political

ARCHITECTURAL SPOTLIGHT:
THE BELFER CENTER

The Belfer Center, on the corner of Eliot and JFK Streets, opened on October 13, 1984 in a dedication ceremony at which U.S. Senate Majority Leader Howard Baker was the principal speaker. This 45,000 square foot building enlarged the Kennedy School's total area by almost 50%.

The Belfer Center, which replaced the original Littauer Center, houses the Alexander Graham Bell Hall, a conference center, two lecture halls, the Harry Starr Auditorium, and the Edwin H. Land Hall. Facilities are also provided for eight executive education programs, three research centers, the Center for Business and Government, the Center for Energy and Environmental Policy, and the Center for Press, Politics, and Public Policy.

The Center's five stories rise above the school's adjoining main building, and features a more intimate version of the highly successful ARCO Forum for Public Affairs. The Forum, which occupies the core of the building's first and second floors, is ringed by study carrels and equipped with carpeted bleachers. This mini-forum had been dubbed "Town Hall" by former dean Graham Allison, and, like its counterpart, serves as a multipurpose facility by providing a setting for smaller panel discussions as well as study spaces and informal meeting areas.

research and study, but would also function as a learning center with which he could be actively involved. Kennedy's assassination on November 22, 1963, tragically interrupted these plans, but only days after the President was laid to rest, his closest aides decided to honor his memory by continuing—and expanding—the project that Kennedy had begun at Harvard.

The Institute of Politics was created three years later, in 1966. The "big plan," as it was called, was intended to combine a library, institute, museum, and school, but the idea was tweaked when met with resistant neighbors who were nervous about the crowds the center was expected to attract. In 1975, Harvard capitulated and moved the museum and library to a second location, but the IOP was there to stay.

Kennedy's advisor and Harvard economics professor John Kenneth Galbraith envisioned the Institute as a forum in which "political fellows" would spend a set period of time conducting seminars, leading discussions, and bringing together undergraduates to analyze politics. The Institute would be created specifically for undergraduates, according to Galbraith, it is "the undergraduates who conduct the most active political discussion at Harvard.

They would be the most interested in the political residents. John F. Kennedy would, I think, have liked the thought of undergraduates being encouraged to a more serious interest in politics."

The Institute of Politics would not be a degree-granting program; rather, it would strive to bring together academia and "practitioners in the work of government," encouraging undergraduates to become involved in public service. Notably, the IOP was founded with the notion that all activities would "be conducted from a completely nonpartisan or from a bipartisan point of view."

The Institute of Politics was off to a promising start. Its Fellows Program invited 10 professionals in politics, journalism, and other forms of public service to spend a year at the Institute of Politics to share their experiences with undergraduates and learn about the state of politics from their perspectives. Its second program of Honorary Associates invited high profile guests who would spend two or three days meeting with students and faculty. Though both programs began around the same time, only one of these programs remained an integral part of the IOP.

On November 6, 1966, Defense Secretary Robert McNamara visited Harvard as the first Honorary Associate of the IOP. His first day went smoothly. He began his second day at the Business School where he had earned an MBA. :ater, while walking out of Quincy House, McNamara was besieged by 800 angry students organized by the Harvard chapter of Students for a Democratic Society (SDS). Some threw themselves in front of McNamara's car to stop

his exit. In an attempt to diffuse the situation, McNamara climbed on top of his car and agreed to answer questions. The crowd, however, would have nothing of it, and McNamara's answers were drowned out by boos and shouts. Growing increasingly frustrated, McNamara shouted at the angry mob: "I spent four of the happiest years at the Berkeley campus doing the same thing as you are doing now. But there was one important difference, I was tougher and more courteous." When the crowd answered him with calls of "murderer" and "fascist," he added, "And I was tougher then and I am tougher now!" This did not exactly extinguish the wrath of the protestors, but it did distract them enough for him to get away; fistfights broke out between supporters and oppo-

KEVIN LIN

HKS Courtyard

FUN FACT

The Fellows Program of the IOP invites six professionals in politics and journalism every semester to share their experiences with students. Each Fellow gets six student liaisons, who work closely with the Fellow during the semester to help run weekly study groups—speaking sessions at which all students are welcome—but most of all to get to know the Fellow with whom they are working. Annissa Alusi '12 was a liaison her freshman year:

"As a liaison for former Iowa Governor Tom Vilsack, I learned about politics through his Study Group, which focused on the risks involved in public policy initiatives pertaining to health care, the economy, energy, and natural disasters. But more importantly, our liaison group bonded with Tom over dinners in Cambridge, pumpkin carving at his apartment during Halloween, going to see the political film *W* as a group, and late nights at pub trivia in the Queen's Head. This not only gave us a chance to bond with him as friends, but also to learn about his life as a politician, his most challenging decisions, why he loves politics, and what he feels our country needs to accomplish over the coming years. Not to mention that we got behind-the-scenes election news from him and his sources. Perhaps the most exciting part of all was when President Barack Obama named him U.S. Secretary of Agriculture. Although Tom of course has his hands full as a member of President Obama's Cabinet, we still remain in contact and hope to have an IOP liaison reunion with him sometime soon."

nents of the Vietnam War while McNamara was guided away by an army of policemen to the IOP.

Dean John U. Munro apologized for the incident and 2,700 students signed an apology letter for the behavior of their peers. The Honorary Associates Program continued to run temporarily, but soon it required more resources than the IOP could afford. In 1977, its core mission was incorporated into the Visiting Fellows Program, which still exists today bringing "distinguished veterans of public life to Harvard for a short stay."

The IOP continues to hold a prominent position on campus, and its Fellows program, Forums, and service organizations are among the best attended events and most active groups on campus.

FUN FACT

Open to all Harvard students, the JFK Forum is a place for political discussion, analysis and evaluation. Some of the biggest names in contemporary history have been welcomed to the Forum, including United States President George H. W. Bush, Archbishop Desmond Tutu, Mikhail Gorbachev, and Muhammad Yunus. Furthermore, all speakers who agree to come to the Forum must also agree to answer questions from the audience. Access to events is always free for Harvard students, although tickets for high-profile guests are awarded by lottery, as their supply is easily dwarfed by their demand.

UNISON AND DIVISION

Along with the creation of the IOP, the School of Public Policy honored the memory of President Kennedy further by changing its name to the John F. Kennedy School of Government in 1966. This broke with a University tradition that prohibited any of its schools from being named after individuals. Indeed, the rule-breaking came at a price—a $10 million donation to the University from the Kennedy family. With a new name, the school required a new look, and in 1979 the school's academic programs, which had been strewn around campus, were consolidated in one location on John F. Kennedy Street, then known as Boylston Street. The ARCO Forum of Public Affairs opened as the premier public speaking venue at Harvard University. The makeover seemed to work, and the school enjoyed huge growth during the 1970s and 1980s, as the faculty grew from 20 members to 100, and the full-time graduate student body increased from 200 to 700.

Dean Graham Allison, in office from 1977 to 1988, deserves much of the credit for the growth of the School. He also made the decision to change the name of the Kennedy School, realizing that the name was no longer an asset for fundraising during the Reagan era. Students who arrived at the Kennedy School in the fall of 1981 found orientation packages with the abbreviation H.S.G.—Harvard School of Government—in place of K.S.G. The media immediately jumped on the change, and President Bok of Harvard University pulled in the reins on Allison, saying he was "surprised and angry" by Allison's strategy. Edward Kennedy publicly accepted Bok's apologies, although in a 1989 interview Kennedy acknowledged that his family had its differences with Harvard over the School of Government. As a *New York Times* article at the time pointed out, "The Irish and Italian politicians on the Cambridge City Council didn't get mad, they got even, changing the name of the street on which the school fronts from Boylston Street to John F. Kennedy Street, so that the name would have to go on the school's stationery, whatever it was called."

More tension arose within the Kennedy School over the discrepancies between practicioners—the lecturers who came from professions in government and journalism—and more traditional academics. Practicioners tended to be popular with their students, but professors criticized them for being exempt from academic criticism, rarely contributing scholarship to their fields, and often overstaying their two- or three-year welcomes, sometimes by decades. It quickly became a game of name-calling and finger-pointing—in other words, a fine display of politics.

HKS TODAY

The Harvard Kennedy School boasts five degree programs, a diverse faculty, and 15 research centers. Leaders from around the world have attended HKS, including United Nations Secretary General Ban Ki-moon, World Bank President Robert Zoellick, President of Mexico Felipe Calderón, Prime Minister of Singapore Lee Hsien Loong, President of Liberia Ellen Johnson Sirleaf, and Chief Executive of Hong Kong Sir Donald Tsang.

SEAN TIERNEY

The IOP Forum in the Harvard Kennedy School

PHILLIPS BROOKS HOUSE ASSOCIATION

One out of every four students at Harvard is actively involved in service. Approximately 1,600 Harvard College volunteers are engaged in one or more service projects through the Phillips Brooks House Association (PBHA), which runs 79 projects serving the Cambridge community and beyond.

The Phillips Brooks House Association was created in memory of Phillips Brooks, a Harvard graduate, Trinity Church preacher, advocate for social service, and lover of humanity. Plans for the building were drafted upon Phillips Brooks' death in 1893, and the Phillips Brooks House was completed on January 23, 1900.

PBHA began as a small enterprise with only six organizations in 1904. Their activities included placing students in settlement houses, organizing clothes and book drives, and financing missionaries to serve in Asia. Although PBHA lost momentum during the two World Wars, it managed a Red Cross center, a lounge for ROTC units, and the Harvard Mission Program, which assisted workers in Albania and Turkey. The concept of sending out volunteers to the communities, however, had not yet emerged.

For PBHA, this concept was realized in the 1950s, when the organization expanded to unprecedented levels. Beginning in 1954, women from Radcliffe College were allowed to participate in PBHA, and throughout the 1960s programs arose that expanded farther into the Cambridge and Boston communities. Unfortunately, the Association's growth was also crippling, as PBHA lacked the financial and organizational structure to sustain its new size. Through the 1970s membership plummeted from almost 1,000 students to fewer than 200, and the next decade was spent restructuring the organization.

FUN FACT

The influence of PBHA has reached much farther than just Cambridge and Boston. In 1954, students formed the Mental Hospitals Committee, an organization that sent volunteers to befriend mental health patients and help them readjust to society. This program served as a model for the National Service Corps, now Americorps.

Similarly, as students became more active participants in public service during John F. Kennedy's presidency, one group, called Project Tanganyika, sent students to Africa to teach English. President Kennedy later modeled the Peace Corps after Project Tanganyika.

In 1973, PBHA became incorporated and began to solicit greater support from Harvard University.

The restructuring of PBHA proved well worthwhile, and it returned in the 1980s larger and more successful than ever before. A million dollar campaign initiated in 1986 allowed further expansion through the association committee, an advisory group composed of alumni, faculty, and community leaders, as well as the development of the Summer Urban Program (SUP), a 12-camp network providing low-cost summer day camps to more than 700 children in Boston and Cambridge.

Greater involvement of the University, however, was both a blessing and a curse, as it meant that Harvard had much greater control over the activities of the Association. In 1995, recognizing that PBHA's current organizational structure stood in the way of its original goals, the PBHA cabinet passed a resolution calling for a "more rational, autonomous structure" for the organi-

ARCHITECTURAL SPOTLIGHT:
PHILLIPS BROOKS HOUSE

Phillips Brooks House, the home base for the Phillips Brooks House Association, was originally built, in 1900, with its front door facing north; after a busy street was built right in front of the house, however, this entrance was blocked off to visitors. Visitors to Phillips Brooks House today enter through the back door.

ALEXANDRE TERRIEN

PBHA Headquarters

zation. A rally was organized on December 7, 1995, at which over 2,000 people supported a student voice in public service activities.

Today, students participate in the PBHA leadership board and work together with College administrators dedicated to PBHA full-time. PBHA itself is now the home to 77 unique public service programs, in addition to 34 programs from the Public Service Network (PSN) that work closely with PBHA and reside within the Phillips Brooks House. Projects range from providing food and shelter to the homeless to teaching dance lessons at underprivileged schools. As the largest student-run organization on campus, PBHA positively impacts not only the lives of the community members it serves, but also the lives of the students involved.

BEYOND
HARVARD

GRADUATING FROM HARVARD

COMMENCEMENT TODAY

Commencement is the day Harvard most resembles the traditional, colonial fantasy its name evokes. Every year, one glorious mid-May morning, Tercentenary Theatre (the grassy square between Widener Library and Memorial Church) is transformed by the solemn and bittersweet academic procession. Familiar faces of friends and faculty are framed by caps and gowns. Degree candidates, alumni, and faculty parade through the Yard to celebrate a new "beginning," as the name of this momentous event so suitably implies. Robes vary in style and coloration by school and degree, which, to the uninitiated, can make the crowd resemble nothing so much as a grand gathering of wizards. In fact, apart from the cell phones and camera equipment (and women), Commencement today looks much like it did a hundred years ago.

Commencement day's Morning Exercises open at 8am with a Senior Chapel ceremony in Memorial Church. Meanwhile, the Harvard Band, gathered on Widener's steps, plays a brass fanfare announcing the arrival of the presidential procession. First to process are the Sheriffs of Middlesex and Suffolk Counties, the University Marshal, the current University President and any former Presidents in attendance, the Fellows of Harvard College, and the Board of Overseers. Next, the Governor of Massachusetts comes along with any candidates for honorary degrees and their faculties. Benjamin Franklin was the first such individual to be honored, in 1753. Since then, recipients have included a number of US presidents, as well as cultural figures like John Singer Sargent, Robert Frost, Walt Disney, and Leonard Bernstein, and international heroes such as Winston Churchill, Desmond Tutu, Mother Teresa, and Nelson Mandela.

BY THE NUMBERS

2	The number of "Bill"s who spoke at Graduation in 2007, Clinton and Gates
3	Legs on the chair that the University President sits on during the Commencement ceremony
170	Harvard Clubs worldwide
27,000	Chairs temporarily placed in Tercentenary Theater for Graduation ceremonies, held outdoors rain or shine

FUN FACT

After an invocation and a performance by the Commencement choir, two seniors deliver speeches: one in Latin and one in English. One advanced-degree candidate then delivers a third speech, also in English. Among the lucky few to have spoken at Commencement are Oliver Wendell Holmes, in 1829, Theodore Roosevelt, in 1880, and W.E.B. du Bois, in 1890. William Weld was the only person in recent Harvard history to deliver two speeches, once for the senior Latin part in 1966 and once for the graduate English part in 1970.

The President's procession walks alongside alumni through ranks of senior speakers, senior class officers, candidates for *summa cum laude*, and current students. After the honorary degree candidates, the Deans and Vice Presidents of the University make their way up the platform. Next come the faculty, ranked according to seniority and wearing academic robes with the silk-lined hoods of their *almae matres*. Finally, former members of the Governing Boards, past professors, former alumni association officers, the President and Orator of Phi Beta Kappa, and the Trustee of the Charity of Edward Hopkins, which awards academic prizes to undergraduates, enter, trailed by the so-called "Ministers of the Six Towns," the clergy of the "Old Cambridge" churches, consuls to Boston, state and federal judges, past honorary-degree recipients, public officials, and other guests.

The procession winds its way through the outdoor quad of "Tercentenary Theatre" (the entire ceremony is held outside, rain or shine) and onto the stage on the steps of Memorial Church. Once on stage, the President settles down in the three-legged Jacobean Chair that has been used at Commencement since it was purchased by President Holyoke in the mid 1700s. One hour and forty-five minutes after the procession first gathered, the ceremony finally begins. The President confers degrees, but diplomas are not awarded until later in the day, at separate ceremonies held in the undergraduate Houses and at the various graduate schools.

HISTORY OF COMMENCEMENT

Tradition plays a key role in Commencement, but much has changed since the first Commencement took place on September 23, 1642, six years after the founding of Harvard. The academic procession that day included the nine graduates, or "commencers"; four so-called junior-sophisters; and eight to 10 freshmen, along with a number of guests from Boston and nearby settlements including ministers, residents, parents, and Native Americans. Orations were conducted by the commencers in Hebrew, Greek, and Latin in the morning, and in the afternoon, commencers disputed in Latin on topics related to "theses philosophicae and philologicae"—basically, the meaning of life, the universe, and everything. In between the two sessions, a bountiful feast was held in the College hall at which the President gave thanks and Thomas Dudley, Governor of Massachusetts, passed around the so-called loving cup or grace cup, from which everyone would sip. It subsequently became tradition for the Massachusetts Governor to attend the ceremony, escorted from the State House to Johnston Gate by a mounted guard.

The early Commencements were festive, raucous affairs, and William Douglass famously claimed that the 1745 capture of Louisburg was "carried on in a tumultuary random Manner, and resembled a Cambridge Commencement." Indeed, those present at the 1703 Commencement consumed fourteen barrels of beer, a barrel of cider, and eighteen gallons of wine. An early 18th-century poem entitled "Satyricall Description of Commencement" described the way "All sizes and each sex the Ways do throng / And black and white ride jib by jole along" to attend Commencement. All this was despite the efforts of Harvard President Increase Mather, a strict Puritan who sought to put an end to the drinking and mayhem. By 1797, the festivities had been carried to such an extreme that a live elephant was brought from Providence, Rhode Island, to be displayed at the Commencement ceremony alongside exhibits of two-headed calves and people dressed up as mermaids and mummies. The Native Americans of nearby Natick were invited to compete with Harvard students in an archery competition, and won.

In spite of its grand history, Commencement has not been held every year since 1642. In 1644, for example, the College determined that no students were ready to enter the next phase of their academic careers. In other years, war or disease have sabotaged Commencement exercises. As a result, the 350th Harvard Commencement was held in 2001.

DRESSING THE PART

Commencement dress code is serious: a tassel of the wrong color or a sleeve of the wrong style, for example, have constituted fashion faux pas since 1902. In 1897, a committee was assembled "to prepare a scheme of gowns, caps and hoods to be submitted to the Board." By 1902, the committee—known as the Intercollegiate Bureau of Academic Costume—had come up with "a scheme for academic dress" still featured in official Harvard dress today.

The new and improved Harvard image adopted different outfits for the different members of the academic community. A bachelor's gown has long-pointed sleeves, the master's gown has long curved sleeves, and the doctor's gown—crimson only since 1955—is faced with three velvet bars on full, round sleeves. Each Harvard academic gown has a crows-foot emblem that is unique to the University. The faculty awarding the degree determines the color of the crow's foot. Bachelors and masters caps have a long black tassel, whereas a doctoral tassel may be gold.

To top it all off it is the hood, which holds the greatest degree of symbolism. Harvard bachelors do not receive hoods at all, while masters' and doctors' hoods are distinguished by length—three and one half feet for masters and four feet for doctors—and are lined with crimson silk. The borders of the hoods are velvet, with different widths indicating different ranks.

If this seems too simple, fear not. There are several hundred colleges and universities registered with the Intercollegiate Bureau of Academic Costume with their own colors and combinations. Harvard Commencement is a catwalk of robes, hats, tassels, and hoods. Don't laugh: as a general rule, the crazier the outfit, the more distinguished the individual.

CLASS DAY

One of Harvard's biggest celebratory and social events, Class Day takes place the day before Commencement and is a less formal celebration of the undergraduate senior class before the pomp and circumstance of the Commencement ceremony. Students attending Class Day enjoy speeches by other students and elected guests. In recent years, these guests have included Amy Poehler, Bill Clinton, Bono, and Hank Aaron; earlier illustrious speakers have included Mother Teresa in 1982 and Coretta Scott King in 1968. As it currently stands, members of the senior class elect four student speakers: two to be serious and two to be funny. The class elects the guest speaker as well, highlighting that the event is meant to celebrate the undergraduate class separately before they join the other graduates of the University.

Class Day dates back to the 1770s, according to Harvard records. The celebration was called Valedictory Day, and involved a series of prayers, orations, and poems. In 1838, Class Day, as it had by then come to be known, took on a more social role. That year, as soon as the morning chapel exercises ended, ladies were asked to go to the green and dance. When inhabitants of Cambridge heard about the dancing, they rushed to join in, and since then, the grass has been kept short on Class Days to facilitate dancing.

The following day, after Commencement, students walk through Johnston Gate for the first time since they entered as freshman. Superstition has it that those who jump the gun and walk through Johnston Gate at any point between these two ceremonies, which bookend their Harvard careers, will end up leaving Harvard without their diplomas.

OFFICE OF PUBLIC AFFAIRS

Bono, of the band U2, speaking at the 2001 Harvard Class Day

AFTER HARVARD

HARVARD CLUBS

After graduating, Harvard alumni are eligible to become members of over 170 Harvard clubs in over 70 countries. The Associated Harvard clubs, established in 1897, serve to keep Harvard alumni connected to the larger Harvard community; members must be graduates, tenured professors, faculty members, or former or current members of the Board of Overseers. The clubs, some of which are over a century old, often have fascinating histories of their own. In the Harvard Club of New York, for example, visitors are greeted by a giant mounted elephant head, shot by Theodore Roosevelt and donated to the club. The Harvard Alumni Association, meanwhile, boasts over 360,000 members.

INFORMATION

OFFICIAL HISTORICAL TOUR OF HARVARD UNIVERSITY

M-Sa 10am, noon, and 2pm
Departs from the Information Office,
1350 Massachusetts Ave., Holyoke Center
During the academic year the tour is given by members of the Crimson Key Society

STATS

Admissions rate for the Class of 2015: 6.2%
Total cost for one year of undergraduate education (tuition, room, board, and student services fee), 2011-2012: $52,652
Undergraduate need-based financial aid in 2011: $154,500,000, distributed among 61% of students
Endowment as of September 2011: $32 billion
Graduate schools: 12
Division I sports: 41

GEOGRAPHICAL BREAKDOWN, CLASS OF 2015

16% New England
22% Middle Atlantic
19.1% South
10.9% Midwest
21.1% Pacific
10.9% International

UNDERGRADUATE CONCENTRATIONS

- African and African American Studies
- Anthropology
    - » Archaeology
    - » Social Anthropology
- Applied Mathematics
- Astrophysics
- Biomedical Engineering
- Chemical and Physical Biology
- Chemistry
- Chemistry and Physics
- Classics
- Computer Science
- Earth and Planetary Sciences
- East Asian Studies
- Economics
- Engineering Sciences
    - » AB in Engineering Sciences
    - » SB in Engineering Sciences
- English
- Environmental Science and Public Policy
- Folklore and Mythology
- Germanic Languages and Literatures
    - » German Literature
    - » German Cultural Studies
    - » Scandinavian Studies
- Government
- History
- History and Literature
- History and Science
    - » History of Science Track
    - » Science and Society Track
    - » Medicine and Society Track
- History of Art and Architecture
- Human Developmental and Regenerative Biology
- Human Evolutionary Biology
    - » Mind, Brain, and Behavior Track
- Linguistics
    - » Linguistics Track
    - » Linguistics with Related Field Track
    - » Mind, Brain, and Behavior Track
- Literature

- Mathematics
    - » Mathematics and Teaching Option
- Molecular and Cellular Biology
- Music
- Near Eastern Languages and Civilizations
- Neurobiology
    - » Mind, Brain, and Behavior Track
- Organismic and Evolutionary Biology
- Philosophy
    - » Mind, Brain, and Behavior Track
- Physics
    - » Applied Physics Option
    - » Biophysics Option
    - » Physics and Teaching Option
- Psychology
    - » Cognitive Science Track
    - » Social and Cognitive Neuroscience Track
- Comparative Study of Religion
- Romance Languages and Literatures
    - » French and Francophone Studies
    - » Hispanic Studies
    - » Italian Studies
    - » Latin American Studies
    - » Portuguese and Brazilian Studies
    - » Romance Studies
- Sanskrit and Indian Studies
- Slavic Languages and Literatures
- Social Studies
- Sociology
- Special Concentrations
- Statistics
    - » Bioinformatics and Computational Biology Track
- Quantitative Finance Track
- Visual and Environmental Studies
    - » Studio Arts and Film/Video
    - » Film Studies
    - » Environmental Studies
- Studies of Women, Gender, and Sexuality

PRESIDENTS OF HARVARD UNIVERSITY

17th Century

	Nathaniel Eaton – Headmaster	1636 – 1639
1st	Reverend Henry Dunster	1640 – 1654
2nd	Reverend Charles Chauncey	1654 – 1672
3rd	Reverend Leonard Hoar*	1672 – 1674
4th	Reverend Uriah Oakes	1674 – 1681
5th	Reverend John Rogers	1682 – 1683
6th	Reverend Increase Mather	1684 – 1701

18th Century

7th	Reverend Samuel Willard	1701 – 1707
8th	John Leverett	1708 – 1724
9th	Reverend Benjamin Wadsworth	1725 – 1737
10th	Reverend Edward Holyoke	1737 – 1769
11th	Reverend Samuel Locke	1770 – 1773
12th	Reverend Samuel Langdon	1774 – 1780

19th Century

13th	Joseph Willard	1781 – 1804
14th	Samuel Webber	1804 – 1810
15th	Reverend John Thornton Kirkland	1810 – 1828
16th	Josiah Quincy	1829 – 1845
17th	Edward Everett	1846 – 1849
18th	Jared Sparks	1849 – 1853
19th	Reverend James Walker	1853 – 1860
20th	Cornelius Conway Felton	1860 – 1862
21th	Reverend Thomas Hill	1862 – 1868

20th Century

22th	Charles William Eliot	1869 – 1909
23th	Abbott Lawrence Lowell	1909 – 1933
24th	James Bryan Conant	1933 – 1953
25th	Nathan Marsh Pusey	1953 – 1971
26th	Derek Curtis Bok	1971 – 1991
27th	Neil Leon Rudenstine	1991 – 2001

21st Century

| 28th | Lawrence H. Summers | 2001 – 2006 |
| 29th | Drew Gilpin Faust | 2007 – present |

*Presidents Hoar through Pusey were graduates of Harvard College.

NOBEL PRIZE WINNING FACULTY

T.W. Richards	Chemistry	1914
George Minot	Medicine or Physiology	1934
William P. Murphy	Medicine or Physiology	1934
Percy W. Bridgman	Physics	1946
Henry J. Cadbury	Peace	1947
Ralph J. Bunch	Peace	1950
Edward M. Purcell	Physics	1952
Fritz A. Lipmann	Medicine or Physiology	1953
John F. Enders	Medicine or Physiology	1954
Frederick C. Robbins	Medicine or Physiology	1954
Thomas H. Weller	Medicine or Physiology	1954
Georg von Bekesy	Medicine or Physiology	1961
James D. Watson	Medicine or Physiology	1962
Konrad E. Bloch	Medicine or Physiology	1964
Julian S. Schwinger	Physics	1965
Robert Burns Woodward	Chemistry	1965
George Wald	Medicine or Physiology	1967
Simon S. Kuznets	Economics	1971
Kenneth J. Arrow	Economics	1972
Wassily W. Leontief	Economics	1973
William N. Lipscomb	Chemistry	1976
John H. Van Vleck	Physics	1977
Sheldon L. Glashow	Physics	1979
Steven Weinberg	Physics	1979
Baruj Benacerraf	Medicine or Physiology	1980
Walter Gilbert	Chemistry	1980
David Hubel	Medicine	1981
Torsten Wiesel	Medicine	1981
Nicolaas Bloembergen	Physics	1981
Carlo Rubbia	Physics	1984
Bernard Lown	Peace	1985

Dudley R. Herschbach	Chemistry	1986
Norman Ramsey	Physics	1989
Joseph E. Murray	Medicine	1990
Elias J. Corey	Chemistry	1990
Seamus Heaney	Literature	1995
Robert C. Merton	Economics	1997
Amartya Sen	Economics	1998
A. Michael Spence	Economics	2001
Riccardo Giacconi	Physics	2002
Linda B. Buck	Medicine or Physiology	2004
Roy J. Glauber	Physics	2005
Thomas C. Schelling	Economics	2005
Jack Szostak	Medicine or Physiology	2009

PULITZER PRIZE WINNING FACULTY

Henry Adams	Biography	1919
Charles McIlwain	History	1924
Mark A. DeWolfe Howe	Biography	1925
Edward Channing	History	1926
Harvey Cushing	Biography	1926
Archibald MacLeish	Poetry	1933
Frederick J. Turner	History	1933
Robert Hillyer	Poetry	1934
Ralph Barton Perry	Biography	1936
Paul Herman Buck	History	1938
Robert Frost	Poetry	1943
Samuel Eliot Morison	Biography	1943
Arthur M. Schlesinger Jr.	History	1946
Walter Piston	Music	1948
Oscar Handlin	History	1952
Archibald MacLeish	Poetry	1953
Archibald MacLeish	Drama	1959
Samuel Eliot Morison	Biography	1960
David Donald	Biography	1961
Walter Piston	Music	1961
Walter Jackson Bate	Biography	1964
Howard Mumford Jones	Nonfiction	1965
Perry Miller	History	1966
Leon Kirchner	Music	1967
Bernard Malamud	Fiction	1967
Bernard Bailyn	History	1968
George F. Kennan	Biography	1968
Mario Davidosky	Music	1971
Robert Coles	Nonfiction	1973
Donald Martino	Music	1974
John E. Mack	Biography	1977

Walter Jackson Bate	Biography	1978
Alfred Chandler Jr.	History	1978
Edward O. Wilson	Nonfiction	1979
Bernard Rands	Music	1984
Paul E. Starr	Nonfiction	1984
Thomas K. McCraw	History	1985
Bernard Bailyn	History	1987
David Donald	Biography	1988
Bert Hölldobler	Nonfiction	1991
Edward O. Wilson	Nonfiction	1991
Laurel Thatcher Ulrich	History	1991
Jorie Graham	Poetry	1996
Samantha Power	Nonfiction	2003
Caroline Elkins	Nonfiction	2006
Geraldine Brooks	Fiction	2006
Paul Harding	Fiction	2010

THE ARTS: HOURS OF OPERATION

Arthur M. Sackler Museum
485 Broadway St., Cambridge, MA 02138   617-495-9400
Open Tu-Sa 10am-5pm.

Peabody Museum
11 Divinity Ave., Cambridge, MA 02138   617-496-1027
Open daily 9am-5pm. Adults $9; senior citizens and students with ID
$7; children ages 3-18 $6; with Harvard ID, Peabody Museum Association membership, or membership or admission to the Harvard Museum
of Natural History free.

The Semitic Museum at Harvard University
6 Divinity Ave., Cambridge, MA 02138   617-495-4631
Open M-F 10am-4pm, Su 1–4pm; closed on holidays and on the Su
before M holidays. Free; donations are appreciated.

Carpenter Center for Visual Arts
24 Quincy St., Cambridge, MA 02138   617-495-3251
Open M-Sa 10am-11pm, Su 1pm–11pm.

Harvard Collection of Historical Scientific Instruments
Science Center 136, 1 Oxford St., Cambridge, MA 02138
                                               617-495-2779
Open M-F 11am-4pm. Free.

Arnold Arboretum
125 Arborway, Boston, MA 02130   617-524-1718
Open daily sunrise to sunset; Visitor Center in the Hunnewell Building
M-F 9am-4pm, Sa 10am-4pm, Su noon-4pm. Free.

Harvard Museum of Natural History
26 Oxford St., Cambridge, MA 02138   617-495-3045
Open daily 9am-5pm.

Harvard Box Office
In conjunction with the Office for the Arts
1350 Massachusetts Ave., Holyoke Center   617-496-2222
Open Tu-Su noon-6pm.

UNDERGRADUATE HOUSES

Adams House
26 Plympton Street

Cabot House
60 Linnaean Street

Currier House
64 Linnaean Street

Dunster House
8 Cowperthwaite Street

Eliot House
101 Dunster Street

Kirkland House
95 Dunster Street

Leverett House
28 DeWolfe Street

Lowell House
10 Holyoke Place

Mather House
10 Cowperthwaite Street

Pforzheimer House
56 Linnaean Street

Quincy House
58 Plympton Street

Winthrop House
32 Mill Street

GRADUATE SCHOOLS

Graduate School of Arts and Sciences
Holyoke Center 350, 1350 Massachusetts Ave.,
Cambridge

Graduate School of Design
Gund Hall, 48 Quincy St., Cambridge

Graduate School of Education
Appian Way, Cambridge

School of Engineering and Applied Sciences
Pierce Hall, 29 Oxford St., Cambridge

Harvard Business School
Soldiers Field, Boston

Harvard Dental School
188 Longwood Ave., Boston

Harvard Kennedy School
(formerly John F. Kennedy School of Government)
79 John F. Kennedy St., Cambridge

Harvard Law School
1563 Massachusetts Ave., Cambridge

Harvard Medical School
25 Shattuck St., Boston

Harvard School of Public Health
677 Huntington Ave., Boston

School of Continuing Education
51 Brattle St., Cambridge

Harvard Divinity School
45 Francis Avenue, Cambridge

ATHLETIC TEAMS AND TICKETING

Men's Varsity
Baseball
Basketball
Heavyweight crew
Freshman Heavyweight crew
Lightweight crew
Freshman Lightweight crew
Cross country
Fencing
Football
Golf
Ice Hockey
Lacrosse
Sailing
Skiing
Soccer
Squash
Swimming and Diving
Tennis
Track and Field
Volleyball
Water Polo
Wrestling

Women's Varsity
Basketball
Heavyweight crew
Lightweight crew
Cross Country
Fencing
Field Hockey
Golf
Ice Hockey
Lacrosse
Sailing
Skiing
Soccer
Softball
Squash
Swimming and Diving
Tennis
Track and Field
Volleyball
Water Polo

Athletic Ticket Office
Murr Center
65 North Harvard St., Boston, MA 02163   617-495-2211
Open M-F 9am-5pm. Tickets available for Football, Men's and Women's
Hockey, Men's and Women's Basketball, and Men's Lacrosse.

TOURS

AT HARVARD

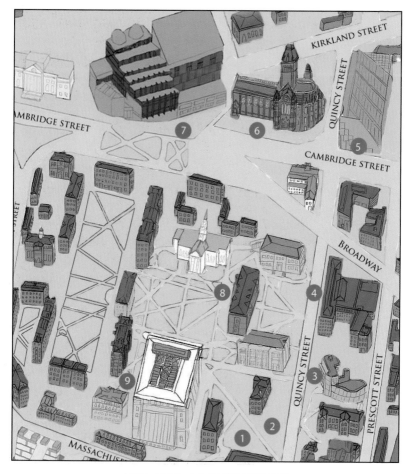

ART AND ARCHITECTURE

1. ALEXANDER CALDER SCULPTURE This light steel sculpture called "The Onion," was completed in 1965 and is on loan from a Radcliffe Trustee.

2. HENRY MOORE SCULPTURE On display in front of Lamont Library and called "Four Piece Reclining Figure."

3. THE CARPENTER CENTER The only building in North America designed by Swiss architect le Corbusier.

4. HARVARD ART MUSEUM Fogg, Busch-Rusinger, Sackler: The three museums in the Harvard Art Museum comprise three distinct collections.

5. GRADUATE SCHOOL OF DESIGN Known as the GSD, centered around Gund Hall where students create in a huge studio space of five levels of terraced desks.

6. MEMORIAL HALL The second largest collection of secular stained glass in the world.

7. THE SCIENCE CENTER Built in 1972, designed by architect, Joseph Lluís Sert.

8. SEVER HALL Designed by famed Boston architect, H.H. Richardson in 1880. The archway over the entrance is a conduit of sound.

9. MARBLE DRAGON STATUE Carved during the reign of Emperor Chia-ch'ing (1796-1820) the ten-foot tall, two-ton dragon carved of gray Chinese marble was presented to the University by Chinese alumni in 1936.

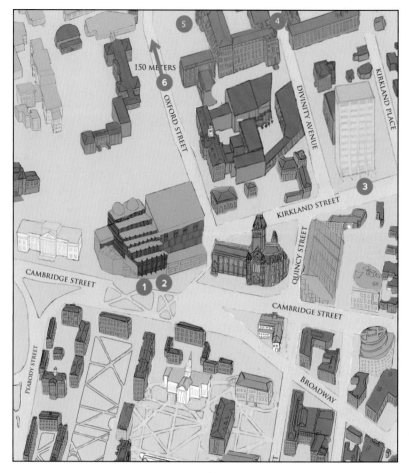

SCIENCE AT HARVARD

1. THE SCIENCE CENTER Houses Cabot Science library, five of the largest lecture halls on campus, two astronomical observatories and countless laboratories.

2. PUTNAM GALLERY Within the Science Center, an exhibition of Harvard's collection of historical scientific instruments.

3. WILLIAM JAMES HALL the tallest building on campus, contains the Social Anthropology, Sociology and Psychology departments.

4. PEABODY MUSEUM Among the first anthropological museums worldwide, houses a uniquely thorough history of human culture.

5. NATURAL HISTORY MUSEUM Accessible through the Peabody Museum or via Oxford St. Home to the internationally acclaimed Ware Collection of Blaschka Glass Model of Plants, known as the Glass Flowers and the world's only mounted Kronosaurus skeleton.

6. NORTHWEST LABS Opened in fall 2008, designed in contemporary style by Craig Hartman and home to a variety of science departments including Neuroscience and Particle Engineering.

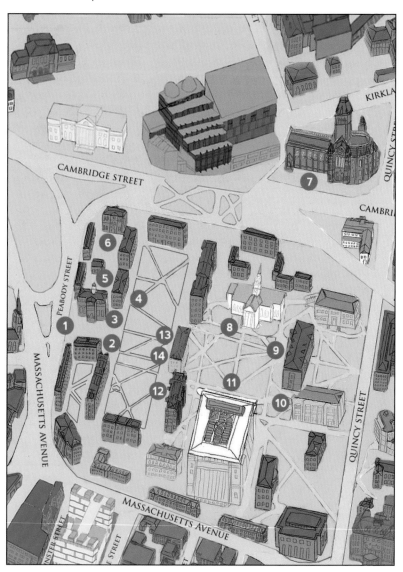

HISTORICAL TOUR OF HARVARD YARD

1. JOHNSTON GATE The oldest and largest gate of Harvard University. Legend has it that if you kiss your college sweetheart under the gate, you are destined to spend the rest of your lives together.

2. MASSACHUSETTS HALL Built in 1720, "Mass Hall" is the oldest academic building on campus and is both a freshman dormitory and home to the offices of the University President.

3. HARVARD HALL The currently standing building is used for lecture classes, however the original Harvard Hall contained the first experimental lab in the colonies and the largest library in the New World but was destroyed in a fire in 1764.

4. HOLLIS HALL Currently a freshman dormitory, because of its proximity to the College Water Pump was the home of the volunteer Fire Engine Society in the 19th century.

5. HOLDEN CHAPEL Originally built as a chapel in 1766, it has since served a variety of purposes including a military warehouse, a fire engine house, chemical laboratory, museum, and now as a classroom.

6. PHILLIP BROOKS HOUSE Referred to by students as PBHA, the home base of most community service organizations on campus.

7. MEMORIAL HALL Built as a Civil War memorial and a space for Commencement. Today, it hosts the largest lecture hall on campus as well as the freshman dining hall.

8. MEMORIAL CHURCH Dedicated on Armistice Day in 1932, though non-denominational, it holds the oldest daily protestant service in the nation.

9. SEVER HALL Designed by famed Boston architect, H.H. Richardson in 1880. The archway over the entrance is a conduit of sound.

10. EMERSON HALL The home of the philosophy department and infamously misrepresented as Barrett Hall in the 1970 film, *Love Story*.

11. WIDENER LIBRARY Built in 1914 in honor of Harry Elkins Widener, class of 1907, it contains approximately one third of the 16 million books in the Harvard University Library System, the largest in the world.

12. WELD HALL Freshman dormitory that President John F. Kennedy resided in his first year at the College.

13. UNIVERSITY HALL The administrative center of the University, originally designed as a multi-purpose building with a dining hall and a gym, in 1969, the Students for a Democratic Society forcefully occupied the premises.

14. JOHN HARVARD STATUE Known also as the statue of three lies: while the inscription on the statue reads "John Harvard, Founder, 1638", he was not the founder, Harvard was founded in 1636 and the figure of the statue is not John Harvard as all his depictions were destroyed in the fire of 1764.

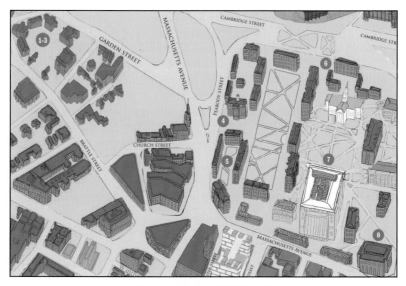

WOMEN'S HISTORY

1. RADCLIFFE YARD Named after Lady Ann Mowlson, born Ann Radcliffe, who established the first scholarship at Harvard in 1643, Radcliffe Yard was the campus of Radcliffe college, Harvard's sister institution.

2. FAY HOUSE One of the earliest buildings of Radcliffe College, now the administrative center of the Radcliffe Institute.

3. SCHLESINGER LIBRARY Contains the largest collection for the study of women in the nation.

4. JOHNSTON GATE Until 1943 women were not permitted in Harvard Yard after dark so Harvard-Radcliffe couples kissed goodnight at Johnston Gate.

5. STRAUS HALL The last freshman dormitory to become co-educational.

6. HARVARD COLLEGE WOMEN'S CENTER Located in the basement of Canaday Hall, a space for all to meet, relax and address specific issues related to women and gender on campus.

7. WIDENER LIBRARY When it opened it 1915 both women students and faculty had to request written permission to stay after hours.

8. LAMONT LIBRARY Completed in 1943, women were prohibited from accessing the library until 1967 because college administrators feared that the "fairer sex" would prove too great a distraction.

INDEX